THE
MOVIES
ON
YOUR MIND

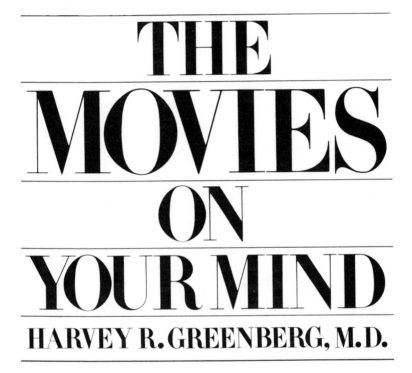

THE MOVIES ON YOUR MIND

HARVEY R. GREENBERG, M.D.

New York 1975
SATURDAY REVIEW PRESS │ E. P. DUTTON AND CO., INC.

Acknowledgment is made to the following:

Avco Embassy Pictures Corp., for permission to quote passages from *8½*, copyright © 1962 Avco Embassy Pictures Corp.

MCA Universal Pictures Corp., for passages from *Bride of Frankenstein, Dracula, Frankenstein,* and *Psycho.*

Metro-Goldwyn-Mayer, Inc., for permission to quote excerpts from the MGM release *The Wizard of Oz,* copyright 1937 Metro-Goldwyn-Mayer, Inc. Copyright renewed 1966 by Metro-Goldwyn-Mayer, Inc.

National Telefilm Associates for passages from *Invasion of the Body Snatchers.*

RKO General, Inc., for permission to quote passages from *King Kong,* copyright 1933.

Simon & Schuster, Inc., for permission to excerpt passages from *Wild Strawberries,* from *Four Screen Plays of Ingmar Bergman* by Ingmar Bergman, copyright © 1960 by Ingmar Bergman.

Warner Bros., Inc., for permission to excerpt passages from the motion pictures *The Treasure of Sierra Madre, The Maltese Falcon,* and *Casablanca* contained in chapters 3, 4, and 5. Copyrighted 1948, 1941, and 1943 respectively.

LIBRARY OF CONGRESS CATALOGING IN PUBLICATION DATA
Greenberg, M.D., Harvey R
The movies on your mind.

Includes bibliographical references.
1. Moving-pictures—Psychological aspects.   I. Title.
PN1995.G67   791.43′0909′353   75-12895

Published simultaneously in Canada by Clarke, Irwin & Company
Limited, Toronto and Vancouver
ISBN: 0-8415-0395-8 (cloth)
0-8415-0396-6 (paper)

"The Rags of Time" originally appeared in a somewhat different version in *American Imago,* vol. 27, no. 1 (spring, 1970). Copyright 1970 by Association for Applied Psychoanalysis, New York, N.Y.

For Rima—who made the pictures move . . .

ACKNOWLEDGMENTS

I wish to thank Gerald Emmanuel Stearn for sharing his formidable knowledge of cinema and American culture with me, thereby enriching *The Movies On Your Mind*. Sanford Teller, who knows more about *Casablanca* than any living soul, contributed invaluable source material on that film. My patients have contributed their free association to the movies on their minds, providing a constant source of illumination about film down through the years. A list of the other moviegoers—family, friends, colleagues, whose insights and opinions have influenced my thinking on cinema would probably be nearly as long as the book itself. . . .

CONTENTS

"One's favorite films are one's unlived lives, one's hopes, fears, libido. They constitute a magic mirror, their shadowy forms are woven from one's shadow selves, one's limbo loves. . . ." (Durgnat)

I

The Movies on *My* Mind

> . . . Mind has triumphed over matter,
> and the pictures roll on with the ease of
> musical tones. It is a superb enjoyment,
> which no other art can furnish us. . . .
>
> Hugo Munsterberg: *The Photoplay*

I was a moviemaniac long before I became a psychoanalyst. It all goes back to childhood, and I blame my mother. I never understood why the other children in my Philadelphia neighborhood always complained that they weren't allowed to see *Frankenstein*—*my* earliest memory is being hauled off to an extravaganza called *The Mad Monster*. It scared my knickers off, but I was irretrievably hooked on the spot.

My mother's tastes were catholic and insatiable—science fiction, musical comedy, grade-"Z" Westerns, four-hanky Joan Crawford epics—we sat wrapt through them all, while my father groaned or snored beside us, an unwilling victim of my mother's moviemania. And as the lights came up:

"How did you like that, Harvey, wasn't that *terrific?*"

"You bet, Mom!"

"How did *you* like it, Murry, didn't it do things to you?!"

1

"It made me acidic. A catastrophe."

So much for the Oedipus complex. I cut the umbilical cord, became socialized, and began flicking out with my peers . . . memorable Saturday afternoons at the ERLEN theater, where eleven cents (they raised the price to twelve cents, precipitating the biggest consumer revolt since the Boston Tea Party) bought a Spy Smasher serial—twenty-one cartoons, a Ken Maynard, Hoot Gibson, or John Wayne oater. Finally, after the Yo-Yo contest, came the Feature Attraction, not one of which I can remember except *Tarzan's New York Adventure* with Johnny Weismuller clambering about the upper reaches of the Empire State Building in a tiger-skin jockstrap. Afterward we would stumble out into twilight reality, eyeballs coagulated, and reel home to pile pot roast on top of the afternoon accumulation of Black Crows and Crackerjacks.

I graduated from junior high school and traveled further afield to the RENEL theater, sister to the ERLEN, but home of Serious Adult Entertainment. By fourteen, my moviemania was serious but not yet terminal, marked by the usual symptoms of anxiety, tension and visual hallucinosis—phantom films on the ceiling—if deprived of RENEL delights for longer than three days.

Then, a disastrous transplantation to Brooklyn where I was bounced out of the Flatbush Midwood by the matinee Movie Matron, that formidable harpy in starched nursing whites, armed with flashlight and body odor—an outrage more humiliating than the pangs of rejected first love. Such barbarism was unknown in the City of Brotherly Love, where if you were old enough to pay, you were old enough to stay. And, when my folks took me to the evening show, I found that the distractions of the Matron were replaced by running subtitles provided by some old crone stationed behind my good ear who was evidently concerned lest some nuance of the action might be missed by her friends within thirty rows:

"HAH LOOKIT WHO'S COMIN INDA WINDA DIDDEN I TELLYA HE WAS NOGOOD WATCHID HE'S GODDA KNIFE SHE DON' SEEYIM" And so forth.

Still, there were the architectural compensations of those long since demolished New York theaters: the rococo magnificence of the average neighborhood house outrivaled the Royal Pavilion at Brighton for sheer absurdity; clouds and stars floated across the ceiling, and caryatids framed the candy stand.

Movies kept me afloat through an acned, reasonably tormented adolescence, since I feared the madhouse consequence of exposing a psychiatrist to the noxious vapors rising from my psyche. Movies sustained me as a card-carrying member of the Silent Generation; I spent most of my college career auditing the Forty-second Street flicks—that was before the tidal wave of porn, before the cashiers had to be shielded by bulletproof glass and before one actually had a better-than-even chance of using the toilet without being robbed, sodomized or murdered.

The transition from university to medical school was accomplished with only moderate trauma, because every step of the way I found fellow somnambulists instantly at the ready to drop scalpel or stethoscope and rush down to the midtown flea-pits to see *Bad Day at Black Rock* or *Creature from the Black Lagoon* for the tenth time. And though I was psychoanalyzed during my psychiatric training, the therapist was never able to relieve my moviemania. The affliction went too deep by this time; besides, I suspected from the tell-tale tremor in his voice whenever I free-associated to *Gone With the Wind* that he too was a victim.

Analyzing my own patients, I soon discovered that whatever their symptoms, most are at least mildly addicted to the cinema, some even as mad for film as their doctor, although they are usually loath to talk about movies at first—often because they don't want to spoil a picture for you. I handily overcame this resistance by reassuring them that it's an occupational hazard to hear about a film I haven't seen. Of course patients also feel ashamed going on and on about a James Bond epic when they should be exploring the Oedipus complex. Nonsense! Cinema is a supremely valid source of free associations, a powerful touchstone into the unconscious. The movies, like waking dreams, interpret every aspect of our lives—the unquiet past, the troubled present, our anxious premonitions of the future, our neurotic conflicts and our inspired gropings towards the light.

These days I regularly use cinema as a Rorschach test. During the first few sessions I ask about favorite films, and invariably some heretofore well-concealed aspect of psychic geography will be thrown into bold relief. Several years ago an adolescent with school-phobia told me that his favorite film was *King of Kings;* he especially enjoyed the part where the Roman soldiers pounded the nails into Jesus' hands. I discovered that his cranium was jammed with homosexual and masochistic fantasies: he was avoiding school because of a tremendous fear—and hidden wish—that a gang of local bullies would beat and rape him. In his daydreams, he would show a Christ-like forbearance and pity for his tormentors, so that they would give up their evil ways and worship, rather than despise him.

Certainly, this is a grossly pathological example of moviemania—but passion for the cinema cuts across age, background, degree and kind of illness. The subtler variations of moviemania are hard to differentiate from average moviegoing. Freud always maintained there was an exquisitely thin line between the norm and the neurotic. Virtually everyone I know, on or off the couch, goes to the flicks. Indeed, a case could be made that total disinterest in film might itself indicate serious psycho-social malfunction.

When reality—or what passes for it—becomes too much to bear, the siren song of cinema is likely to prove irresistible, especially by one whose overdeveloped imagination requires more stimulation than the sluggish environment provides.

Sufferers from acute cinema addiction go on binges. Some view anything, anytime, anywhere, especially after being traumatized. A horny, uptight recent divorcé slinks into the hard-core porn houses. A timid shipping clerk, brutally put down by a sadistic boss, devours three Spaghetti Westerns in a row, discharging his pent up aggression while Clint Eastwood mauls the opposition. The flickout binge ends with the addict returning to the debatable rewards of workaday life slightly disoriented and ashamed, but unlike the alcoholic, no worse for wear—indeed, usually much comforted by the relapse.

One encounters chronic moviemania in rigid, inhibited types who feel exquisitely uncomfortable when forced into close interpersonal contact. Safe only in well-defined social situations, intolerably anxious if called upon to improvise, these people sleepwalk through the day's routine and only come truly alive at second hand, as proxy participants in the adventures of their screen idols. (Walker Percy's elegant novel *The Moviegoer* describes such a case.) And at the furthest antipodes of moviemania, in the land of schizophrenia, dwell a few shattered souls whose entire lives have come to revolve around the cinema. Their chief human relationships are with the ticket-lady, the candy-seller, and the usher.

Not too long ago, while vacationing on a tiny Greek island, I watched the entire population turn out for *Hello Dolly!* The islanders came by donkey, bicycle, scooter; the aged and infirm were carried on litters down from mountain villages. The theater was the town square, the seats were chairs from the local cafes, the screen a bedsheet flapping in the hot August wind. The print was lousy, the Greek subtitles barely decipherable, and Barbra Streisand sounded like Donald Duck, but the audience went wild, and time after time the projectionist stopped the picture and ran a scene through again.

It was then that I began meditating seriously on the complex purposes that urge so many around the world to the cinema. The compulsion must run very strong and very deep, for men have dreamed of making pictures move since the dawn of recorded time, and from the day Lumière first showed crude filmstrips of commonplace events to Parisians at the turn of the century, we have trooped to the movies in droves. Now that cinema has entered our homes via TV, moviemania is an even more universal, if more solitary, phenomenon. Psychoanalysts believe that behavior is *overdetermined*—that no single cause produces any one psychological effect. Too many influences play upon us to allow behavior to be reduced down to a facile common denominator. I hazard that there are numerous, articulating explanations for the cinema's vast appeal to the psyche.

The earliest filmmakers plunked a camera in front of the action and let it grind away. The results were theatrical, and after the initial novelty wore off, curiously flat. Within a few years basic shooting and editing techniques were developed—close-up, fade-out, flashback, dissolve, intercutting, etc.—and refined by master innovators such as Griffith, Eisenstein and Pudovkin. Cinema came to look at life very much like the human eye does, as the moviemen grew ever more adept at arranging the camera's "perceptions" to mimic the intelligence guiding the human lens and retina. Hugo Munsterberg wrote in 1916:

> . . . attention turns to detailed points in the outer world and ignores everything else; the photoplay [does] this when, in the close-up, a

> detail is enlarged and everything else disappears. . . . Memory
> breaks into present events by bringing up pictures of the past: the
> photoplay [does] this by its frequent cutbacks [flashbacks]. . . .
> Through our division of interest, our mind is drawn hither and
> thither. We think of events which run parallel in different places.
> The photoplay can show in intertwined scenes everything which our
> mind embraces. . . . *The photoplay tells us the human story by
> overcoming the forms of the outer world—namely space, time, and
> causality, and by adjusting the events to the forms of the inner
> world, namely attention, memory, imagination and emotion.* . . .

This happy correspondence between human and movie eye makes
cinema the one art form that most consistently reflects back to us our
own unique style of organizing experience, constantly recording what
it is like to be at once within the world and within oneself. We willingly surrender control over our lives for a brief hour or two and are
whirled away from ourselves—sometimes light years away, to remote
times and fabulous regions, but the camera remains an extension of
personal and familiar vision. We let the movies take up where we have
left off: they seem to think like us and therefore it is amazingly easy to
let them think—and live— *for* us.

Movies cater to the universal desire for omnipotence that curiously
enough stems from the very time in childhood when we are mostly
helpless and dependent. The hungry infant wails, mother appears as if
by magic to nourish and protect. The impression soon develops that all
you have to do is yell and the world will dance to your tune. Of
course, reality quickly compels us to recognize the limitations of this
irrational but highly seductive mode of thinking—but the recognition
is grudging at best. Man never gives up his secret hope for total, ef-
fortless control over his world. We are thus forever prone to a curious
kind of mental juggling: I pay my bills, or at least worry about paying
them; I fill up the gastank so my car will keep running—on the other
hand, I'm already planning how to spend the proceeds from the mil-
lion-dollar lottery, although I haven't bought my ticket yet, and of
course, I know I will never die.

Movies fulfill Huey Long's promise—making every man a king, offering up a feast of sight and sound we would otherwise be unlikely to
savor in a single lifetime on a limited expense account. We are exposed to terrifying peril, overwhelming natural and unnatural catastro-

phes. We charge with the Light Brigade, Martians zap us with ghoulish rays, Krakatoa erupts—and we live on to tell the tale.

Movies bestow omniscience as well as omnipotence. The characters are confined within the screen's narrow dimensions. The man going to the gallows in *Intolerance* does not know his pardon is achingly near. The besieged settlers cannot know that the Seventh Cavalry will come riding over the hill in a moment to rescue them. The sleeping villagers will never know that Gorgo, the resurrected dinosaur, is about to stamp them out of existence. *We* know and foresight sharpens enjoyment:

> *We* are the Immortal Gods, watching the screen characters live their anguished lifetime-in-90-minutes lives. . . . Art doesn't really make the artist immortal, but it makes the audience *feel* immortal. (Durgnat)

Siegfried Kracauer believes that today's moviegoer particularly relishes this illusion of superhuman power because of "the increasing difficulty for the individual to account for the forces, mechanisms and processes that shape the modern world, including his own destiny." I doubt it. Poets, novelists and playwrights have been trying to scratch our omnipotent itch for centuries and in times more stable than ours. The movies do a better job, simply because they are not limited by the restrictions of proscenium or printed page.

Our innate voyeurism is also immensely gratified at the movies. As children we are barred—often humiliatingly—from watching what grownups *really* do in and out of the bedroom. The stealthy, disrespectful camera lets us eavesdrop upon the intimacy of lovers unrebuked, or observe the awful rites of the Death-goddess Kali unpunished. Again and again we find ourselves where we really have no right to be—in boudoir or bank vault—and we get away with it!

I have touched upon only the barest fraction of the secret strivings evoked and satisfied by cinema. The ambience of the theater, the awareness that no one can get to you for the next two or three hours, everything conspires to create a passive state in which ordinarily disregarded and forbidden fantasies can play themselves out. One grows intensely suggestible, and the screen is the master hypnotist! Watching a film on television can never hope to duplicate this experience. The picture is too small, the effluvia of daily life are too close at hand, and the all-important attitude of total absorption is constantly jangled by the raucous demands of intrusive commercials to wipe out diseased breath and watch out for ring-around-the-collar.

Like the theater, the psychoanalyst's office is dim, hushed. The patient stretches out upon the couch. Freed of the world's rush and gab, thoughts wander where they will. The unconscious presses invincibly to the surface. The analyst's attention hovers evenly over a seemingly random flow of half-forgotten memories, associations, dream fragments. He weaves this tangled web into a succinct observation that links the past with the present. Now, peculiarly receptive, the patient will experience insight and, hopefully, liberation from conflict.

At the cinema, consciousness is similarly lulled. Vision is directed within, then drawn outward again to the screen; the mind coils subtly between the seductive images; personal and cinematic fantasy interpenetrate. Past conflicts are processed—but never in the psychoanalytic sense, for conscious insight is not the intention. Instead, our deepest terrors and longings are mimed, simultaneously expressed while they are denied. C. B. DeMille's spectaculars, for instance, gave legions of puritanical voyeurs a good excuse to watch Delilah romping in the near-buff. For one ticket, the audience got both sermons *and* tits!

The stars indulge in the pleasures we have disowned, suffer our common sorrows and our tedious problems—transformed into strange scenarios. We glorify and identify with the stars who, like gods, live on through repeated deaths, to be reborn in the imagination of one generation to the next, conferring upon us a taste of their insubstantial immortality. A cheap catharsis—no Antigone at the RKO PANACEA—but potent beyond belief.

Movies are complex phantasmagorias, manufactured and merchandised by an ulcer-ridden conglomerate of dedicated artists, workaday technicians and shrewd hucksters who probably consume more psychoanalytic time and keep more therapists in Jaguars and golf shoes than any other labor force in the nation. They do not hesitate to manipulate public taste—often shamelessly—but are equally manipulated by the public's half-formed yearnings, by obscure cultural imperatives

Hollywood both molds and obeys. The ongoing resonance between maker and consumer is mostly subliminal. Occasionally, however, a film comes along that reveals this feedback system strikingly.

The counterculture had been slouching towards Bethlehem for several years prior to *Easy Rider,* but directly after it was released, America seemed truly up for greening, as the teenage and college population were outdone by hordes of weekend hippies and other unlikely followers of the ''groovy'' life-style in frantic efforts at getting stoned, hairy and freaked-out on instant, incoherent intimacy. *Easy Rider* did seem to retransmit previously inchoate cravings for freedom. There's a collective gasp in response to such a film: ''So *that's* what's happening!'' followed by a wave of social reaction—changes in dress, behavior, speech, sometimes shortlived and frivolous and confined to one subculture, but occasionally far more lasting and decisive than we would care to realize. For who really knows or can measure how deeply, how enduringly, movies *move* us?

If cinema is a species of dream or fantasy within the public domain, then it is legitimate for the professional decipherer of restless dreams and errant visions—the psychoanalyst—to interpret film for us.

Psychoanalytic study of the cinema has been quite spare compared with similar investigations into the other lively arts. Freud himself seemed absolutely disinterested in the movies, even though by the time of his death many of the screen's masterpieces had already been produced. Hugo Munsterberg, a German psychologist and philosopher, was far more discerning in his appreciation of film aesthetics than Freud and his followers; a rabid fan of all things American, Munsterberg gained a brief ascendance as a Kissinger-like doyen of the Harvard intellectual set, only to be shamefully discredited by his adopted land in the wave of anti-Teutonic sentiment that swept the United States during World War I.

The critic Parker Tyler undertook pioneering voyages in the forties, at a time when cinema criticism was still for the most part fixated at the ''Gee whiz, I liked that!'' level. He wrote that ''Hollywood is but the industrialization of the mechanical worker's daylight dream . . . extended ritualistically into those hours reserved by custom for relaxation and amusement. . . .'' Tyler noted ''the tendencies of screen stories to emphasize—unintentionally—neuroses and psychopathic traits discovered and formulated by psychoanalysis.''

There is a pleasant assortment of books—see the bibliographies in my chapters—by other writers who aren't psychoanalysts, but nevertheless possess an unmistakable talent for probing beneath the smooth surface of cinema and coming up with unexpected psychological truths. I've especially enjoyed the work of Pauline Kael, Barbara Deming, Raymond Durgnat and Robin Wood.

Psychoanalysts themselves (myself included) have interpreted a few films, but their efforts are usually buried in professional journals—heavy going, indeed. The one authoritative source still remains *The Movies* by Martha Wolfenstein and Nathan Leites. Although their work is restricted to American and European films of 1945, their observations, notably pithy and incisive, are completely applicable to films made today. They discovered, for instance, that movies are pervaded by the "false appearance" by which some unconscious forbidden wish is portrayed, then safely disavowed, thus saying in effect— "Of course that never *really* happened because the *real* explanation is. . . ." By ascertaining what the scenario is reassuring us never happened, one finds some intensely pleasurable yet reprehensible wish has been cleverly acted out for our delectation, a wish we have probably harbored, and felt the pangs of conscience if ever we thought of satisfying it in reality!

Armed with such techniques, the psychoanalytic sensibility can unravel motivation and defense, interpret meaning within a single film, illuminate the *oeuvre* of a director, trace the obsessive pull of the ever popular genre films—horror, science fiction, Westerns—so often imperiously dismissed as egregious trivia by the self-appointed apostles of high art. We are enabled to perceive the exquisite meshing of individual and collective fantasy, as the timeless myths of personal and cultural history are reinvented on the silver screen.

Movies on Your Mind is a sampler of these possibilities, designed to heighten the understanding and enjoyment of the dedicated buff, or anyone who has ever thought there is more to cinema than idle entertainment. My chapters cover nearly 100 movies produced during the past four decades. Some are analyzed in great detail, others in passing or *en genre*. My selection is wildly undefinitive—from Bogart to Bergman, from *Frankenstein* to Fellini, from *The Wizard of Oz* to *2001*—choices dictated by private preference, the vagaries of personal nostalgia, and the burden of restrictive accessibility. I deal chiefly with American movies in this book and would hope to get more deeply into foreign films in the future.

A word of caution—pictures and their stars are not patients! The individual in therapy fleshes out the analyst's suppositions with a thousand details acquired over months and sometimes years of treatment. Films last no longer than two or three analytic sessions, hence psychological conclusions about plot and character must be highly inferential, especially when certain crucial childhood events that are principal grist for the analytic mill are rarely furnished. We will never know how James Bond took to toilet training, or if Sam Spade sucked his thumb.

There is also more, infinitely more, to patients and pictures than the analysis thereof. Analysts have often been guilty of reducing subtle, exuberant art down to a few dreary rubrics—penis envy, anal eroticism, breast fixation—with disastrous, or merely inane results. Psychoanalysis remains only one dimension of film criticism; movies can evoke in the unaware analyst a kind of exegesic delirium, a madness to interpret from his own point of view, and soon, as Durgnat mordantly observes: "no film is felt to be 'about' its subject matter. Its specificity, concreteness, consequently its richness of detail dissolve into a sort of spiritual soup [making] nonsense of all the differences between one culture and another, one person and another, one film and another. . . ."

Therefore let the analyst be as humble in the halls of art as in the office; one has, after all, a limited provenance in either locale. Most psychoanalytic film criticism, no matter how skillful, has also frequently entertained a specific literary bias, focusing on script line while ignoring the images, that are "so much a part of the cinema's dramatic—not just grammar—but spelling" (Durgnat). Unfortunately the nuances of a visual medium often exasperatingly defy capture by the written word. Stills are of questionable value—they *stop* motion as decisively as the printed page. I have tried to move your imaginary forces in my essays, so watch the films I've "treated" with these meditations in mind, to fathom what Richard Schickel has called "the unconscious movie, the one neither maker nor viewer are consciously aware of, that expresses the attitude, desires, neuroses shared by both parties. . . ."

Bibliography

DURGNAT, RAYMOND. *Films and Feelings*. Cambridge, Mass.: The M.I.T. Press, 1971. See pp. 135, 16, 67 and 226.

KRACAUER, SIEGFRIED. *Theory of Film*. The Oxford University Press, 1960. See p. 171.

MUNSTERBERG, HUGO. *The Photoplay*. New York: Dover Publications, Inc., 1970. See pp. 74, 95.

TYLER, PARKER. *The Hollywood Hallucination*. Introduction by Richard Schickel. New York: Simon & Schuster, Inc., 1944. See pp. vii, 141, 203, 237.

———. *Magic and Myth of the Movies*. New York: Simon & Schuster, Inc., 1970.

WOLFENSTEIN, M., and LEITES, N. *The Movies*. New York: Atheneum Publishers, 1970. See p. 15.

II

The Wizard of Oz
—Little Girl Lost
—And Found

> The treasure which you think not worth taking
> trouble and pains to find, this one alone is the
> real treasure you are longing for all your life.
> The glittering treasure you are hunting for day
> and night lies buried on the other side of that hill
> yonder. . . .
>
> B. Traven: *The Treasure of
> the Sierra Madre*

In 1939, MGM delivered two of the all-time movie greats—*Gone With
the Wind* and *The Wizard of Oz*. Both pictures spoke directly to the
American heartlands and were instant box office smashes; the heroine
of each is a gutsy teenager (Scarlett O'Hara is sixteen at the start of
GWTW, Dorothy Gale about thirteen in *Wizard*) whose serene life is
shattered—in Scarlett's case by the hammerblows of fate during the
Civil War, in Dorothy's by a concussion sustained during a savage
Kansas twister. Each young lady has her mettle fiercely tested in a
succession of compelling trials and tribulations: Scarlett emerges from
economic and romantic disaster in post-bellum Georgia older and no

wiser—bullheaded, scheming as ever. But Dorothy Gale returns from her Oz-dream only a few moments older, and—as we shall see— matured far beyond her years.

Dorothy's "trip" is a marvelous metaphor for the psychological journey every adolescent must make. Contrary to popular misconception, psychoanalysts do not believe that the core of personality is fixed, immutable, in earliest childhood. Those years are certainly crucial, but we remain open to change and healing every day of the rest of our lives. At no other stage of development is this more true than adolescence, when the enormous thrust of physical, intellectual and sexual growth literally propels the youngster out of the family nest. Simultaneously, the half-buried conflicts of childhood are resurrected to be resolved or haunt us forever. A poignant and infuriating mixture of regressive and progressive tendencies, the adolescent is exquisitely vulnerable to further emotional injury and terrifically capable of self-repair.

With the onset of puberty, the parents, previously viewed from below as supreme authorities, are now confronted at eye level—and who ever enjoyed *that* view? After all, if one admits that one's progenitors are simply human, then the very human wish to be cared for and protected indefinitely must go out the window. This possibility terrifies the adolescent, until it is recognized that realistic power can be acquired over one's affairs, that one is neither omnipotent nor absolutely helpless in shaping personal destiny. Before this saving recognition is firmly rooted within the psyche, the quixotic teenager will alternately badger his folks with outrageous demands to be treated like the ruler of the nursery, or else rake them with withering blasts of contempt and go out questing for substitutes to redeem their "failure," some super-hero to worship and imitate.

These substitutes take many shapes, and are traded in with bewildering frequency: rock stars; sports and other media idols; teachers; gang leaders; these are all sought with one idea in mind: the "hero" is put back on the pedestal vacated by the parents, endowed with a special mightiness—athletic, romantic, spiritual, etc.—to remedy the sense of a perceived lack within the self. In other words, *everyone wants a Wizard during adolescence,* but the wanting will cease when the youngster begins to tap his own unique abilities.

Forswearing childhood wishes, giving up worn-out attachments to one's parents, produces a profound feeling of loss, a deep sorrow that is an important ingredient in the periodic ''blues'' afflicting teenagers so inexplicably. The inner vacuum may loom as large as outer space, until it is filled by solid new relationships away from the family. This takes time; in our particular culture, which grants its youth a great deal of leeway for experimentation, one may be well into the twenties before the establishment of satisfying peer relationships and the consolidation of identity can occur. It is comforting for an adolescent to have the real parents around during this period of subtle psychic shifts, to know that one *can* go home again to touch comfortable emotional bases. But when the youngster must re-mourn a mother or father *already* lost, the tendency to cling to an idealized image of the dead parent increases and the pain of letting go and growing up can be intolerable.

Such is the case with Dorothy Gale, who throughout *The Wizard of Oz* is desperately trying to come to terms with her orphanhood. Neither the film, nor the L. Frank Baum classic, explains how, when, or in what sequence her parents died. Permit me to speculate, on the basis of my analyses of a number of grown-up Dorothies, that her father died first—probably before her eighth year, thereby impelling her into an extraordinarily close relationship with her mother. When her mother passed away, Dorothy suffered an overwhelming spiritual wrenching. Every sign in *Wizard* points to enormous desolation over parental loss, more specifically over maternal loss, and terrible dread of its repetition.

It is a perverse paradox that the mother, giver of life, is unconsciously perceived at the very beginning of life as the destroyer of life. Insofar as we can fathom the mental activity of the very young child, it appears that the infantile mind splits the image of mother in twain. The Good Mother nourishes and cherishes, the Bad Mother abandons and devastates. This primitive doubling is often found in religion. The Hindus, for instance, believe the Mother-goddess Kali is the source of fertility as well as the harbinger of death and chaos.

In folklore and fairy tale, the Bad Mother is the witch who snares the children strayed from home, then enslaves or murders them. To the unconscious, which thrives on opposites, the Bad Mother kills either by abandonment or binding so close that one strangles in her clutches. (Often, the victim is devoured, the ultimate "closeness"!) The Good Mother is the bounteous fairy godmother, the lovely gossamer queen who makes everything copacetic with a wave of her wand.

Good and Bad Mother are, of course, *one and the same*. The child, given time, growth and understanding, comes to appreciate that Mom isn't abandoning because she cannot be around constantly to gratify every whim. But a host of natural shocks compromise the ability to integrate and reconcile the Good and Bad Mother-images within. Maternal death is the most severe of these: the mother who dies is blamed by the child; she is supremely bad for leaving the child so exposed and vulnerable. *Mutatis mutandis,* the child also believes that it was bad and drove mother away; kids are pathetically prepared to take the burden of death and divorce upon themselves: if I was bad, then if I am good, maybe it will be all right again. . . .

At the dawn of adolescence, the very time she should start to distance herself from Aunt Em and Uncle Henry, the surrogate parents who raised her on their Kansas farm, Dorothy Gale experiences a hurtful reawakening of her fear that these loved ones will be rudely ripped from her, especially her aunt (Em—M for Mother!). Dorothy is seriously hung up on her ambivalence towards Em: she wants Em to be the Good Mother, but frets that Em will turn Bad, die, go away forever. Dorothy's fear goes hand in hand with her rage—rage at the abandonment by her dead mother, displaced upon her equally guiltless aunt.

The voice of her conscience cries: *How can you be so wicked, so ungrateful? It wasn't mother's fault she had to go! Doesn't Em always do her best?* So, to keep her dead mother all good, all giving, and safe from her wrath, Dorothy takes the bad potential of the mothering figure and projects it wholesale into a fantasy of a malevolent persecutrix—a witch!—one can't have any trouble hating. But if this pseudo-resolution persists, it must only perpetuate her problem by reinforcing her ambivalence. For it is only when she can view Em and all the grown-ups in her life for who they really are, not as wizards *or* witches, that she will be able to join them as a mature adult herself.

The drama of Dorothy's search for her authentic, autonomous self is delightfully played out during her adventures in the Land of Oz.

The opening scenes of *Wizard* are shot in listless black-and-white, rendering the Kansas landscape absolutely prosaic. Dorothy and her little dog, Toto, come hurrying down the road:

> DOROTHY (*breathlessly*): She isn't coming yet, Toto—did she hurt you? . . . We'll go tell Uncle Henry and Aunty Em!

The farm is bustling: an old incubator has broken down, Em and Henry are laboring desperately to save some newly hatched chicks. Dorothy spills out her story: Toto got into Miss Gulch's garden, chased her cat, Miss Gulch hit him with a rake. Em is abstracted, can't be bothered with such foolishness. Dorothy wanders over to the pig-pen where three farmhands—Zeke, Hickory and Hunk—are bickering. They can't spare Dorothy more than off-handed advice. Hunk tells her to use her head—"*it's not made of straw*"—don't walk home near Miss Gulch's house, then Toto won't get the chance to bother her. Zeke tells Dorothy not to "let that old Gulch heifer bother ya—she ain't nothin' ta be afraid of—*have a little courage, that's all!*"

She balances precariously on the railing, falls into the pen and is almost trampled. Zeke pulls her out and collapses with fright at his own bravery. Out of patience, Em rousts the boys back to work, sternly chiding Dorothy to find a place where she won't get into more trouble. Crestfallen, Dorothy muses: "Do you suppose there is such a place, Toto? There must be . . . far, far away . . . behind the moon, beyond the rain . . ." and sings the famous "Over the Rainbow." (This lovely song was almost removed by studio pundits who thought audiences would find it unrealistic to have the heroine singing in a barnyard.)

Just as the first dream recalled in therapy often encapsulates a person's entire neurosis, just as the first words uttered by a patient coming through the office door often strikes the theme of an entire analytic session, the opening sequences of *Wizard* adroitly capture Dorothy's central preoccupation with whether the child within her will be cherished or abandoned, and whether the adult stirring within her can dare to leave the nest. Toto, her dog, becomes an extension of herself—perky, mischievous, nosing into things that don't concern him, forever *running away* when he should stay put. He has been bad, and that manifestly bad woman, Miss Gulch, may be coming to take him from the farm. The incubator is broken, the newborn chicks are threatened by the failure of their mechanical womb and Em and Henry are struggling to help them survive. Dorothy herself nearly perishes, and is rescued by an obviously weak, cowardly man. The characters are deftly sketched in: Aunt Em, harried, decisive; Uncle Henry, kind but vague; the three handymen, lovable bumblers all. The farm is a matriarchy, Em obviously rules the roost. Dorothy, rejected by Em and everyone, conjures up a place where happiness springs eternal and the dreams you dare to dream *do* come true. . . . One recalls the many myths of Utopias overflowing with lavish sustenance granted on nothing more substantial than a wish—the Big Rock Candy Mountain, or the German *Schlaraffenlandt,* where preroasted chickens obligingly walked themselves into your mouth.

Dorothy's fantasies are interrupted as Miss Gulch sweeps in on her bicycle with a court order for Toto, and proclaims that she'll take the whole farm if she doesn't get him. Dorothy's identification with the mutt is underscored: she offers to take Toto's place, and when Miss Gulch refuses, she cries—"You go away, or I'll bite you myself . . . *you wicked old witch!*" Em and Henry put up only token resistance, and Dorothy is forced to part with Toto. Henry is particularly ineffective, mumbling a few inarticulate words of small comfort. *After* Dorothy runs out sobbing, Emily dresses down Miss Gulch, the Good Mother contending with the Bad. Henry stands silent. In Dorothy's realm, as I have suggested, it would seem that power resides on the distaff side.

As Miss Gulch pedals away, the redoubtable Toto leaps out of the basket and scoots back to Dorothy's room. Without a moment's hesitation she packs her things and takes off. Ostensibly, she is worried that Gulch will return to claim her pound of pooch, but actually Toto's escape has given Dorothy the excuse she needed to spread her wings and quit the farm.

Just down the road, the runaways encounter an engaging old carny faker, toasting hot dogs near his wagon: PROFESSOR MARVEL— ACCLAIMED BY THE CROWNED HEADS OF EUROPE—LET HIM READ YOUR PAST, PRESENT AND FUTURE!!!'' The "Perfesser" easily reads her very obvious plight: "They don't understand you at home . . . they don't appreciate you . . . you want to see other lands—big cities, big mountains, big oceans!" He sits her down before his crystal ball—". . . the same genuine authentic crystal used by the priests of Isis and Osiris in the days of the Pharaohs of Egypt, in which Cleopatra first saw the approach of Julius Caesar and Mark Antony, and so on. . . ." While Dorothy has her eyes closed, Marvel rummages through her basket, comes up with a picture of Em, and describes a painful vision: "A woman . . . her face is careworn . . . she is crying . . . someone has just about broken her heart . . . someone she loves very much . . . someone she's taken care of in sickness . . . she's putting her hand down on her heart . . . she's dropping down on the bed. . . ."

Rather cruelly (or so I've always thought), Marvel addresses Dorothy's dread both of losing and hurting her aunt. Strangely enough, all too often the child will believe that the sheltering parent can be harmed if *it* grows up and goes away. The more intense the relationship between mother and child, the more the child is likely to be worried about the ill effects the rupture of the charmed partnership will have upon *both* parties. Dorothy is evidently only too willing to believe that her absence can kill Em, so she starts back down the road for home immediately after Marvel's "revelation." From our first glimpse of them, Dorothy and Toto have been ping-ponging back and forth between the safety of the farm and the mysterious, seductive world that lies outside the fence. . . .

Now Dorothy's fear of separation becomes a desperate reality. As she draws near the farm, a tornado twists evilly in the gray distance. The wind rises to an insane howl. Em, screaming hysterically for Dorothy, is dragged down into a storm cellar by the menfolk, and Dorothy is left utterly alone and unprotected. Calling after Em, she stumbles back into her room. A shutter flies loose and smacks her temple; she drops, unconscious upon the bed. Intriguingly, *she* has taken Em's place in Marvel's prophecy, suffering for having made Em suffer, paying for her "badness" by being brought to the brink of death, the ultimate separation.

The house rises dizzily into the twister's spout. Dorothy awakens, peers out the window and sees, whizzing merrily by, an old lady in a wheelchair (undigested memory of Em's "sickness"?), a cow, two gentlemen rowing a boat, and Miss Gulch, pedaling furiously. In the twinkling of an eye, Gulch metamorphoses into the witch of every child's darkest nightmare, and flies off on a jet-propelled broom, cackling hideously.

The house descends with a sickening jolt. Dorothy opens the door in the sudden stillness and, as a female choir sings wordlessly, she whispers—in what has to be one of the great understatements of cinema—"Toto, I have a feeling we're not in Kansas anymore!"—as she steps into a Technicolor Fairyland.

We are, and we aren't, for this is the landscape of the dream. Freud found that dreams take the characters and events of the preceding day—down to indifferent details—and weave them into a strange, meaningful tapestry. The characters of Kansas reality reappear in the dream Dorothy dreams, while she lies unconscious during the tornado, clad in the costume of her fantasies. Miss Gulch undergoes the first such transformation.

Glinda, Good Witch of the North, arrives in a giant soap bubble, resplendent in diaphanous gown, carrying the obligatory wand. Dorothy's farmhouse, she explains, has fallen on the Wicked Witch of the East, who held the little people of this fabulous country, the Munchkins, under her sway. Is Dorothy a Good Witch, or a Bad Witch? The nagging issue of Dorothy's goodness or badness is raised regarding her culpability in the Witch's demise—actually, it is her responsibility for hurting Em by running away that still plagues her conscience.

The Midget Munchkins pop up, applaud Dorothy as the national heroine, sweep aside her story that the Witch died accidentally (as on the farm, no one *ever* seems to listen to her!). The Munchkins make a big huff-and-puff about verifying the termination of their oppressor's rule; the Witch must be proven "morally, ethically, spiritually, physically, positively, absolutely, undeniably and reliably—*dead!*" Their obsession again reflects Dorothy's troubled conscience and her anxiety that the Bad Mother will be resurrected to punish her.

After the Munchkin coroner's verdict—"She's not only merely dead, she's really quite sincerely dead!"—the town breaks into wild rejoicing: "Ding, Dong, the Witch Is Dead!" The Munchkins are the little children held captive by the Bad Mother, a collective symbol for the child Dorothy, who by releasing them from bondage has unchained herself and become a Good Mother in the bargain. Munchkin babies dressed like fluffy chicks stir awake in a floral nest, recalling the nestlings Em labored so lovingly to rescue.

Just as the festivities have reached a pitch of manic glee, there is a burst of hellish smoke and flame, and *another* Witch materializes—the sister of the deceased and even *more* Wicked, if that's possible. She holds Dorothy accountable, and is about to take vengeance when Glinda reminds her of the ruby slippers, still upon her sister's feet that protrude grotesquely beneath the farmhouse. As the Witch goes for them, they are whisked in a trice onto Dorothy's feet. The Bad Mother has returned, but Dorothy has warded her off by acquiring her power! Temporarily foiled, the Witch vanishes sulfurously after an ominous warning: "I'll bide my time . . . my fine lady, it's true I can't attend to you here and now as I'd like, but just try to stay out of my way, just try . . . I'll get you, my pretty, and your little dog, too!"

Glinda tells Dorothy it might be better for her to clear out, the town isn't big enough for her and her new enemy. Dorothy wants to leave the territory, too—but how to get back home? The governance of Oz, like the Gale farm, has appeared matriarchal until now: Glinda directs Dorothy to follow the Yellow Brick Road that leads to a masculine source of supreme authority, the mysterious Wizard in the far-off Emerald City.

Glinda departs by bubble express, and Dorothy exclaims: "My, people come and go so quickly here!" No one more so than she! *Dorothy* can't stay put—wherever she is, there soon develops a compelling reason for being elsewhere. This restless rushing about catches the curious adolescent propensity for not getting pinned down too long in any single place, relationship or philosophical position, so that many different approaches to life can be kept open. It would seem that Dorothy is afraid of entrapment by the Witch; in fact, her anxiety over being caught and done in by a Bad Mother is the flip side of her *own* infantile dependency upon Em, her *own* desire to be fixed in place forever, a helpless, clinging and unproductive parasite.

As she proceeds along the Yellow Brick Road, Dorothy joins up with a Scarecrow, a Tin Man, and a Cowardly Lion. She is intuitively drawn to these unlikely fellow travelers: "You're the best friends anybody ever had . . . and it's funny, but I feel as if I've known you all the time. . . ." She has; they are the farmhands, Ozzified. Each appears to lack some crucial portion of his spiritual or physical anatomy: the Scarecrow—a brain; the Tin Man—a heart; the Lion—his courage. Alone, each is helpless. The Scarecrow on first meeting is literally hung up—on a pole. The Tin Man is rusted into immobility and the Lion so paralyzed by timorousness that the sheep he counts to fall asleep scare him awake. Joined with Dorothy into a tottering team, each functions better, but still imperfectly.

Virtually every male in Oz or Kansas is presented as weak and damaged in some fashion, while the women, for good or ill, are far more capable. Uncle Henry obviously defers to Em's judgments; the farmhands follow his lead. I would speculate that Dorothy's real father was perceived quite as ineffectual or—more likely—that the tragedy of his death is engraved upon her mind as a paradigm of masculine failure. (One sees this in real life cases regularly.)

Dorothy, like all teenagers, wonders if her abilities to cope with the world aren't somehow defective. In her half-formed state, neither adult nor child, it is easy for her to believe that she is not brainy, gutsy or sensitive enough to cut the mustard. An adolescent girl, embroiled with her mother in unprofitable squabbling dependency, will regularly turn to her father as a source of identification and strength, as well as other men, young and old, in her wider circle. I do not downgrade the role of other women in providing an "out" from the bind with mother, but the upsurge of sexuality during puberty reawakens the girl's earlier sexual feelings for her father, and creates a special urgency in her need for him or substitutes for him. (Note also that Dorothy *has* no other women with her on the farm to dilute the intensity of her relationship with Em.) There is no Dad for Dorothy, only poignant memories of him, and the surrogates who don't really fill the bill. So off she goes with her damaged friends to find the great Pa in the sky, to connect up with the Mighty Wizard and heal her sense of loss.

The Witch, determined to stop them, puts a field of poppies in their way and croons a cracked lullaby. Narcotic fumes overcome Dorothy, Toto and the Lion (who is throughout portrayed as the weakest and most childish of the company). Scarecrow and Tin Man call for help; Glinda waves her wand, and a bracing snow falls, awakening the victims. The Bad Mother has attempted to lull the children into fatal passivity—speaking of the perils of dependency, poppies are the source of opium!—while the Good Mother, Glinda, allows *her* children to go down the path towards fulfillment.

The entrance to the Emerald City is kept by an officious bureaucrat—a duplicate of Professor Marvel—who refuses to admit them, until he discovers that Dorothy is wearing the ruby slippers. "That's a horse of a different color!" he declares, and opens the gates. The Wizard's domain is executed in greenish art deco, a la Buck Rogers. A friendly cabby, another Marvel look-alike, drives them through the city as his horse goes through all the hues of the rainbow—for he's the horse of a different color! (Dreams frequently convert abstract ideas into visual puns.) At the Brush-Up Factory, the Scarecrow is newly stuffed, the Tin Man regalvanized, the Lion, Dorothy and Toto combed and curried in preparation for their audience with the Wizard.

Throughout these scenes the dwellers of the Emerald City speak a veddy upper-class British, with the exception of the cabbie, who has a mock-Cockney dialect. Living in the land of Oz is exceptionally "refeened," but it is dangerous to travel there. Let us remember that America in 1939 stood on the verge of a fateful re-entanglement with the affairs of foreign states. A strong suspicion of the stranger across the sea pervaded our country, and I do not doubt that *Oz* spoke very directly to our native isolationism and xenophobia. Dorothy's yearning to cease her wanderings would be echoed several years later by thousands of young men transplanted to equally unfamiliar shores!

At the Wizard's sanctum, the friends meet a Marvel-lous majordomo more contentious, if possible, than his fellow at the gate: "Orders are, nobody can see the great Oz, not nobody, not nohow!" But Dorothy melts his heart: "Professor Marvel said she was sick, she may be dying, and it's all my fault . . . I'll never forgive myself, never, never, never!'' The majordomo dissolves into tears—he, too, had an Aunt Em. He ushers them down a long tunnel into a vaulted chamber that always reminded me of my first glimpse of Radio City Music Hall at age five. Amidst the crash and roar of baleful music, spurts of green smoke, an enormous fanged face suspended in midair addresses the suppliants in stentorian tones. The Wizard's features are Transylvanian, his rhetoric Agnewesque, but the voice is unmistakably that of the ''Perfesser'':

> MARVEL (*to Tinman*): You dare to come to me for a heart, do you, you clinking, clattering collection of collaginous junk!!! (*to Scarecrow*) And you, Scarecrow . . . you have the effrontery to ask for a brain, you billowing bale of bulky fodder!!!

The Lion faints dead out. Dorothy rebukes the Wizard (note that she always rises to the occasion, despite her fears), and the ''great and powerful Oz'' silences her peremptorily; he will grant every wish when Dorothy's team brings him the Witch's broomstick. He thus proposes a stringent test of the very qualities they believe they lack, especially ingenuity and courage.

A Freudian somewhat more high church than myself would tag the broomstick and the ruby slippers as—what else?—phallic symbols. From the more traditional analytic viewpoint, Dorothy would blame her sense of imcompleteness upon an imaginary lost penis. And for those who still would have it that love conquers but Oedipus wrecks, Dorothy's quest for the phallic broomstick at another level could classically be interpreted as indicative of a long repressed wish to take father away from mother. The Witch thus becomes the maternal rival of the Electra complex, retaliating because of Dorothy's ambitions to oust her and take her place as father's lover. Em and Henry are the logical replacements for her dead parents in Dorothy's Electra configuration. (In Greek mythology, Electra urged the murder of her mother, Clytemnestra, upon her brother Orestes, in revenge for Clytemnestra's complicity in the death of her husband, Agamemnon).

I do not categorically deny that these elements exist in Dorothy's psychodynamics—it is a keystone of our philosophy that motivation and behavior rarely admit of simply one cause—but, as I've suggested, Dorothy's search for a strong, competent male ''rescuer'' seems to stem most pointedly from the pressure to divest herself of her pathological dependency upon Em-Mother, rather than to compete with Em for Henry. Fewer women than Freud imagined actually have fantasies of wanting a penis, but all women—as their male counterparts—seek realized independent selves.

Cut to the haunted forest near the Witch's castle. Dorothy and company are assaulted by a squadron of flying monkeys, their bluish features fixed in mirthless death's-head grins. They swoop down, snatch up Dorothy and Toto and bring them to the Witch's lair, leaving the three helpers temporarily *hors de combat*. With Dorothy finally on her own turf, the Witch threatens to drown Toto if Dorothy doesn't come across with the goods. But when the Witch tries to take off the ruby slippers, they zap her with magical voltage. Just as he escaped Miss Gulch, Toto leaps out of his basket and scoots out of the castle. Exasperated, the Witch turns over an hourglass filled with blood-red sand to count out her captive's last precious minutes, and stalks away. At the edge of the precipice, Dorothy calls for her dearest protector:

DOROTHY: I'm frightened, Aunty Em, I'm frightened!
EM (*by some arcane TV, she's on the Witch's crystal*): Dorothy . . . where are you? Please, it's Aunt Em, we're trying to find you. . . .
DOROTHY: I'm here in Oz, Aunty Em—I'm locked up in the Witch's castle . . . and I'm trying to get home to you. Oh, Aunty Em, don't go away . . . I'm frightened, come back!!!

Em's face, filled with concern, blurs into the Witch's—her voice wheedling, then viciously mocking: "Come back, Aunty Em, come back . . . I'll give you Aunty Em, my pretty, ah ha ha ha ha hah hah!!!"

The Witch's contorted features fill the screen and wink out. Dorothy recoils in terror—as did I and my friends as kids. See how intimately bound together is the Good Mother and the Bad: for a brief, nightmarish instant Em and the Witch have fused identities. This scene, I have found, is peculiarly troubling to most children, no doubt because it captures so effectively our archaic terror of the mother's destructive potential.

Toto, meanwhile, has found the three companions and leads them to the castle. They overcome the sentries, don their uniforms and smuggle themselves inside. Just as the hourglass runs out, they break into Dorothy's cell and liberate her. An alarm is sounded and after a mad pursuit by the Witch's minions, they are hemmed in on all sides, at the Witch's mercy:

> WITCH: The last to go will see the first three go before her—and her little dog, too! How about a little fire, Scarecrow?

She takes up a torch and sets the Scarecrow alight. Throughout the film, he is the only traveler who actually suffers harm to his person. The Witch previously tried to incinerate him when he first met Dorothy, and her flying monkeys literally *destrawed* him, distributing him wholesale over the landscape. By virtue of his flimsy construction, he is the most vulnerable to total annihilation; our deepest fears of death center around this awful sundering of the self by a titanic, overwhelming force, symbolic of the catastrophic power of the Bad Mother.

Dorothy flings a pail of water over Scarecrow. The Witch is drenched too, and, shrieking piteously, she dwindles away to nothing. (Note that, like her sister, she is eliminated by Dorothy "accidentally"—disavowing any malevolent intent on Dorothy's part.) The Witch joins a long succession of horror and science fiction ghoulies whose seemingly invincible destructiveness is counteracted by some absurdly simple remedy, easily at hand. The Martians in *The War of the Worlds* are destroyed by ordinary bacteria; the animated shrubbery in *Day of the Triffids* dissolve in saltwater. We can always end our nightmares just as easily, by waking up and hauling ourselves out of harm's way. In *Wizard, aqua vitae* does the trick, plain water, Adam's ale, a primal symbol of rescue and rebirth. Once more, Dorothy has unintentionally committed an ambiguous murder of a Bad Mother and, in the bargain, become a kind of Good Mother herself. The Witch's henchmen, like the Munchkins, now worship her as their Bolivar, and present her with the defunct tyrant's broom. Dorothy has, in fact, freed *herself,* but must still be enlightened as to the true meaning of her liberation.

When she returns to the Emerald City, the Wizard balks at seeing her, indulges in windy rhetoric, and is then unmasked when Toto pulls aside a curtain to reveal a very ordinary mortal, an exact replica of Professor Marvel, undisguised for the first time in Oz, frantically manipulating Frankensteinish dials and levers:

> WIZARD: Pay no attention to that man behind the curtain . . . the
> . . . er . . . Great Oz has spoken . . . er. . . .

With a gasp, they realize that Oz is a humbug, an outrageous fraud!

> DOROTHY: You're a very *bad* man!
> WIZARD: Oh, no, my dear, I'm a very good man. I'm just a very *bad* wizard. . . .

Dorothy's unconscious saw through Marvel's carny flummery back in Kansas, but consciously, she needed to have him on a pedestal. In her dream, immediately after the Witch's demise the Wizard is cut down to size. Her God has feet of clay, he turns out to be just another "failed" parent—but what his magic lacks he makes up for with plain old jay-hawk horse sense. He addresses the friends in turn, wittily healing each's "defect." To the Scarecrow, he says there's nothing special about a brain; where he hails from, there are universities "where men go to become great thinkers, and when they come out they think deep thoughts—and with no more brains than you have!" But they *do* have diplomas, so he awards Scarecrow a "Th.D."— Doctor of Thinkology, whereupon the Strawman promptly spouts a pythagorean theorem!

The Lion, explains the Wizard, is merely a victim of disorganized thinking. He confuses courage with wisdom—inferring that it's OK to be afraid, how you handle your quaking is what counts: "Back where I come from, we have men we call heroes. Once a year they take their fortitude out of mothballs and parade it down the main street . . . and they have no more courage than you have!" But they *do* have medals, so Lion receives the Triple Cross "for conspicuous bravery against Wicked Witches," to remind him of what he performed to save his loved ones under fire, despite his timid soul.

The Wizard can't imagine why Tin Man wants a heart—"Hearts will never be practical until they can be made unbreakable . . . back where I come from there are men who do nothing all day but good

deeds . . . they are called phil . . . philo . . . er, good deed-doers
. . . and their hearts are no bigger than yours!'' But they *do* have testimonials, so the Wizard gives Tin Man a heart-shaped watch with a
loud tick, gently admonishing him that ''a heart is not judged by how
much you love—but by how much you are loved by others. . . .''

The Wizard's wisdom is as therapeutic as any dispensed from behind the couch: you have always had what you thought you lacked,
and have already proven it. Do not delude yourself by seeking an impossible standard, but look within to find your own strength, sensitivity and sagacity. Medals, diplomas, testimonials, are only superficial
rewards, the world's imprecise recognition of qualities best appreciated by yourself and those who love you. If you are open to love, purpose and meaning will unfold in good time. Ripeness is all.

But what of Dorothy? The Wizard has already figuratively brought
her home to herself, for his homely advice to her alter egos has shown
that she has heart, pluck and wit enough to make a successful voyage
through life. It only remains to transport her literally. He reveals his
identity: a circus balloonist whose vehicle was snatched by the winds
and carried to the Emerald City years ago where he was instantly
acclaimed ''Wizard deluxe.'' Throughout his reign, he has kept the
balloon ''against the advent of a quick getaway,'' and with it he and
Dorothy will return safely to Kansas.

Cut to the balloon, prepared for flight. The Wizard, Dorothy and
Toto in the gondola. The Wizard addresses the cheering crowd, nominates Scarecrow to take his place as ruler of Oz, to be assisted by Tin
Man and Lion (the voice of reason rules, one notes), Then Toto, perennial runaway, jumps out of Dorothy's arms to chase a cat. Dorothy
goes after him, but the Wizard can't control his vehicle and it floats
away, leaving Dorothy stranded, apparently no better off than before.
The dream thus repeats the loss of her father when his strength is most
needed, and also emphasizes that the Wizard, his prestige punctured,
is only human. The Wizard-father's removal puts her squarely back in
the hands of the mother (reduplicating, as I have theorized, the original sequence of loss), but it is the Good Mother who now puts in a
final appearance:

> GLINDA: You don't need to be helped any longer—you've always
> had the power to go back to Kansas. . . .

SCARECROW: Then why didn't you tell her before?
GLINDA: *Because she wouldn't have believed me . . . she had to learn it for herself. . . .*

Hesitantly, like a patient groping towards insight, Dorothy describes what she had learned during her dream of Oz:

DOROTHY: . . . it wasn't enough just to see Uncle Henry and Aunty Em . . . and it's that if I ever go looking for my heart's desire again, I won't look any further than my own backyard, because if it isn't there, I never really lost it to begin with. . . .
SCARECROW: But that's so easy . . . I should have thought of it for you.

No, Glinda repeats, *she had to find it out for herself*—and not by an act of sheer intellect. As in analysis, the head must be connected to the heart.

Dorothy exchanges tearful farewells, says she will miss Scarecrow most of all. She clicks the slippers together three times, murmuring—"There's no place like home," and awakens in black-and-white Kansas reality, back in her bedroom, surrounded by Em, Henry, the farmhands and Professor Marvel. The sands that ran out in the castle pictured the imminence of actual death:

HENRY (*to Marvel*): She got quite a bump on the head . . . we kind of thought there for a minute she was going to leave us.
DOROTHY: But I did leave you . . . I was gone for days and days. . . . It wasn't a dream . . . you were there, but you couldn't have been, could you? . . . I remember that some of it wasn't very nice . . . but most of it was beautiful . . . but anyway, Toto, we're home . . . home . . . and this is my room, and you're all here . . . and I'm not going to leave here ever, ever again . . . because I love you all, and, oh, Aunty Em . . . there's *no* place like home!

In these final scenes, Dorothy's account of what she learned in Oz may sound a trifle pat and sentimental: daydreams are fine, but are ultimately no substitute for the familiar. There is, however, a deeper truth here, couched with deceptive simplicity, the truth of Glinda and the Wizard. To paraphrase T. S. Eliot, our beginnings inform our endings. If we do not understand who we are, from where we have come, who we have identified with along the way and why, we will never know what we may be. Dorothy—like all adolescents—has looked to surrender *her* power to some mighty power outside herself that will relieve her of the responsibility of forging her own identity. In so doing, she risks being swallowed up by her own passivity and dependency. But at the conclusion of *Oz* she relinquishes her Wizard, lets him float back over the rainbow, and returns under her own steam to the people within the perimeter of her unfolding who can help her actualize a considerable potential.

Dorothy, I would stress, is no more "neurotic" than anyone else in her circumstances. She is a lost child, driven too close to her aunt by an overwhelming early tragedy. That very closeness has grown into a formidable obstacle to her emotional growth. By consolidating her relationships with the rest of the Gale household, she will surely loosen the tie to Em, will gradually turn her affection from her small world to the people in the wider world outside her doorstep, a world that has seemed until now as scary and enchanting as Oz. One notes that Dorothy has a special place in her heart for Hunk, the Scarecrow in Oz. He is the kind of man a grown-up Dorothy is often drawn to. Her down-to-earth uncomplicated approach to things nicely complements his somewhat abstracted "braininess."

Like *Finnegan's Wake, The Wizard of Oz* comes full-circle to begin again. What has passed is yet to come. Dorothy is, in fact, barely out of her childhood, so it is absolutely appropriate for her to want to go home in order to travel away again, secure from fear. If we take the entire film as one extended fantasy, the tornado that whirls her, Gale-force, to Oz, is emblematic of her adolescent *rite de passage,* of the death of her child self and the rebirth of a newer, lovelier Dorothy. The Yellow Brick Road, from this perspective, points the way down the rest of her days, into a future brimming with promise.

Epilogue

Today *The Wizard of Oz* seems as fresh and alive as ever, an incomparable blend of cinematic crafts—the fabulous *mise-en-scène* created by the wizards—mostly unknown and unsung—of the MGM production staff, the lyrics and music of E. Y. "Yip" Harburg and Harold

Arlen, and a brilliant adaptation of L. Frank Baum's classic by Noel Langley, Florence Ryerson and E. A. Woolf. Victor Fleming directed a miraculous ensemble of thespians, each of whom created a role now uniquely identified with the player: Ray Bolger's wildly flexible Scarecrow; Bert Lahr's Lion—half beast, half Canarsie; Jack Haley's Tin Man with a Hahvahd Yahd accent; Billie Burke's pixillated Glinda; Frank Morgan's genial Wizard. (W. C. Fields declined the role—not enough money for him, which was all to the good. Fields had the requisite patina of fraudulence—enough for three Wizards!—but his innate hatred of children would have cast a pall over the part.) Margaret Hamilton, the prototypical Wicked Witch, is actually the kindest lady imaginable. A former kindergarten teacher, she's helped develop a radio network for hospitalized veterans, organized storytelling groups at the Los Angeles Children's Hospital and still acts today.

Then there was Judy—Judy Garland, catapulted over the rainbow into instant stardom. She was sixteen when *Wizard* was made. Her breasts were bound to make her look younger. Originally the moguls wanted Shirley Temple. When that dream didn't come true, Garland was transformed into an absurd double, with bobbed nose, capped teeth and a blonde fright wig. Somebody saw the light after early rushes, and let Judy play Dorothy according to her own instincts, which were never truer. She had a strong affinity for the part, and her life gives us some of the reasons. Her own father had died just a few years earlier. The loss profoundly affected her. Dorothy's bond with Em was only a pale shadow of Garland's tormented relationship with an aggressive stage-door mother she both deeply needed and resented. Later, she was to write: "Mother was the worst . . . the real life Wicked Witch of the West . . . sometimes it seems I've been in bondage since I was a fetus . . . I became a thing instead of a person."

Studio honchos took up where mother left off. They lifted her from the obscurity of a nickle-and-dime vaudevillian, made her the darling of millions, but every move was dictated for her in advance. As she grew up she fought desperately and self-destructively to be free, free of mother, the moguls, the doubts and fears that assailed her about her viability as person and performer. Still she sang on, through recurrent cycles of artistic, romantic, and financial disasters and triumphant comebacks. At age forty-five, she cried: "Finally I am loved! This is it! For the first time in my whole life I'm happy, really happy!" Three months later, she was dead of an accidental overdose. She sought her Wizard through five marriages, in the waves of adulation that washed over the footlights, and we shall never know if she found him.

Bibliography

Quotations from Judy Garland and Mickey Rooney are from *Screen Greats Series #9*. Barven Publications, 1972. See pp. 20, 57.

MORELLA, J., and EPSTEIN, E. *Judy, The Films and Career of Judy Garland*. New York: Citadel Press, 1970.

ROHAUER, R. *A Tribute to Mervyn LeRoy*. Gallery of Modern Art, 1967.

THOMAS, L. B. et al. *The MGM Years*. New York: Columbia House, 1972.

"A Wonderful Witch of Oz," interview with Margaret Hamilton. *Focus on Film #3* (May-August, 1970). See pp. 40–52.

III

The Treasure of the Sierra Madre —There's Success Phobia in Them Thar Hills!

> I reckon if earth was worth as much as gold,
> men would kill each other for a handful of dirt. . . .
>
> Gary Cooper, in the film *Garden of Evil*

A college senior, refused entrance to medical school, shoots himself. An executive, passed over for promotion, plunges into acute alcoholism. After her fiance deserts her, an attractive young woman imagines that people in the street are whispering that she is a prostitute, unfit for marriage. These tragedies are, after all, quite explicable—the victim's life has been rendered empty and devoid of purpose by the failure to achieve some intensely desired ambition.

It is less generally known that *achievement itself* can be as potent a precipitant of psychic upheaval as failure! In an essay entitled *Some Character Types Met with in Psychoanalytic Work,* Freud described individuals "wrecked by success"—whose neurosis broke out directly *after* some long sought goal had been reached. He argued that success in these cases might be unconsciously equated with the gratification of forbidden Oedipal wishes: thus, an apparently innocuous personal advancement for the adult would symbolically represent the child's murderous triumph over the same-sexed parent, to possess the parent of the opposite sex. Freud postulated that the accession to prestige and power for those wrecked by success was accompanied by intolerable remorse and anxiety, as if they had committed the Primal Crime of incest-murder. Although Freud never mentioned it, Oedipus himself can be considered as the archetypical "success neurotic"; ignorant of his past, he fulfills the Oedipal fantasy of every child, slays his father, beds his mother, then brings on his ruin at the highest pinnacle of fame by relentlessly forcing the exposure of his unwitting culpability.

In my own practice I have often found success problems originating even earlier in childhood than the Oedipal period (dated at about age four); in these cases, success unconsciously portends the rupture of the life sustaining tie that has bound the child to an overprotective mother. The neurotic adult then feels that his advancement has promoted him out of his depth, leading to overwhelming feelings of helplessness and vulnerability at having to face the harsh world unprotected.

Freud thought that "success neurosis" * was a relatively rare phenomenon, but the impression of most clinicians today is that it occurs far more commonly than he ever imagined. I think we all potentially have a bit of success anxiety, whether we choose to recognize it or not. In psychoanalytic practice one encounters a rather amazing number of symptoms and inhibitions at least partly related to fear of succeeding—curiously including the fear of *failing* that frequently masks success phobia!

Several of Freud's cases lived only on the printed page: they were characters from literature. He cited Shakespeare's Lady Macbeth and Rebecca West, the heroine of Ibsen's *Rosmersholm,* as typical victims of success. To these, I will now add Fred C. Dobbs, as played by Humphrey Bogart, the grimy protagonist of John Huston's classic film *The Treasure of the Sierra Madre.*

Treasure is much more than a clinical vignette of a diseased personality driven mad by gold. It is, by turns, the story of a young man's

---

* The victim may develop a full-fledged psychosis rather than a neurosis if the underlying personality is sufficiently disturbed.

coming of age, of an aging man's search for his last resting place. It is a rousing adventure tale, a subtle commentary on the capitalist mentality, and a document of cultural collision more vivid than most anthropology texts. But I am always drawn back to Dobbs himself, to this mean spirited, vicious, yet strangely sympathetic figure. . . .

It is 1920; the place—Tampico, a Mexican boomtown on the edge of newly discovered oilfields. Fortunes are daily made and lost; the native population has been overmatched by a motley crowd of drifters, grifters, ex-soldiers and soldiers of fortune, products and rejects of the American dream. A caste system as rigid as the Raj's decrees that a white man without suitable work must starve, and starve with dignity, for if he shines shoes or peddles lemonade, no fellow *gringo* will hire him, and the "natives" will hound him to his grave.

The film opens on the hero's hands, tearing up a lottery ticket. The camera pulls back, revealing Dobbs' unshaven, wolfish countenance. He has lost again, surely the latest in a long chain of defeats. He stares at a half-smoked butt smoldering in the street, wrestling indecisively with his pride. A street urchin spies it, and without a second thought grabs it up. Disgruntled, Dobbs decides to panhandle an affluent American in white (John Huston), and treats himself with the proceeds to coffee and cigarettes at a dingy outdoor cafe. Through the medium of Dobbs' bumhood, one is made subliminally aware of Tampico's alien, inimical milieu: the constant blare of a *mariachi* band, the soft insistence of an unfamiliar tongue, tropical heat and filthy streets.

A boy tries to sell Dobbs another lottery ticket; in a burst of rage Dobbs flings a glass of water in his face—"Get away from me, ya little beggar!" Actually, Dobbs is the beggar, the lad has a job! The vendor persists, and Dobbs is persuaded to buy a one-twentieth share: the numbers on the ticket add up to thirteen—a sure winner! . . . Dobbs is clearly down and out, a man who has lost control over his life, yet still a bitter wooer of fate, a great believer in cracked omens.

Dobbs grouses in the park with a young American, Curtin (Tim Holt) about deteriorating local economics, then puts the bite on the man in the white suit again. This time, he treats himself to a haircut and shave. The barber invites him to inspect his handiwork with a florid wave; Dobbs regards his seedy, slicked up reflection in the mirror with absurd appreciation. It is one of those instants that tells more about a man's character than an entire battery of psychological tests.

Outside, he approaches White Suit again, but this time is roundly
rebuked:

> WHITE SUIT: Such impudence never came my way—early this after-
> noon I gave you money, while I was having my shoes polished I
> gave you more money, now you put the bite on me again!
> DOBBS (*obsequiously*): I never knowed it was you . . . I never
> looked at your face, I just looked at your hands and the money you
> gave me.
> WHITE SUIT (*handing him a peso*): This is the very last you get from
> me. Just to make sure . . . here's another peso. But from now on,
> you have to make your way through life without my assistance!

Dobbs cuts no pitiable character here and White Suit is not as arrogant as many a complacent philanthropist in his shoes. He addresses
Dobbs' parasitism: despite his quirky pride, it is much easier for him
to beg than he is willing to admit. He conveys a subtle conviction that
he has every right to what he receives—and more.

Dobbs is not troubled overmuch by White Suit's admonition. His
next mark, Pat MacCormack, is an entrepreneur who fast-talks him
into signing on with an oil-rigging outfit; Pat's line tempts Dobbs as
much as the lottery boy's. He joins a group of haggard men at the
ferry, meeting up again with Curtin, the young American from the
square. After several months of backbreaking labor the two return to
Tampico, and are left high and dry at the bar where Pat was supposed
to pay them off.

They spend their last centavos on a night's lodging at a dismal
flophouse, filled with other disinherited Yanks who gather around a
grizzled old prospector, Howard (Walter Huston). In contrast to the
gloomy demeanor of the listeners, Howard is brisk and lighthearted.
He's evidently gone everywhere the hunger for buried treasure could
take a man, has witnessed much evil and more suffering along the
way, without ever losing his good humor, shrewdness or enthusiasm.
He holds the played-out Americans enthralled—especially Dobbs:

> HOWARD: Gold in Mexico? Why, sure there is—not ten days from
> here, there's a mountain waiting for the right guy to discover a
> treasure! . . . I tell you, if you was to make a real strike, you
> couldn't be dragged away . . . not even the threat of miserable

death'd keep you tryin' to add ten thousand more. . . . I know what gold does to men's souls . . . ah, long as there's no find, the noble brotherhood will last, but when the piles of gold begin to grow, that's when the trouble starts!

Several days later, Dobbs and Curtin lounge in the park and turn over the old man's words. Dobbs says gold can be a blessing as well as a curse—it certainly wouldn't change *him* for the worse! Then they spot Pat MacCormack strolling out of a hotel, dressed to the nines with a lovely señorita on his arm. He invites them smoothly into the bar where he bilked them, and at the first opportunity flings whiskey in their eyes, but is beaten senseless in a brutal brawl. Dobbs extracts what they are owed from Pat's well-stuffed wallet and flings the rest contemptuously over his body. Flushed with victory, he proposes to Curtin that they go prospecting: "This is the country where the nuggets of gold are just cryin' for you to take 'em out of the ground, make 'em shine in coins, on the fingers and neck o' swell dames!" (Though he has little education and less sensitivity, there is a rough poetry in Dobbs; odd turns of his expression stick persistently in the mind.) His voice takes on a religious fervor: he is utterly blind to the gold fever already raging within. His friendship for Curtin has a spurious ring, founded insecurely on shared tribulation, the recovery of the swindled pay, and the defeat of their common enemy.

Dobbs fantasizes maximum reward for minimum effort: Curtin observes they know nothing about prospecting, so they decide to go to Howard for help. Dobbs is skeptical about taking him along—"He's too old, we'd have to pack him on our backs!" Howard has been waiting for just such an opportunity to wager his savings on one last gamble. But, even with his contribution, they are still short of funds. Dobbs is instantly depressed, then as quickly elated when the lottery boy appears to inform him he holds a winning ticket with a 200-peso prize. Dobbs flings his winnings into the pot:

DOBBS (*to Curtin*): If we make a find, we'll be lightin' our cigars with hundred dollar bills; if we don't, the difference between what you put up and what I put up ain't enough to keep me bein' right back where I was this afternoon, polishin' a bench with the seat o' my pants. Put 'er there, partner!

Framed by their handshake, Howard eyes them knowingly; he has seen it all before, the vows of undying comradeship, the empty joviality. He reads Dobbs to the core, but keeps his counsel. . . .

Cut to the third-class compartment of a train rattling into the interior. Howard explains over a map that they must stay far off the beaten track—he alludes to the dangers they may face, but his companions treat their expedition like a schoolboy outing. The train lurches to a halt, and a horde of desperadoes swoop down; the Americans take guns out of their packs: henceforth they will never willingly part with weapons. Dobbs trades fire with the bandit *El Jefe* (Alfonso Bedoya), a disreputable rascal sporting a gold hat and flashing gold teeth. *El Jefe* will be Dobbs' nemesis: he cuts both a frightening and ludicrous figure, the very personification of indifferent evil, the dark side of the golden promise.

The bandits are driven off; a conductor, passing through the car, says nonchalantly: "Big boulder on the track so train stop . . . bandits get big surprise because soldiers on the train waiting for them— not many passengers get killed. . . ." His offhanded attitude serves notice that they have penetrated into territory where the value of life is negligible.

They arrive at the sleepy town of Durango; Howard picks supplies and mules with a practiced eye, steps cheerily into the wilderness, his callow companions in tow. Huston made the actors push their lines here, so that an air of exhilaration pervades these scenes. Days later, the old man is still going at a jaunty clip, but the excitement of the others has waned considerably:

> CURTIN: If I'd known what prospecting meant . . . I'd've stayed in Tampico and waited for another job to turn up. . . .

Dobbs stumbles on gold-streaked rocks—"a mother-lode!," he cries, as he sprinkles water eagerly about. Howard examines the "find" with jaundiced eye: "Pyrites . . . fool's gold . . . next time you fellows strike it rich, holler for me before you start splashin' water around—water is precious . . . sometimes it can be more precious than gold!" He gives a crusty wink, and they are off again, through howling windstorm, drenching rain and steaming jungle. Steadily the old sourdough plows on, bristling with vivacity, supremely knowledgeable and apparently tireless. In the evening, irritatingly fresh as a daisy, he dines with relish on the meanest of fare, while the younger men collapse, too exhausted to eat:

> HOWARD: Hey, fellers, want some beans? Goin' through some mighty rough country tomorrow—*you better have some beans! Mighty good beans!!!*

Howard could be an ancient Taoist sage, flexible, infinitely adaptable, conforming to the vessel of his environment like water. His pliancy is counterpoised against Dobbs' driven insensibility to nature and his fellow man. The mercurial Dobbs is at the mercy of every whim of circumstance, oscillating, as we have seen, between wild elation and childish despair. Whatever his conscious aspirations, one discerns in the man an invincible pull towards failure. Next morning, he says he's ready to "give up . . . leave the outfit . . . everything, behind . . . go back." Howard looks up from some soil he's sifting:

> HOWARD (*mocking*): What's that you say, go back—well, tell my old grandmother! My, my, my—what great prospectors! Two shoe-clerks reading the magazine about prospectin' for gold in the land of the midnight sun, south of the border and west of the Rockies! . . . Let me tell you something, my two fine fellows, you're so dumb, there's nothin' to compare ya with, you're dumber than the dumbest jackasses. (*He breaks into an uproarious little jig.*) *You're so dumb ya don't even see the riches you're treadin' on with your own feet!!!*

Dobbs and Curtin had thought him mad; now all their fatigue and pessimism drain away. But their toil in the finding of the treasure is nothing compared with the labor to come. As Howard points to the face of the mountain, the camera follows his hand in a long panning shot: "Here ain't the place . . . it comes from some place further up . . . up there . . . *up there!*" Brave music heralds the ascent to the prize, and peril, waiting above.

Cut to Howard, panning by a stream. His partners are amazed that gold in its natural state looks like common sand—and would be worth as much, one infers, were it not for the lunatic cupidity that sets such value on it. Huston will make much of this ambiguity by emphasizing the gold's gritty quality throughout the film.

The men build a rough-hewn mine and sluiceway, and the earnings mount up. One fateful evening, while the day's find is about to be weighed, Dobbs somberly asks: "When are we gonna start dividin' it up?" Curtin doesn't get the point, Howard does: being responsible for Dobbs' goods is no pleasure, even though he believes he himself is the most trustworthy; older and slower, he's less likely to run with the bindle. Dobbs takes instant offense: "Only a guy who's a thief at heart would think *me* likely to do a thing like that!"

> HOWARD: After we save a couple hundred ounces, it'll be a nuisance carryin' little bags hangin' from our necks, and each of us will have to hide his share of the treasure from the other two (*chuckles*) and having done so will be forever on the watch that his hiding place is not discovered.
> DOBBS (*even angrier*): What a dirty filthy mind you've got!

One perceives the early stirrings of Dobbs' success anxiety, and his paranoia. While the exact cause of paranoid disorders is still not fully understood, the clinician is struck regularly by the paranoid's preoccupation with the uses and abuses of power. Perhaps because they have suffered so frequently from the most devastating criticism in childhood, paranoids are exquisitely sensitized to the potential for exploitation and humiliation in human affairs—and, intriguingly, are usually themselves exceptionally manipulative and minimizing. The paranoid reduces the complexity of relationships down to a single issue—who is powerful, and who powerless. Equality and mutual concern are out of the question; intimacy and trust are frightening, because they open the way for greater abuse when one's guard is down. Far better to rely on the rankling certainty of ill-treatment, and prepare requisite countermeasures in advance.

Freud theorized that paranoids were homosexuals at heart, that their secret homosexual wishes were particularly laden with revulsion and fear. Hence, the desired object of the same sex is converted into a persecutor: "I, a man, cannot possibly *love* him, I *hate* him, because *he* hates and attacks me!" These speculations are disputed today, but most therapists accept Freud's premise that the fundamental psychic defense mechanism in paranoia is *projection:* one's own unacceptable impulses are broadcast into the outside world, fastened onto some other person or agency, who is then designated as the villain.

Thus it is *Dobbs* who is a thief at heart, *Dobbs* who has a dirty, filthy mind. He is a mediocrity, well aware, if unconsciously, of his incompetence, obsessed with his impotence, ridden with testy pride. When a little wealth comes his way, he wants more, wants all of it, in fact, with his partners under his thumb and ultimately out of the way. In true paranoid fashion, these murderous intentions are projected upon Curtin and Howard. *They* want to do him in and steal his treasure, not vice versa. (Freud said that in every paranoid delusion there is a germ of truth; no doubt, in some dark corner of their souls, Dobbs' partners lust after their neighbor's "goods," but their sinister thoughts will not father evil deeds.)

Consider that Dobbs has been daily painfully reminded of Howard's expertise, and his own ineptitude. Has the old man taken the place of the original Old Man—the cruel father who perhaps downgraded and competed with Dobbs as a child? Dobbs functioned with his insane competitiveness in check, as long as he was on the bum, leading a marginal existence and contending with actual oppressors like Pat MacCormack. But the acquisition of wealth, presaging the achievement of *real* power over others, destroys Dobbs' tenuous adjustment. As his treasure increases, so does the jealousy of imaginary persecutors, waiting to wreak bloody vengeance upon him. Howard cannily observes the mad glow of greed in Dobbs' eyes as the gold is shared out. Like Tiresias, he has foreseen all, yet no more than the blind prophet can he halt the march of awful consequence.

Months of toil pass in swift montage. Dobbs is nearly killed by a cave-in. Curtin hesitates outside the mine, wrestles with his conscience, then rushes in. Dobbs declares: "I owe my life to you, partner!" But his gratitude is short-lived. One evening, the partners fall to meditating on the uses of their hard-won riches. Howard thinks of setting up a small business, enjoying a peaceable old age far from the heartbreak of prospecting. Curtin—more sensitive than we would have thought—dreams of his days as a fruit-picker, when he drank and sang with fellow workers in the mellow evenings; he imagines owning his orchard. . . . "It must be grand, watchin' your own trees put on leaves, come into blossom . . . watchin' the fruit get big and ripe on the boughs. . . .'' Dobbs' fantasies are narrow as his soul—a hot bath, fancy duds, a willing woman, a lavish meal in "a swell cafe . . . order everything on the bill of fare, and if it ain't just right—or mebbe even if it is—I'm goin' to bawl the waiter out and make him take everything back!'' The shoe's on the other foot, for once he will be the victimizer, not the victim.

Howard wants to put a limit on their earnings; Dobbs objects violently.

> CURTIN: There's no use making hogs of ourselves. . . .
> DOBBS: Hog, am I? . . . I'd be in my rights if I demanded half again as much as you get . . . there's no denyin' I put up the lion's share of the cash, is there?

Curtin has touched a raw nerve, Dobbs becomes all the more defensive for having his rapacity revealed. Disgusted, Curtin offers to repay him, with interest. Caught in a web of his own spinning, Dobbs backs down, trying to maintain the fiction of his fairmindedness. But his festering suspicion has infected them. True to Howard's prophecy, that night they cannot sleep for the checking and rechecking of their caches against each other's fantasied depredations.

Next morning, Dobbs' paranoia is in ghastly bloom; he refuses to go to the village for provisions, convinced that the others have conspired to rob him while away. He draws his gun on Curtin when the latter unwittingly traps a Gila monster in the crevice where Dobbs has hidden his goods. Curtin dares Dobbs to put his hand under the rock. With Howard looking on, Dobbs moves his hand tentatively, but lacking the courage of his screwball convictions, hastily withdraws it. Curtin uncovers and destroys the venomous reptile, but he has also publicly exposed Dobbs' craziness and cowardice, a humiliation for which Dobbs will never forgive him.

Curtin travels to the village; there, two members of the gang that attacked the train have been caught by the *Federales*—Mexican mounties. After a cursory interrogation, they are summarily shot. A lean Texan, Cody (Bruce Bennett) tries to draw Curtin out about the "paydirt" in the mountains. Tight-lipped, Curtin replies he wants no company, but Cody trails him back to camp, where his arrival is sourly greeted. Dobbs orders him to make tracks at daybreak. Howard offers Cody grub silently:

> DOBBS (*snarling*): Help yourself . . . we don't let guys starve to death . . . tonight you're our guest, but tomorrow morning, look out, no trespassin' around here, y'know—*beware the dogs. . . .*

Dobbs accurately diagnoses his spiritual condition. *Homo homini lupus,* wrote the ill-tempered philosopher, Thomas Hobbes: "Man is a wolf to man"—unless checked by the constraints of civilization. Dobbs in the wilderness has regressed to Hobbesian man at his ugliest. In the morning he abuses Cody for taking water to make coffee; Cody mildly observes—"I thought I was amongst civilized men who wouldn't begrudge me a little fresh water. . . ." Dobbs howls— *"Who's not civilized???"* and pummels him to the ground. We have repeatedly seen Dobbs' temper explode when he is confronted with some unpleasant feature of his inner or outer life—e.g., against the lottery vendor who reminded him of his beggar status, or against Curtin when the latter addressed Dobbs' hoggishness. His retaliation against Cody is particularly vicious: the malignant aggression barely held in check before has slipped further from his conscious control, always an ominous sign in a poorly put together paranoid.

Cody refuses to descend to Dobbs' level. He says he has discovered the mine, and offers them three choices—kill him, run him off, or deal him in. Calmly analyzing the assets and liabilities inherent in each possibility, he concludes it would be best for all if he joined them, especially since he wants nothing of past profit, only a share of what's to come. Howard, struck by the Texan's fairness, leans towards bringing him in. Dobbs' position is predictable: "Fred C. Dobbs ain't a guy likes bein' taken advantage of—do the mug in, I say!" Heavily, Howard asks Curtin to cast the deciding vote. Poised uneasily between the two moral polarities of his companions, Curtin throws in with Dobbs.

They draw their guns, but Cody mutely points down into the valley, towards a horde of mangy *bandidos* making their way up the mountain. There is no question now of killing the Texan—he means an extra gun. They take up defensive positions; soon Dobbs is staring at his nemesis again, *El Jefe* from the train robbery, much the worse for wear. Initially, in their famous dialogue, *El Jefe* is egregiously congenial, but when Dobbs rubs him the wrong way, he is instantly aroused to mindless rage. He is Dobbs' primitive double, without even the gringo's sketchy scruples:

> JEFE (*demanding Dobbs' gun*): *Oiga,* señor, we char *Federales*—
> y'know—the montid poliss?
> DOBBS: If you're the police, where are your badges?
> JEFE: Botchess? We ain' got no botchess! We don' nid no botchess!!
> *I don' haff to show dju any stinkin' botchess!!!*

Dobbs plugs him through his hat. *Caramba! El Jefe* beats a hasty retreat, then returns with a malodorous *compadre;* both flash toothy, untrustworthy smiles:

> JEFE: Look here, *amigo* . . . we don' wanna get you gon fer nothin'
> . . . I chaff a gold watch with a gold chain . . . they worth at leas'
> two hondred pesos—I 'change it fer y'gon. Y'better take it, thatza
> good bizness for you!!
> DOBBS: You keep your watch, I'll keep my gun!
> JEFFE: O, Dju kip it? Dju will kip it??? We won' get it???? *I'll show*
> *you!!!*

He goes for his gun, Howard blasts the watch to smithereens. Double *caramba!* The desperados, realizing that they are facing more than a lone man, withdraw cravenly, then the entire raggedy battalion attacks. The Americans beat them back, but at a price—Cody is killed. As the second and certainly fatal assault is mounted, the *Federales* charge into the valley and the bandits, caught in a potential crossfire, quit the field.

The partners' exhilaration dissipates as they look down on Cody's corpse. In his effects they find a poignant letter from his wife. Cody emerges as a devoted husband and father, who gave up a precious peace for the pursuit of gold.

> CURTIN (*reading*): . . . I have never thought any material trea-
> sure, no matter how great, is worth the pain of these long separa-
> tions . . . the country is especially lovely this year . . . the upper
> orchard looks aflame, and the lower like after a snowstorm . . . I do
> hope you are back for the harvest . . . it is high time for luck to
> start smiling upon you, but just in case she doesn't, remember we've
> already found life's real treasure. . . .

Cody's presence is brief, but authoritative. Despite his fatal passion, there was a manly rectitude and self-respect about the Texan. Saving himself, all the visitors to the Sierra Madre are rootless and disaffected. *El Jefe* and Dobbs are the worst of these men on the perimeter of society, but even Howard, the best of them, has led a disordered, marginal existence.

One has noted the striking absence of women in the film until now. Prior to Cody's appearance, they have been treated as degraded objects, treasure to be gotten with treasure, recipients of animal lust, nothing more. Pat MacCormack has a Mexican lady of easy virtue on his arm in Tampico, Dobbs yearns after whores, Howard says it's better not to torment oneself with thoughts of women in the wilds, Curtin is absolutely silent on the subject. Cody lays down his life for these alienated men who would have gunned him down. His bequest to them is the richness of his relationship with his wife. Although we never meet her, she is as crucial a character as her husband.

The critics have objected that her letter is banal and beside the point, yet I find it neither trivial nor irrelevant. Her words will call these adventurers, fallen far away from the possibilities of love, out of their spiritual wilderness, out of their obsessive moiling in the sterile earth, if they but have grace enough to listen. It is no accident that shortly after this scene the partners—even Dobbs—grow weary of their work and decide to pack up. Howard wants to take another week to break down the mine, put the mountain back in shape:

> HOWARD: Make her appear like she was before we came . . . we've wounded this mountain, it's our duty to close her wounds, it's the least we can do to show our gratitude. . . .
> CURTIN: You talk about that mountain like it was a real woman!
> DOBBS: She's been a lot better to me than any woman I ever knew!

The ruined piece of nature is likened to a raped woman. Howard redeems his moral lapse in assenting to Cody's execution by healing the mountain's wounds, rather than continue to treat it as an object of crass exploitation. Thus, he places himself squarely back on the side of life, and indirectly admits the influence of the letter. After a moment of hesitation, the others join him. They share complicity in deadly intent upon Cody, and have also been obscurely moved by his wife's testament. For Dobbs, the redemption will be temporary, the softening of his malice transitory. But we are given a rather surprising glimpse into a possible source of his perennial mistrust. The inanimate mountain treated him better than any flesh and blood woman— including, perhaps, his mother, the first failed source of warmth and trust.

One notes that Dobbs has pulled together psychologically since combatting real enemies instead of the straw men of his delusions. The certainty that he will be free of the enforced closeness with his partners now that the adventure is ending no doubt improves his relationship with them, and his fragile emotional equilibrium. Paranoids like Dobbs generally do better when they can be isolated or keep moving on. Intimate bonds become a scarifying trap wherein, according to their twisted perceptions, they can be manipulated, abused and finally destroyed.

The mine is dismantled, the burros loaded up, and as they leave each waves an affectionate—"Thanks, Mountain!" That evening, by the campfire, Curtin says he has decided to give some of his gold to Cody's wife and son; Howard readily chips in, but Dobbs, back in character, won't part with an ounce—"You two guys must've been born in a revival meeting!"

Four peasants suddenly emerge from the jungle; the startled Americans are relieved to find their visitors come on a mission of mercy. The leader's little son fell into the river earlier in the day, and still cannot be awakened; perhaps the *gringos,* being educated men, would know what to do. Howard accompanies them to their village; in a scene sculpted in lamplit *chiaroscuro,* the peasants look on, *indio* faces solemn as the centuries, while the gruff old man kneels over the comatose child, performing artificial respiration, the motions of which acquire, in this primitive setting, the beauty of some arcane ritual. The boy stirs, groans—even for a sophisticated viewer it is a miraculous moment. Howard the healer has even more profoundly reasserted his alliance with the forces of generativity.

In the morning the villagers restrain the Americans from leaving; it is an affront to the saints if "El Doctor" is not properly feasted. Dobbs cannot comprehend the motive of their hospitality, and very nearly gets himself killed. Howard decides to stay with the Indians for a few days, then makes a terrible misjudgment, letting his partners take his gold on to Durango rather than trusting in the peasants' honor. "I'll bet you remember this the next time you try to do a good deed!" chortles Dobbs. Howard's detention has vindicated his dog-eat-dog philosophy, and provides the necessary spur to his latent criminality. For Dobbs, unknowingly, has used Howard as an auxiliary conscience: with him gone, Dobbs' madness and badness reach malignant fruition.

Deprived of the old man's natural leadership, alone for the first time, Dobbs and Curtin quickly fall to bickering. Curtin can admit their dependence on Howard, but that would be too humiliating for Dobbs. Red threads of lunatic resentment and incipient treachery begin to appear in his chronic grousing: ". . . ain't it always *his* burros that won't march in line . . . he knew what he was doin' when he turned 'em over to us!" Dobbs not surprisingly soon works himself up to a sufficient pitch of self-justification to legitimize running off with Howard's goods. Curtin refuses, Dobbs turns on him wildly: "You're not puttin' anything over on me—I see right through you—for a long time you had it in your mind to bump me off at the first opportunity, so you could take not only the old man's goods but mine in the bargain!" Of course, this is *exactly* what Dobbs has in mind.

Dobbs tries to gun down his "persecutor," but Curtin disarms him. To convince Dobbs of his good intentions, Curtin returns the gun, minus ammunition. Unfortunately, trying to argue a paranoid out of his delusions usually only strengthens them. It is also not impossible that Curtin's rather moving declaration of good faith speaks to Dobbs' repressed homosexual feelings for this handsome youngster, which he must then repudiate all the more by keeping Curtin a despised enemy. When Curtin suggests they separate, Dobbs counters that if he leaves first, Curtin will attack him from behind (another homosexual reference?!); if Curtin goes first, he'll surely ambush Dobbs later on.

> CURTIN: Why wouldn't I do it here and now if I meant to kill you?
> DOBBS (*triumphantly*): 'Cause you're yella—ya haven't got nerve enough to pull the trigger when I'm lookin' ya straight in the eye!

Bewildered by this weird but typical circular logic of the paranoid, unwilling to act out Dobbs' persecutory delusions by murdering him, Curtin can see no way out but to keep awake and outlast him until

Durango. Although armed, he becomes, in effect, *Dobbs'* prisoner—a not uncommon occurrence in the relatives of a paranoid who lack the resolve to leave or commit the patient, and instead remain enmeshed and tormented. Dobbs clearly enjoys the ensuing game of cat-and-mouse, wearing Curtin slowly past the edge of exhaustion. When Curtin gives himself up to delicious slumber, Dobbs quickly filches his gun, kicks him awake, pushes him off-camera into the brush and guns him down.

Dobbs has won! He has the Treasure, and from precisely this instant of success his mental deterioration alarmingly accelerates. Fearing that Curtin still lives, he returns to the body but cannot fire again, tosses the gun away. He lies down by the campfire and meditates on his evil deed:

> DOBBS: Conscience—what a thing . . . if you believe you got a conscience, it'll pester ya to death . . . but if you don't believe ya got one . . . what can it do to ya?

And the campfire rises behind his haunted face like an inferno!

The scene is intriguingly reminiscent of Richard III's last evening before Bosworth Field, when the ghosts of those he slew in his course to the English throne rise up and assail his guilty soul.

> RICHARD: O coward conscience, how dost thou affect me! . . .
> My conscience hath a thousand several tongues,
> And every tongue condemns me for a villain.

Another victim of success, Richard loses his cunning directly after winning the crown; all his schemes henceforth founder, and he dies ignominiously!

Next morning, contemplating Curtin's burial, Dobbs cannot stomach the viewing of his victim: "What if his eyes are open . . . lookin' at me?" Recall how Dobbs accused Curtin of not having enough guts to look *him* in the eye and kill him! When he musters courage to return to the bush, he finds to his horror that Curtin is gone. Sensing his sanity slipping away, he tranquilizes himself into believing a tiger devoured the corpse.

In fact, Curtin has dragged himself during the night to the Indian village, where Howard is basking in the lap of luxury. He binds up Curtin's wounds and listens tolerantly to the young man's tale: "Well, I reckon we can't blame him too much. . . . Mebbe if I'd've been young and been out there with either of you, I might have been tempted, too." They ride off in pursuit, with a posse of the villagers.

Dissolve to a shot of a dead burro; nearby, Dobbs, gaunt with thirst, fatigue and despair. He stumbles towards a trench, tumbles into the fetid water and drinks deep. Then he spies another reflection joining his in the water: looming over him, *El Jefe*, who has traveled a road as long and bloody to their final encounter. *El Jefe*'s tattered state mirrors Dobbs': they are brothers in bestiality.

Dobbs clambers out of the trench; the other *bandidos* hem him in like raggedy Eumenides, plucking at his clothes as *El Jefe* inquires gaily: *"Oiga,* amigo—hey, did I know you from some place? . . . you the guy in the hole, the wan who won' give us the rifle, hah hah hah hah!!!" Horrified, Dobbs marks his nemesis face-to-face for the first and last time, and grasps his utter aloneness: he has cut himself off from his true friends, and left himself naked to these merciless predators.

One sees repeatedly in clinical practice how the paranoid is tragically compelled to force the very ruin he fears—an unhappy end often uniquely in accord with his delusions, as, for instance, the insanely jealous husband who drives his wife out of a marriage and into the arms of another man by his relentless suspicions.

Dobbs maintains he is a poor hunter going to sell hides in Durango. "We can sell those burros for just as good a price as dju can!," laughs *El Jefe*. Dobbs draws, forgetting that he carries the gun Curtin had unloaded. The hammer clicks impotently, the bandits rush upon him, hooting derisively, and Fred C. Dobbs goes down forever under their ruthless machetes. Hardly has the life ebbed out of him, when his corpse is stripped. The burros run away, and after a comic chase are rounded up in the courtyard of an old mission. Searching through the hides, the bandits find the sacks of gold dust; after splitting them open, they can only conclude that Dobbs meant to swindle an unwary buyer by weighing down his hides with sand; they have completely accepted his story, and were just as willing to murder him for his merchandise, or the shoes on his feet.

When they get to Durango, the mules are quickly recognized as those sold months ago to *los Americanos*. The bandits are caught red-handed in Dobbs' rags, and are hustled off to the firing squad. *El Jefe* is unregenerate to the end. A brave rogue, he rates his life worth less than the spit he showers, viper-like, upon his captors. He stops the execution to retrieve his hat, sets it on his head at a jaunty angle, and faces the guns of the *Federales* with aplomb.

Now a bristling northern wind rises, tumbling the dead *Jefe*'s sombrero over his fresh grave, past Howard and Curtin and the Indians as they ride into town. The people tell them Dobbs is dead, but his possessions recovered in good order. Relief changes to dismay when they find the sacks are gone. As at the beginning, the turn of destiny's wheel is heralded by a little boy, who could be the twin of the lottery hawker in Tampico—he says he heard the bandits speaking perplexedly of *"los sacos"* left at the mission. The Americans ride back furiously through the howling wind, back to the ruins where the sacks lie scattered about, ripped, empty, the rare and worthless earth mingled and whirled about by the uncaring elements. Howard is struck dumb; then he recovers his composure and rises magnificently to the occasion, transcending defeat with howls of sidesplitting laughter that mock the raging wind. Curtin looks at the old sourdough as if he had taken leave of his senses, but Howard is as clearheaded as when he danced his jig at the Treasure's finding:

> HOWARD: O, laugh, Curtin, old boy—it's a great joke played on us by the Lord or fate or nature or whoever you prefer . . . but whoever or whatever played it certainly had a sense of humor! . . . The gold has come back to where we found it—it's worth ten months of suffering and labor, this joke is!!!

Howard waves at the mountain, both collapse helplessly against a shattered wall, roaring with mirth.

Afterward, Howard decides to stay with the Indians: "I'll be worshipped and fed and treated like a high priest for telling people things they want to hear; good medicine men are born, not made!" He gives Curtin his share of what the burros, tools and hides will bring, if he returns to Dallas to meet Cody's widow at harvesttime. They mount up, shake hands, and ride away from each other, the mountain towering above them in long shot; then, in close-up, an ugly cactus and a torn sack in the swirling dust. . . .

Before they part, Curtin declares: "Y'know, the worst ain't so bad when it finally happens—all I'm out is a couple hundred bucks—not very much compared to what Dobbsy lost!" In fact, his fortunes have immeasurably improved. In Tampico, the protagonists lived amongst the legions of the lost, disengaged from the natural ties of friendship and family. At the conclusion of their abortive enterprise, Howard and Curtin have both found their way back to an appropriate place in the life cycle. Howard becomes a venerated elder statesman, adoptive father to his tribe. Curtin, who gave every evidence of floundering in a perpetual adolescence, has assimilated Howard's wisdom and grit. Howard has been a good father to this prodigal son. (Curtin's case thus reminds one of Dorothy Gale, who sought the Wizard along the perils of the Yellow Brick Road, and came home to herself.) With the old prospector's guidance, Curtin returns to his homeland, reaffirming his love for the soil. The implication is clear that he will replace Cody in the arms of his widow. By discharging a debt of honor to another Good Father who saved him, Curtin links himself to the succession of generations and, one may speculate, resolves his Oedipal struggle (the bandits executed his conflicted death-wish towards Cody, leaving Curtin guiltless, indeed obligated to marry the older man's wife).

For Howard and Curtin, the journey to the magic mountain has yielded profit out of failure, profit vastly greater than the vanished Treasure of the Sierra Madre. But Dobbs, voyaging into the wasteland of his soul, with only the clamor of inner demons for company, has been consumed by the golden delusion of corrosive power.

Some critics believe *Treasure* has not worn well with the years. Andrew Sarris, American architect of *auteurist* theory, is one of the film's—and Huston's—more notable detractors. *Treasure* has been particularly criticized for the bogus quality of the studio-built exteriors, while it has been generally ignored that Huston, pioneer of on-location work, fought tenaciously with the moguls to bring in as much Mexican footage as possible. These scenes, especially the early shots of the streets of Tampico, project through Ted McCord's grainy photography a masterful feeling for time and place that has rarely been equalled.

While one may quibble over *mise-en-scène,* the enduring excellence of script and acting is unquestionable—at least to this critic. Huston received a well-deserved Oscar for his screenplay, as did his father for the crowning achievement of a distinguished career in his portrayal of Howard. Indeed there is hardly a performance in the film that isn't memorable, down to the smallest role. Like most buffs, I admit an inordinate fondness for Alfonso Bedoya—Caliban in sombrero—as *El Jefe,* and have long since committed his lines to memory.

Bogart's work has not, I believe, received its just due. The critics found him competent, but out of character. (James Agee: "The only trouble is that one cannot quite forget that this is Bogart, putting on an unbelievably good act. . . .") On the contrary, Bogart was peculiarly suited for Dobbs; the part is quite consistent with the Mr. Hyde aspect of Bogie's screen persona. Rick Blaine in *Casablanca,* Philip Marlowe in *The Big Sleep,* are by outward appearance alienated, cynical, even cruel—but the tough facade always proves penetrable, revealing a sensitive man behind the pitiless armoring. In Bogart's Dobbs, the armor altogether becomes the man. It took an actor well-acquainted on and off camera with this emotional carapace, with the fear of showing oneself weak and vulnerable, perhaps even with the nearer reaches of paranoia, to make the wretched misfit Dobbs so believable and pitiable that he even acquires a narrow tragic dimension. Of paranoia and the Bogart hero, more in our next two chapters.

Bibliography

AGEE, J. *Agee on Film;* Vol. 1. New York: Grosset & Dunlap, 1969. See p. 293.

NOLAN, WILLIAM F. *John Huston, King Rebel.* Los Angeles: Sherbourne Press, 1965.

TOZZI, R., ed. *John Huston, A Pictorial Treasury of His Films.* ("Hollywood's Magic People" series.) New York: Crown Publishers, Inc. (Crescent), 1973. See pp. 51–57.

TRAVEN, B. *The Treasure of the Sierra Madre.* New York: The New American Library, Inc. (Signet), 1963.

IV

The Maltese Falcon —Even Paranoids Have Enemies

> The only effective kind of love interest is that which creates a personal hazard for the detective . . . a really good detective never gets married. . . .
>
> Raymond Chandler: *Casual Notes on the Mystery Novel*

> *"I guess somebody lost a dream," the intern said. He bent over and closed her eyes. . . .*
>
> —— : *The Little Sister*

The grip of the detective mythos upon the collective imagination is as acute now as in the forties—the Golden Era of Hollywood's hard-boiled private eyes, when the tough shamus-like Sam Spade and Philip Marlowe ruled the screen and the airwaves, sidestepping danger with a wisecrack, adoring secretary ever poised with pencil at the ready to take "the notes from my latest caper, sweetheart!"

Psychoanalytic inquiry into the immensely popular genre has been both sparse and highly conjectural. Pederson-Krag has suggested that the private eye symbolizes the curious child bent on ferreting out the secrets of grown-up sexuality. The "crime" he seeks to unravel is actually the Freudian Primal Scene—parental intercourse—which analysts believe can be imprinted upon the untutored mind of the young as an act of unparalleled violence when the partners are misperceived as being locked in a mortal combat. Like many analytic intrusions into aesthetics, this theory is singularly hard to prove or disprove, since its author offers no supporting evidence whatsoever, either from detective literature or the therapy of detectophiles.

I have found the observations of Dr. Leo Bellak far more well reasoned, especially since this noted analyst appears so obviously to be an aficionado. Bellak conceives that the detective story satisfies its enthusiasts on multiple levels: the reader identifies both with criminal and sleuth; with the criminal, because our Freudian Id, that vast reservoir of primitive aggressive and sexual impulses, recognizes no social restraints and will stop at nothing to have its wishes savagely fulfilled; alternatively, with the sleuth, as an embodiment of the Dr. Jekyll side of the personality, the Superego, in that the detective is an extension of the inner voice of conscience, an idealized figure endowed with superhuman intelligence, implacably allied with the forces of law and order. (The English expert, Edmund Bergler, also postulated that one might, if masochistic enough, even identify with the victim!)

Bellak believes detective fiction gratifies an inherent pleasure at having tension skillfully manipulated, increased, then suddenly reduced following the elucidation of the mystery and capture of the criminal. In an uncertain life brimming with unpredictable trauma, it can be uniquely entertaining to undergo carefully planned anxiety, with the promise of certain relief when the book is finished or the movie ends. The mystery buff confronts danger selectively, not willy-nilly—and it is, after all, not *his* danger, but another's! Since we are inherently problem-solving creatures, we also enjoy what Bellak calls the "closure satisfaction" at the riddle's resolution, digging the *gestalt* of the crime.

Psychoanalysts have principally addressed the so-called "English" school of detection—wherein the sleuth is upper class by origin or lifestyle (Sherlock Holmes, Lord Peter Wimsey), the victim and criminal are likely to share an identical Church of England background, the story is laid out in a setting of implacable gentility, replete with rose gardens, high tea, and humble servitors, and motivation is likely to be less important than the elegant Chinese puzzle-box of the murder. Sleuthing follows conventions as strict as Robert's Rules, and even the perpetrator gives at least the outward show of gentility.

I sing of another school of detection, one with its own unique but far less elegant conventions. It developed out of the American pulp magazines of the twenties and thirties, in a crisis-ridden post-bellum era of prohibition and economic depression; it thrived not on decorum, but on violence, corruption and the sheer will of its protagonist to endure and to prevail in the end, with his skin and precarious integrity intact, and a desperate truth revealed. . . .

The writers who created the tough American private eye are mostly unsung and forgotten now; their tabloid style left a great deal to be desired, but what they lacked in technique was more than recovered in the acuteness of their vision into the shadowy side of a ruthlessly competitive and materialistic culture. Ernest Hemingway and John O'Hara owed them much, and out of their ranks came a few truly great innovators—such as Dashiell Hammett, an ex-Pinkerton operative who transformed the mystery novel from a pallid teatime affair into a social document of overwhelming power. Now the ''how'' of killing was subordinated to the ''why'' residing in the dark turnings of the heart and the unquiet past. Raymond Chandler, Hammett's equally famous inheritor, wrote that Hammett ''gave murder back to the kind of people that commit it for reasons, not just to provide a corpse, and with the means at hand, not hand-wrought dueling pistols, curare and tropical fish.''

Hammett's 1929 masterpiece, *The Maltese Falcon,* captured perfectly the essence of the private eye's peculiar, seamy milieu. Hollywood flubbed with two inane editions of the novel, first in 1931 under the original title, then in 1936 as *Satan Met a Lady.* In 1941, a fledgling director named John Huston assembled a memorable cast and undertook a third remake: this time, Humphrey Bogart played Sam Spade, and played him to the hilt. A remarkable success financially and artistically, Huston's film took the American detective off the printed page, launched him on an odyssey that saw his character finally elevated to the status of existential hero, a close cousin to Camus' *The Stranger*.

I find it oddly appropriate to use another brand of sleuthing—psychoanalysis—to follow Spade as he goes about the intricate business of digging up the human wreckage left in the Maltese Falcon's wake. The private eye as analyst *manqué*—the analyst as shamus *manqué!* Both professionals keep their personalities anonymous and enigmatic. Both prize the truth above all else, but the truth is never easily known, it hides beneath the surface of an ambiguous reality, where character and event never merely signify themselves and no one is who or what he claims to be. For the analyst, the truth is concealed by the chimera of unconscious defense and resistance, by repression and amnesia forged over a lifetime, persisting against the patient's better judgment, and keeping him ill. For the detective, the truth is likely to be buried out of conscious malice, greed or guilt, and he traces it out to *his* direst peril. . . .

The Maltese Falcon begins with a slow pan over the Golden Gate Bridge, across a gray San Francisco skyline. The detective is an urban animal, a facile manipulator of the lackluster paraphernalia of city life—taxicabs, telephones and desk clerks. The action typically unfolds in California, at the farthest perimeter of the barely civilized American frontier. The brief opening pan is as much as we shall see of the metropolis' exterior rush and glamor; instead, we will move amidst the traumatizing rawness of the underground city, descending into a claustrophobic world of alleyways and seedy hotel rooms, inhabited by permanent transients, where no blade of grass or bit of uncluttered sky relieves the blight cast by the overweening lust for profit and power.

The offices of Spade and Archer, Private Investigators, are spartanly furnished. The shamus, in his living and working quarters, will invariably eschew the decorative for the (barely) functional, indeed he positively revels in the dilapidation of his environs. Spade is alone, self-possessed even at rest, competently rolling a cigarette. Enter Effie Perine (Lee Patrick), his secretary, a wholesome and direct young woman as much a part of the iconography as revolver and trench coat.

She ushers in a new client, ''Miss Wonderly'' (Mary Astor), a fur-clad brunette radiating desperation, and a teasing insincerity. Spade, like the analyst, is a good listener, draws her out easily. . . .

Wonderly is trying to find her younger sister, Corinne, who ran away with a man named Floyd Thursby while her parents were in Honolulu. Corinne vanished after writing that she had come to San Francisco. She left only General Delivery as an address. Wonderly followed her, hoping to retrieve her before the parents' return. She met Thursby at the post office, picking up her last letter to Corinne. He refused to take her to her prodigal sister, but made an appointment to meet her that evening at her hotel.

While she is spinning this unlikely yarn, Spade's partner, Miles Archer (Jerome Cowan), enters and gives a silent whistle of apprecia-tion. Miles appears ''about as many years past forty as Spade is past thirty.'' An aging gigolo with a certain coarse cunning, he is clearly not the brains of the outfit. Spade briefs him, tells Wonderly they'll trail Thursby back to Corinne and ''if she doesn't want to leave him . . . well, there are ways of arranging that.'' Eyelashes aflutter, Won-derly emphasizes Thursby's violent proclivities; Archer gallantly vol-unteers his personal services, to Spade's amusement.

Wonderly gives them $200, a stiff retainer in 1941, and exits. Her convoluted tale would make any red-blooded American salivate like Pavlov's dogs—an innocent girl duped by an evil seducer, a glamor-ous, helpless rescuer, presumably well-to-do parents and the promise of a fat fee. But Spade's intelligence races ahead of the damsel's too obvious distress, probing for a different, hidden purpose. Archer, on the other hand, has been thoroughly gulled.

> ARCHER: Oh, she's sweet!—maybe you saw her first, Sam, but I spoke first!
> SPADE (*ironically*): You've got brains—yes you have! . . .

Dissolve—to a terse shot of Miles approaching the camera. His ex-pectant smile gives way to disbelief, a shot roars out and he staggers back. . . .

Dissolve—A call from the police jangles Spade awake in his apartment. His reaction to Miles' death is remarkably even; blinking the sleep out of his eyes, he phones Effie with the news and tells her to notify Iva, Miles' wife—"keep her away from me!"

Dissolve—The scene of the crime; Spade glances over a broken fence at his partner, sprawled brokenly below on rocks beetling over surf. Detective Tom Polhaus (Ward Bond) greets him. Cop and shamus are old acquaintances and adversaries. They rehearse the details of Archer's death, Spade holding rigorously to his professional detachment. Miles was shot at the end of a blind alley, fronting on the ocean; he fell over the fence—his coat was burnt by the blast, his gun still on his hip, unfired.

Spade curtly refuses to view the remains, won't tell Polhaus more than that Miles was tailing Thursby. The decent policeman pronounces Miles' epitaph gruffly, one city dweller trying to puzzle out some meaning in the random, savage passage of another stranger:

> POLHAUS: It's tough him getting it like that, ain't it? Miles had his faults, just like any of the rest of us, but I guess he must have had some strong points too, huh?

Spade only grunts ambiguously. Wonderly's hotel tells him that she has left without a forwarding address. Back home, he is visited by Polhaus and his superior, Lieutenant Dundy. The cops run a typical Mutt and Jeff routine, Polhaus awkwardly amiable, Dundy oozing suspicion from every pore. They reveal that Thursby has just been gunned down, and Spade is now involved in *two* murders! Dundy taps Spade's chest with a thick finger, and Spade, uncharacteristically, blows his cool— *"Keep . . . your . . . paws . . . off . . . me!!"* then quickly recovers, sidesteps the grilling and eases them out.

Next morning in his office Spade is accosted by Iva Archer, an overripe woman slightly past her prime who he has obviously been bedding for some time with waning enthusiasm. She collapses into his arms, asks weeping if he murdered Miles—"Be kind to me, Sam!" He laughs harshly; she's using him, half-hoping he is the killer, and he'll have none of it. Turning mock solicitous, he dismisses her with a dubious promise to see her later. Effie is distressed but not terribly surprised to hear her boss is under suspicion, not, one guesses, for the first time. His disordered life holds few secrets from her, but he evades her concern. It is a scene that has been played out between them on many occasions; he accepts her technical assistance, treating her as the obedient extension of his expertise, but he will not tolerate her—or anyone else—invading his territory, questioning the risks he insists upon taking.

The migratory Miss Wonderly resurfaces—phones Spade to come to her at another hotel, under another name—LeBlanc. She blames herself ostentatiously for Miles' death, admits her story of the previous day was a lie, her two identities are lies, too; she is neither Wonderly nor LeBlanc, but plain Brigid O'Shaughnessy. Spade is not particularly upset at this news—''We didn't exactly believe your story—we believed your two hundred dollars!'' As for Archer, Spade says he had a large life insurance policy, and a wife who didn't like him—no need for remorse!

Brigid throws herself on his mercy: Thursby betrayed her after she engaged him in the Orient to protect her—from some obscure danger that still threatens her. When he tries to pin her down, she is as slippery with him as he was with the police. ''You won't need much of anybody's help,'' he says, admiringly, ''You're good—chiefly your eyes, I think, and that throb you get in your voice, when you say, be—*generous*, Mr. Spade.'' Then, curiously, he relents; he takes $300—most of her cash—over her protests, leaves with the warning that she admit no one until his return.

What draws him to her, since he so clearly pegs her for an artful schemer? Not simply her obvious physical charms. There are certain men who cannot accept woman as helpmeet and bed partner both. It is inconceivable to them that a ''good'' woman can have ''bad'' sexual feelings, therefore they split the feminine image in two. The basis for this cleavage is the unconscious need to negate childhood incestuous desire for the mother, one's first beloved—since if mother is denied her natural sexuality, it then becomes easier to deny the sensual claim upon her. Clinically, one often discovers that the sufferer from the so-called ''Madonna-Whore complex'' has, in fact, been exposed to a mother who puritanically discouraged healthy displays of sexuality in her little boy. Typically, such a little boy, grown into a neurotic adult, will go unaroused or frankly impotent with his wife, who represents a newer version of his mother, but will become a sexual quarterback with prostitutes, or with a mistress from a different, usually lower, social class.

Effie is Spade's Madonna!—a permanent fixture in his turbulent life, self-sacrificing, energetically devoted to his welfare. She could almost be his wife, were it not for the fact that she holds about as much sexual attraction for him as her typewriter. But shady ladies of uncertain reputation *do* turn him on, especially when their criminal tendencies come candy-coated in cloying helplessness. Iva Archer is a lesser example of the breed: Brigid is a *nonpareil!* And, beyond her allure as degraded love-object, she also holds the key to two murders—of which Spade himself now stands as prime suspect stemming directly from his entanglement with her. He must bind himself to her devious cause, so that the work of detection—*and* his ultimate liberation—can be accomplished!

Back at the office, Effie hands Spade a card reeking of gardenias—another client, one Joel Cairo (Peter Lorre), a fulsome Levantine of overblown appearance. Effie calls him "queer" outright in the novel; in the film, Spade's bemused reaction to the scented card and Lorre's mincing portrayal leaves no doubt about Cairo's inversion.

He offers Spade $5,000—"on behalf of the rightful owner" to recover "an ornament that . . . shall we say . . . has been mislaid, a statuette, the black figure of, er, a bird . . . I am prepared to promise that—what is the phrase? (*a knowing roll of the eyes*)—'No questions will be asked'!" Then, when Spade's back is turned, the little man pulls a gun and demands to search the office. The detective easily disarms him and punches him out. A search through his pockets uncovers multiple passports, a perfumed handkerchief that elicits another quizzical glance at the victim—but no $5,000.

Cairo awakens and makes straight for a mirror: "Look what you did to my shirt!" he whines, absurdly, then resumes negotiations as if nothing had happened. Spade allows Cairo to believe he can get the statuette—like a good analyst, he practices silence when ignorant, since you rarely get into trouble keeping your mouth shut, especially if the other party is under considerable pressure to keep his open. Cairo thinks he has outsmarted Spade, since he has divulged little about the bird, and nothing about the "rightful owner"—unaware that the detective had never heard of the Falcon until his new "client" spilled the beans. Cairo maintains his first offer was in good faith: he will put down a retainer, the rest to follow later:

CAIRO: You will take, say, one hundred dollars?
SPADE: No—I will take, say, *two* hundred dollars!!

He returns the gun, and breaks up with genuine amusement when Cairo immediately aims the weapon at his chest and demands once again to search the office: "Sure . . . g . . . go ahead I won't stop ya!!" Spade loses nothing here: the one who sought to manipulate the shamus has been cannily exploited. In his last match with Brigid, Spade knew he was also being manipulated, and left her convinced that she had engaged his sympathy. (She *has,* a little, but Spade is aware of this, too!) Cairo has also been lulled into assuming Spade is on his side—purely for profit. From both, Spade takes more money than they are willing to part with, not out of greed, but to underscore that he has the competitive edge. They have started the game, but he will most certainly play it out to his satisfaction, and by his own rules.

Spade leaves the office, picks up then shakes a clumsy tail by a diminutive, pinch-faced young thug, Wilmer (Elisha Cook, Jr.). At Brigid's, Spade casually reveals he has met Cairo. She reacts with equally studied nonchalance until he mentions the black bird and the sum Cairo was ready to pay. Bitterly, she says she can't raise that kind of money—"if I have to bid for your loyalty . . . what else is there I can buy you with?" He takes her face in his hands, kisses her with a curious expression of despair, as if he were giving up, or giving in. . . .

Brigid has admitted she is base—"bad, worse than you could know!" She seems the least likely candidate to deserve what little good faith remains in Spade, and it is damned little. Yet she continues to tantalize him, a diamond on a dustheap. From the start, Spade has been keeping a curious set of double-entry mental books on her. He senses her treachery, yet cherishes the illusion that she is as helpless, as vulnerable, as she would have him and the world believe. He knows better, but simultaneously seeks to redeem his sour expectation of betrayal.

Brigid begs for his patience again, asks him to set up an interview with Cairo at his apartment, for she is apparently mortally afraid of the Levantine. They leave, and Spade is doubly shadowed; Iva Archer watches furtively from her car as he and Brigid enter his building. Inside, Spade peers through the curtains at Wilmer, standing idly under a streetlamp. Cairo arrives, greets Brigid with too-elaborate courtesy. Brigid promises the Falcon back within a week—Thursby hid it, and now she is anxious to dispose of it after his violent end. Their elliptical conversation is studded with references to "the Fat Man" and "the Boy outside."

> BRIGID: But you might be able to get around him, Joel, as you did that one in Istanbul, what was his name?
> CAIRO: You mean the one you couldn't get to—!!

Uproar, pandemonium!!! Brigid swings on Cairo, he slaps her back, Cairo draws a gun, Spade belts him, Cairo howls—"That is the *second* time you've laid hands on me tonight!!" It is never explained what sets Brigid and the Levantine going at each other like bargain-basement shoppers fighting over the last girdle; I suspect that the anonymous boy from Istanbul was somehow involved in nailing down the Falcon, that Cairo mixed business with pleasure, developed sexual designs on the lad and Brigid came between them. . . .

Dundy and Polhaus return at this inopportune moment. Spade blocks them at the door, blandly denying Dundy's accusation that he murdered Miles to marry Iva. Cairo screams for help, Spade smoothly ushers them in—to find Brigid and the Levantine brawling again. Cairo accuses Spade of entrapping and brutally interrogating him with his henchwoman; Dundy, delighted with the mayhem, wants to book them all. Spade explains that Brigid is an operative—they were indeed questioning Cairo—and he tells enough about the little conspirator to make it obvious that involving the police will compromise Cairo's freedom to chase down the Falcon.

Cairo, befuddled, now balks at pressing charges, then Spade abruptly shifts gears, tells the cops they've been flummoxed—he put his "friends" up to staging a fracas to give the law a hard time for bugging him. The wily shamus dances around Dundy's ponderous rec-

titude like a picador jabbing a particularly dense bull. Goaded beyond
endurance, Dundy slugs him; Spade's objectivity seems to fracture—
as when Dundy touched him previously. Aware that he has gone too
far, Dundy departs grumpily with Polhaus, Cairo slithering out between them.

> BRIGID: You're absolutely the wildest most unpredictable person
> I've ever known. Do you always carry on so high-handed?

Spade's performance was high-handed, but *never* wild; an icy lucidity reigns over these pranks and storms. Cairo has been intimidated,
the police thoroughly bewildered, and Brigid enormously impressed.
For all his outrage, it appears that Spade deliberately provoked Dundy
into striking him, guessing that the lieutenant would wilt after a
mindless muscular display.

When Spade tries to elicit more about the Falcon from Brigid, she
fobs him off with another of her tangled histories: she was promised a
large sum to steal the bird in Turkey. Cairo and Thursby were in on
the heist. She and Thursby discovered Cairo meant to keep the Falcon
for himself, so they absconded with it instead. Then she found
Thursby had no intention of sharing the profits either.

> SPADE (*half-smiling*): You *are* a liar . . . was there any truth in that
> yarn?
> BRIGID (*smiling*): Some . . . not very much. . . . Oh, I'm so tired
> . . . of lying and making up lies, and not knowing what is a lie and
> what is the truth. . . .

It is quite possible that this is the one and only time Brigid is being
truthful. She lives poised on the edge of reality and fantasy, and her
success as a schemer lies precisely in the vividness of her daydreams
for her. She almost believes she *is* Wonderly or LeBlanc, *haut monde*
instead of *demi-monde*. She fantasizes that she is a passive victim of
scheming men—her lie to Spade about a wealthy sister seduced and
menaced by Thursby is another edition of this central fantasy; Corinne
is a projected image of an imaginary self, which as we shall see, is
quite at variance with her actual, criminal self.

She stretches out languorously on the couch, Spade bends over her, his expression again a curious riddle of pain, anger and tenderness. The camera drifts away from them and through the open window; rustling curtains frame the young gunman, loitering in a pool of lamplight, the peril implicit in Brigid's sensual promise. This confrontation, as the last, ends with Spade accepting her body in lieu of the truth. The acceptance is provisional.

In the novel, Spade spends the night with her. Huston omitted, for the sake of the Hays office, a sequence of Spade tiptoeing out of the apartment the next morning. Instead, there is a direct cut to Cairo's hotel. The deletion—admittedly a sop to the censor—nevertheless works tellingly: it reinforces the curious blurring in the passage of time as the texture of intrigue has thickened. One has lost track of the hours or days elapsed since Spade was awakened by the news of his partner's murder, and it has become increasingly difficult to separate day from night, particularly since most of the action takes place indoors under thin, artificial light. As the case gathers momentum, the detective neither slumbers nor takes more substantial food than black coffee and cigarettes. He is completely immersed in and nourished by the ugly business at hand: it is in this prolonged sleepless night that he comes authentically alive.

Spade spots Wilmer in the lobby of Cairo's hotel. Guessing a connection between Wilmer and "the Fat Man" from Brigid's enigmatic conversation with Cairo, he tells the boy he wants to see his boss, and has the hotel dick roust the little gunsel out. Wilmer cuts a comic and malevolent figure. Dressed in an overcoat two sizes too large, pockets abulge with gats, he is incapable of a line that hasn't been cribbed from a "B" gangster flick—"Keep askin' for it, and you're goin' to get it—*plenty!*" Spade openly insults him, just as he incited Dundy.

Cairo enters the lobby much the worse for wear. The police booked him after they left Spade's, grilled him thoroughly, but he adhered to Spade's ridiculous story. Now he wants no further dealings with the detective, since their business invariably winds up with such consistent disrepair to his person and haberdashery.

At his office, Spade finds Brigid, distraught as usual. Her apartment has been ransacked while she was away. He packs her off to Effie's place for safekeeping, then sets up appointments with two callers—the District Attorney, and a Mr. Gutman, who claims he received Spade's message from "the young man." Wretched Iva interrupts, begging forgiveness for sending over the police last night in a paroxysm of jealousy. Miles' widow is completely peripheral to Spade's intentions now, either as a lover or as a significant piece of the mystery. Spade has already pondered and rejected the possibility that *she* murdered Archer. He dispatches her impatiently, and goes off to test his mettle against the elusive Fat Man.

Kasper Gutman (Sydney Greenstreet), a vast penguin in cutaway coat and striped trousers, greets Spade at his hotel suite with effusive *bonhomie*, placing his hands familiarly on the detective as he guides him to a chair, a drink and a cigar. Gutman sets the tone of a business conference between straight-shooting men of the world, surrounded by masculine accoutrements, but he is patently criminal and only less obviously homosexual, a degenerate old queen of ambiguous nationality. (In the novel, he travels with a daughter, Rhea, eliminated in the screenplay, thus emphasizing the Fat Man's homosexuality.)

We have seen that Spade places the highest premium on his physical and emotional inviolability. He cannot abide being touched and *man-handled*; he would not suffer Dundy to lay a finger upon him, yet permits Gutman impressive liberties with his person. But he had clearly defined a habitual stance of non-cooperation with the policeman and was secure in defying Dundy's clumsy intrusions. Gutman's attack must be parried differently. To get the better of the Fat Man, Spade must seem *conspiratorial* and *seduceable*.

Gutman's methods are informed by the subtly eroticized competitiveness of the gay bar. He will not cease trying to swindle and outfox Spade. Ostensibly, his chicanery is aimed at acquiring the Falcon, but unconsciously Gutman craves a more sensual victory. He wants to *screw* Spade literally and figuratively, and if the detective dies as a result, why, that will give an added, climactic pleasure!

Gutman speaks in orotund Wildeian aphorisms, savoring his words as if each were a pearl of Iranian caviar:

> GUTMAN: Well, sir, here's to plain speaking and clear understanding . . . I distrust a close-mouthed man. He generally picks the wrong time to talk and says the wrong thing . . . talking's something you can't do judiciously unless you keep in practice . . . I'll tell you right out, I'm a man who likes to talk to a man who likes to talk!

Spade affirms that he acts for himself, not for those who sought to hire him, and infers that no one really knows the nature or value of the bird except the Fat Man himself. Gutman chuckles voluptuously: thinking he holds trump cards, he refuses further information unless Spade will reveal the bird's whereabouts. Spade throws a tantrum, worthy of a drag-queen in high pique, smashes a glass, his voice cracking with hysteria as he storms out—"You've got 'til five o'clock, then you're either in, or out, for keeps!" In the hall, he grins faintly as he regards his trembling hand. Murder surely waited inside amidst the cigars and suave speech. He goes down one elevator, just as Cairo steps out of the other, neither seeing the other. . . .

Bryan, the District Attorney, next tries to back Dundy's muscle with the power of his office. A bespectacled, iron-jawed type, Bryan is easily foiled. He can't grasp Spade's unwillingness to cooperate if he's got nothing to conceal. Spade replies with the essence of his *Weltanschauung: "Everybody has something to conceal!"* He maintains insolently that he can only clear himself by finding the killers on his own, free from the bungling law, and exits abruptly, leaving the D.A. choking on his words, much as he left Gutman. It is integral to Spade's style to provoke an opponent and break his rhythm, with some mercurial piece of behavior. Consistently, he leaves turmoil behind him as he proceeds to the next turn of the maze.

Wilmer is waiting for Spade outside his office: the Fat Man wants to see him again. As they go down the hotel corridor, Spade slips behind the youth and immobilizes him. He hands Gutman Wilmer's brace of pistols: "A crippled newsie took them away from him, but I made him give them back!" Gutman roars appreciatively and gestures his bungling bodyguard into another room. Then, he sits Spade down and relates the Falcon's past with the eloquence of a natural actor, pausing only to replenish the detective's glass several times.

The bird is a sinister metaphor of rapacity; fashioned in 1539 from purest gold and rare jewels in the coffers of the crusading Knights of Malta ("We all know that the Holy Wars to them were largely a matter of loot. . . ."), it was meant as a gift for Charles V of Spain, but fell into the hands of pirates. It then disappeared and reappeared in various locales, acquiring in its bloody passage a coat of black enamel. After seventeen years Gutman traced it to a Russian general, one Kemidov, in Istanbul. When he refused to sell it, ''I sent some— ah—agents, to get it. Well, sir, they got it—and I haven't got it—heh, heh—*but I'm going to get it!''*

Gutman offers Spade $50,000 or a quarter of the Falcon's sale price. His flabby hand fondles the detective's knee as he reverently speculates on the bird's real value—a quarter of a million—a million—who can say? Spade's speech thickens; he lurches to his feet, takes a few unsteady steps. At the Fat Man's bidding, Wilmer enters, trips the detective and kicks viciously at his prostrate body; Cairo emerges from the bedroom and the conspirators hurry out.

Several hours later: Spade heaves himself into painful consciousness,* calls Effie, finds that Brigid never arrived at her home. He searches the suite, finds a newspaper shipping page with an encircled notice: ''5:30 P.M.—*La Paloma*—from Hong Kong.'' For once, he has been bluffed—Gutman only brought him back to neutralize him!

Spade rushes to the docks, where the *La Paloma* lies in flames, no one aboard. He returns to his office, and is briefing Effie when a gaunt, seafaring man staggers in, clutching a crudely wrapped parcel: Captain Jacoby (Walter Huston, conferring his blessing on his son's first endeavor in his cameo role), the master of the *La Paloma*. He groans—''the bird. . . .'' and dies. ''We've got it, angel, we've got it!'' Spade exults. He has parlayed a few scraps of information into possession of the Falcon and is now the potential master of all those who want the bird!

The phone rings—Brigid crying for help, then her muffled scream! Spade, in no great hurry, gathers up the package and tells Effie to call in the police, but not to mention the Falcon. After checking his acquisition at the baggage office of a bus terminal and mailing the stub to himself, Spade cabs to the address Brigid gave over the phone—a vacant lot, more ''hooey'' thrown in his path. As he enters his apartment, Brigid glides breathlessly into his arms (she is chronically breathless—Huston got the effect by making Mary Astor race around the set between takes). He opens the door, the light flicks on, revealing Wilmer behind him, guns drawn, Gutman and Cairo seated.

---

* An obligatory sequence in the detective genre—the unexpected knockout, followed by a fuzzy-headed, blurred-focus recovery.

"Well," says Spade without missing a beat, "are you ready to make the first payment, and take the Falcon off my hands?" Gutman hands him $10,000—less than the original fee, but "genuine coin of the realm; with a dollar of this, you can buy ten dollars of talk!"

Money is not the principal issue to be resolved. Spade says he needs a fall guy, for unless there is a believable suspect in the murders, his neck is as good as in the noose. "Let's give them the gunsel," he blandly recommends—"He actually did shoot Thursby and Jacoby, didn't he?" Wilmer blanches with rage, Gutman assures him the idea is utterly repugnant, Wilmer is like a son to him (a concubine more likely!). But he is intrigued by Spade's guarantee that the police won't listen to Wilmer in their eagerness to nail down a conviction (Spade, of course, has made a shrewd guess about Wilmer's guilt).

If the Fat Man refuses to part with his minion, Spade nominates Cairo. Incensed, the Levantine suggests they frame Brigid. Gazing dispassionately at the quaking woman, Spade says he is open to *that* possibility, too. When Gutman affably threatens to torture the Falcon's location out of him, Spade studies his alternatives with the same detached pragmatism:

> SPADE: If you start something, I'll make it a matter of your having to kill me—or call it off . . . (*reflectively*) the trick from my angle is to make my plan strong enough to tie you up, but not make you mad enough to bump me off against your better judgment. . . .
> GUTMAN (*amazed*): By *Gad,* sir, you *are* a character!!

Spade is willing to stake his pain threshold, even life itself: the risks are too high for the Fat Man to risk such a gamble. Gutman and Cairo withdraw behind the latter's bejewelled fingers to assess Spade's initial suggestion. "Two to one they're selling you out, sonny," Spade sneers. Wilmer rises, rigid with fury, and Spade knocks him cold. He then promises to have the bird delivered in the morning, but only if Gutman fills him in on the details of the killings—"so I can be sure the parts that don't fit are covered up. . . ." Gutman, unaware he is playing right into Spade's hands, spills the whole dirty business:

Brigid left the Falcon with Jacoby in Hong Kong and came to San Francisco with Thursby. When Gutman couldn't win Thursby over because of his unswerving loyalty, he was murdered by Wilmer to intimidate Brigid. Cairo pursued his treacherous confederates from Turkey to Hong Kong, thence to America. After he fell afoul of Spade, he decided to throw his lot back in with Gutman, thus establishing a precise alignment of homosexuals on one side of the "dizzy affair" and straights on the other.

Cairo discovered the *La Paloma* docking notice after Spade had met the Fat Man, remembered that Brigid and Jacoby had been seen together in Hong Kong. The detective was called back and drugged to keep him out of the way, so Gutman could surprise Jacoby and Brigid. The *La Paloma* was fired accidentally by Wilmer's inept search—"no doubt he was careless with matches." Brigid agreed to give up the Falcon at Gutman's hotel, was let go and never showed up. The gang then dashed to Brigid's apartment; Wilmer plugged the captain as he went down the fire escape, but the rugged seaman still escaped. Brigid was "persuaded" to confess she had sent Jacoby with the package to Spade; she was forced to lure Spade away with a phony SOS, but by that time Spade already had the goods, so the gang returned to Spade's apartment to settle their score with him.

By his own account, Gutman's a total bust as a Machiavellian: he and his companions are a sorry bunch of second-rate chiselers. Wilmer's inadvertent arson of the *La Paloma*—the bad boy playing with matches—is a ludicrous paradigm of their inveterate bungling. It is Brigid who emerges as the Dragon Lady of the piece, Brigid who deceived Gutman and Cairo in Istanbul, and, who thereafter, every step of the way, has had every man connected with the caper dancing to her tune, with the possible—just barely possible—exception of Sam Spade.

Gutman looks down at Wilmer endearingly: "I want you to know I couldn't be any fonder of you if you were my own son. . . . Well, if you lose a son, it's possible to get another—there's only *one* Maltese Falcon!" Brigid has been holding the envelope containing the $10,000; Gutman takes it from her and counts only nine bills! Spade, after brief consideration, says—"You palmed it!" and threatens to search the Fat Man if he doesn't own up. "Yes sir, that I did," replies Gutman merrily: "I must have my little joke now and then. And I was curious to know what you'd do in a situation of this sort!"

Spade has separated Gutman from his *amour propre,* Wilmer. The

Fat Man's childish prank, botched thoroughly, is actually a spiteful attempt to drive a wedge between Spade and his "beloved," to repair Gutman's loss and humiliation. Spade, although he completely mistrusts Brigid by now, will not give Gutman the satisfaction of thinking he can be divorced so easily from her.

Effie delivers the package and leaves. Spade places it on a table; the conspirators cluster around like vultures at feeding time. Gutman, eyes moist, undoes the cord—"Now—*after seventeen years . . .*"—extracts the black bird from its wrappings, caresses it lasciviously. He unclasps a knife, peels a shaving back from the Falcon's ebony surface, then another—and another; his face suffused, he hacks robot-like at the statue, his glazed vision fixed upon a terrible recognition: the Falcon is a leaden forgery! "You and your *stupid* attempt to buy it," howls Cairo—"Kemidov found out how valuable it was. . . . You—*imbecile!* You—*bloated idiot!!! You fat*—" and he collapses, blubbering.

Gutman tugs at his collar, then quickly recovers his composure. He has spent seventeen years in his quest—another year is an additional investment of only "five and fifteen-seventeenths per cent." On to Istanbul! Cairo, despite his imprecations, is instantly ready to follow, but Wilmer has glided out behind them. Gutman demands the $10,000 back at gunpoint; Spade coolly extracts a single bill—"time and expenses"—hands him the rest. Gutman tries to cozen Spade into joining the Turkish expedition—"You're a man of nice judgment, and many resources!" and failing, toddles out, bequeathing to Brigid "the *rara avis* on the table there, as a little—heh, heh—memento!"

Directly Spade is on the phone to Polhaus, turning the lot of them in. Then he addresses Brigid with convincing urgency. Gutman will talk once caught; they'll surely be implicated if he doesn't have *all* the answers. Pleading and bullying, he leads her through a labyrinth of lies, to the last pieces of the mystery:

Brigid wanted Thursby out of the way before the *La Paloma* docked, so she hired Spade and Archer, and told Thursby he was being shadowed. She hoped that Thursby, fearing for his life, would kill or be killed by Miles. In the former event, she would tip off the police and have Thursby arrested, rendering him *hors de Falcon.* But Thursby balked—apparently he was never the paragon of violence she painted. Spade reasons she then borrowed Thursby's gun and lured the lecherous Archer to his death:

> SPADE: Miles hadn't many brains, but he had too many years experience to be caught like that . . . up a blind alley with his gun on his hip and his overcoat buttoned . . . but he would have gone up there with you, angel. . . .

This would have concluded her business with Spade and Archer, but when Thursby was independently murdered, she knew Gutman was on her trail again.

> SPADE: You needed another protector, somebody to fill Thursby's boots . . . so you came back to me. . . .

Brigid sobs wildly: she would have come back anyway, for from the first she loved him.

> SPADE (*flatly*): Well, if you get a good break, you'll be out of Tehachapi in twenty years—and you can come back to me then. I hope they don't hang you, precious, by that sweet neck . . . *I'm going to send you over!*

Brigid tries to laugh away his chilling words, but her face darkens as she grasps his cruel resolve:

> SPADE: You're taking the fall—*I won't play the sap for you!* (*He shouts, his reserve finally snapped.*) I don't care who loves who!!!
> . . . I won't walk in Thursby's—and I don't know how many other's—footsteps. You killed Miles, and you're going over for it . . . when a man's partner is killed, he's supposed to do something about it . . . when one of your organization is killed, it's bad business to let the killer get away with it . . . bad for every detective, everywhere. . . .

Finally, he cannot let her off the hook, because "all of me wants to regardless of consequence . . . and because you counted on that, the same as you counted on that with all the others!" A poignant note of triumph trembles in his voice. To her venal insinuation that he would never have betrayed her if the Falcon were real and he had received full fee, he retorts—"Don't be too sure I'm as crooked as I'm supposed to be. That kind of reputation might be good business, bringing high-priced jobs, and making it easier to deal with the enemy."

Polhaus and Dundy arrive—Gutman and his accomplices have been taken. Spade gives them Brigid, the weapons Wilmer and Cairo left behind, and the thousand-dollar bill. One sees that money has little intrinsic interest for Spade; he will very likely be required to yield up the retainers Cairo and Brigid paid him, and even if he were allowed to keep the few hundred dollars, the sum hardly justifies the risks he has taken.

Dundy escorts Brigid out the door. Polhaus looks down at the statuette, trying to fathom the ancient signet of greed.

> POLHAUS: What is it?
> SPADE (*grimly satisfied*): The stuff that dreams are made of. . . .

He picks up the Falcon and walks into the hall. Brigid, manacled to Dundy, stares fixedly ahead, her face drained of emotion as the elevator gate closes upon her, harsh promise of a heavier captivity. The lift slowly descends as Spade, too, goes down the stairs, the fatal bird cradled in his hands.

Spade's entrapment of Brigid causes him exceptional agony, despite his disclaimer that it will cost only a few nights' sleep. Brigid represents to the detective what Freudians would call a "narcissistic object choice"—much of himself Spade dearly prizes is mirrored in her—her lucidity, her steely self-control (despite the phony fragile facade), her knack for gauging character and using her soundings to the best advantage. Above all, she reflects Spade's *criminality*—exponentially raised!

Leo Bellak speculated that the compulsive mystery buff is drawn to the genre to gratify unconscious criminal impulses. Frequently, in the detective novel, the shamus *himself* must engage in shady practice to prove that he is on the side of right (usually because the police are too corrupt or inefficient to do their job). Thus, he often becomes the chief suspect, and his employer classically is likely to be the real perpetrator.

Spade's explanation that he dissembles a crooked reputation the better to bilk an innominate "enemy" is a masterpiece of self-deception. Every brigand he brings to justice proves to Spade that he is not a rogue: if a man derives such kicks from tweaking the law by the nose, if he freely chooses to spend so many of his days consorting with knaves and rascals, one must be highly suspect of the knavery within him. Brigid has long since passed permanently over the line that Spade dares cross only transiently, to grapple with malefactors and reaffirm his ambiguous morality. Brigid would have wedded him forever to her culpability had he not brought her low—but ultimately, it is Miles' murder that sticks in his craw and makes him send her "over."

Archer's death has the resonance of Oedipal crime—the murder of the father-rival to enjoy the mother's favors. Although by indicting Brigid, Spade shows himself innocent to the blaming world, he must stand half-convicted in his own unconscious. For all his brave talk about upholding the sacred confederacy of detectives, he bedded Iva Archer, violating the integrity of the partnership, an impressive indicator that the fantasy of eliminating Miles was never far from his mind. One regularly finds in the analysis of men who lust after a colleague's wife that the lady in question symbolizes the forbidden mother, and the colleague is a substitute for the father the patient still seeks to displace. The obligations of partnership or professional association symbolize the incest barrier the child once longed and dreaded to penetrate.

An unacknowledged struggle for stud supremacy has existed between Spade and Archer. Miles smugly believes he has stolen away a glamorous new client. While it could be argued that Spade could not have actually foreseen Miles' murder, his intuition, razor-sharp— surely informed him that Brigid meant trouble, yet without a warning he allowed Archer the illusion of victory, permitting him to take over Brigid's affair. Spade won—he always wins—but for once he got more than he bargained for, and Miles went to his doom!

Spade loses interest in Iva immediately after Miles is dead. Admittedly, he may have been tiring of her before. Admittedly, Brigid has piqued his lust and his curiosity. But his estrangement from the widow basically may well stem from anxiety over full ownership of the fruits of Oedipal combat. With Miles out of the way, by the way, Spade *does* become sole owner of the agency. The corpse is hardly cold before Spade dispassionately orders the signs in the office altered to show his name alone; then he sets out on the new firm's first business—tracking down his partner's killer, thus denying his unrecognized complicity.

Ernest Jones believed Hamlet procrastinated avenging his father's murder because in his heart he knew he was capable of the killing, an incest-ridden patricide. The inner perception of guilt that dictates Hamlet's delay is replaced in *The Maltese Falcon* by the maze of external circumstance, the twists and turns of plot that prevent the hero from identifying the murderer and exacting retribution. Unlike the Melancholy Dane, Spade will go on to draw breath in this harsh life, haunted by realistic remorse even though he has revenged the partner-father's death.

Archer not only is his partner's *victim:* he is his *stand-in,* his patsy, as well. He *bought* Spade's death, and must be repaid. Barbara Deming has speculated that the tough-guy hero of forties' cinema endures the assaults upon his person to demonstrate that he can survive where others have been annihilated: "The hero takes the hopeless case, enters the deadly embrace, to prove himself that he can emerge intact . . . until [the] self is tried, this hero is no one, is no where. . . ." Thus, the shamus can be classified as a *counterphobic*—someone who denies fear by rushing to meet it head on. I suggest that the detective's phobia is that of *death* itself!

Again and again, Spade must signify that death shall have no dominion over him. He affects a studied indifference to Miles' killing, does not want to see the body, brushes aside expressions of sympathy—he strives to blot out the essence of Miles' *deadness* by displacing his concentration upon the *puzzle* behind his death. After Jacoby expires on his rug, Spade says resentfully—"Why couldn't he have stayed alive long enough to tell us something?" The cadaver itself could be just so much meat!

Spade's need to assert his mastery over danger and death constitutes a crucial ingredient in his outrageous provocations, whether he is inciting Dundy and Wilmer openly, or the Fat Man subtly. He regards a shaking hand outside Gutman's door with a mixture of admiration and numb relief, for he has unbalanced an adversary and cheated the reaper. His "set-ups" of Gutman very nearly succeed in getting him killed. Gutman could easily have had Wilmer dispose of him after he was drugged, but perhaps he wanted Spade alive as a possible source of assistance if the *La Paloma* did not yield up the Falcon. Later, Spade assents to torture rather than yield, outfacing Gutman, and again denying death has any terror for him.

With Wilmer's betrayal and the Falcon's recovery, Gutman once more could have elected to murder Spade before opening the package, recovering his $10,000 and insuring Spade's silence. And he could just as easily have done him in *after* the bird was proven fake. That Gutman lets Spade survive is a testament to the fear and respect the detective has inspired, plus Gutman's conviction that Spade is implicated too deeply to incriminate him.

Throughout the caper, Spade repeatedly confronts enemies bent on putting something over on him or getting something out of him. His antennae exquisitely sensitized to the possibility of exploitation, our hero always succeeds in turning the tables, putting something over or getting something out of his foe. The enemy may be overt or disguised, as expert in the coercive arts as a Borgia or clumsy as a two-bit gunsel, upright and uptight or down and dirty, on one side of the law or the other, but always dedicated to sending him to the death he owes, whether by due process or hoodlum violence. Spade deals deftly with each opponent, changing style chameleon-like to match the moment and the man, relishing the competitive game for its own sake as much as for the actual work of detection.

Finally, Spade's most formidable adversary in the "dizzy affair" is a woman. After Brigid hires him he wards off multiple onslaughts of masculine aggression to seize the Falcon and embrace her at the mystery's core. Brigid and the Falcon are equivalent: glittering birds of prey who have passed through the hands of one man after another, promising each successive owner supreme power, but bringing only ruin and destruction; Brigid is lethal as the Sphinx, that other half-woman, half-monster of antique origin who tore men apart unless they could resolve her riddle.

I have noted that Brigid's attraction for Spade is compounded out of her beauty, out of his identification with her, out of the aura of sticky helplessness she radiates that he professes to scorn, and out of his itch to master her guile and bring her to heel. Whatever the causes, Brigid succeeds where all others have failed; she has engaged what passes for tender feelings in Spade. She has awakened something akin to love in his stony spirit—but then he perceives the skull-smile mocking him behind those imploring lips. Knowing how she has served Miles, Jacoby, Thursby, he sees that she will certainly be *his* death unless he can disengage himself. The vindication of his faith in her double-dealing brings a hollow triumph. He has lain with his death, half-surrendered to the lure of oblivion, then freed himself at the precipice to take up once more his alienated existence. The analysis of the thanatophobe often uncovers the secret desire to die, to rejoin the mother in blissful union, returning to the womb of life to lie unborn and forever fulfilled.

In sum, Spade contends successfully with a series of hostile father surrogates, gains the mother in Brigid, then recoils from her clutches. One finds in certain paranoids that the father, whose image is prefigured by various imaginary persecutors, has paradoxically posed less of a threat to the patient's integrity in childhood than the first source of woe—a mother intensely intrusive, suffocating, destructive of her child's bids for autonomy and independence. It is as if the paranoid is telling us in a psychotic context that he stands a better chance of survival slugging it out with his father, than confronting the desperately needed and feared Witch-Mother, the death-goddess of myth and nightmare—Medusa, the Harpies, the Furies, the Sphinx are her adumbrations. The prolonged dependency upon mother in the earliest era of psychic and physical development carries such a constant and horrific threat of sundering of the self for those unfortunates burdened with a Harpy-Mother that closeness with every person thereafter—father, siblings, friends or lovers, will inevitably be fraught with humiliation and manipulation at best, or utter extinction at worst. Protection of the damaged self against the wounds inherent in human contact becomes of paramount importance, so that the risks of that first, frightening relationship will never be repeated.

One doesn't have to be frankly delusional to be paranoid—although it helps! There are milder forms of paranoia, quite compatible with the outward appearance of normality—especially in an environment filled with actual danger! It is enough to be chronically suspicious, to aver that things are never what they seem on the interpersonal scene, to keep eternally vigilant for the hidden message, the double-meaning, the iron fist concealed in the velvet glove and, armored against intimacy, to treat each newcomer as ill-meaning until proven otherwise.

We know next to nothing about Spade's past and his forebears—so we can only wonder if his early life experience would conform to the model described above, and later produce a paranoid life-style. Spade has chosen work in which *he* plays the role of the perpetual intruder, yet keeps his own privacy sacrosanct. He lives alone, has nodding acquaintances in connection with his work, but no evident binding male companionship. Hammett implies previous sexual liaisons: none have been durable, and although he has been capable of suffering somewhat with their loss—"a few nights' sleep"—it has evidently been more important to keep himself free from encumbrance.

Women find him attractive: his evasiveness will particularly stir up more than a few masochistic types and, let's face it, the man has style! He is physically prepossessing, has an attentive, courtly veneer replete with sexist "darlings," "sweethearts" and "angels," which he well knows how to use to keep his chauvinism and distance intact. His most substantial relationship is with his secretary. As inferred, Effie plays the dependable, asexual wife-mother, an office Penelope to Brigid's evil Circe. Spade returns from adventures and infidelities to Effie for a touch of warmth, but ultimately he denies her meaningful participation in his life. Both in the novel and the omitted last scene of Huston's scenario, it is tragically evident that she has sickened of his appalling coldness.

In our eagerness to romanticize the private eye, in our vicarious identification with his toughness, shrewdness and, yes, his self-sufficient loneliness, we have denied the barrenness of the wounded self that directly articulates with the very qualities we admire. During his quest for the Falcon, Spade eschews friendship, flirts with and rejects both homosexual and heterosexual entanglements. His career must be his sole sustenance, a profession that validates his misanthropy, mistrust and withdrawal. Pathetically, he invokes the lonely brotherhood of detectives, arrayed against a faceless "enemy" to grant a meager semblance of communion with others. The circle comes full round, and with his next case he will again resume the empty struggle against his inevitable mortality.

Bibliography

BELLAK, L. "On the Psychology of Detective Stories and Related Problems." *Psychoanalytic Review,* vol. 32 (1945). See pp. 403–407.

CHANDLER, RAYMOND. *The Simple Art of Murder.* New York: Ballantine Books, Inc., 1972. See p. 16.

———. *The Little Sister.* New York: Ballantine Books, Inc., 1971. See p. 280.

———. "Casual Notes on the Mystery Novel" in *Writing Detective and Mystery Fiction,* edited by S. Burack. Boston: The Writer Inc., 1945. See pp. 81–89.

DEMING, BARBARA. *Running Away from Myself.* New York: Grossman Publishers, 1969. See pp. 140–171.

HAMMETT, DASHIELL. *The Maltese Falcon.* New York: Random House, Inc. (Vintage), 1972.

MCARTHUR, C. Discussion in *Underworld, U.S.A.* New York: The Viking Press, Inc., 1972. See pp. 84–87.

NOLAN, WILLIAM F. *John Huston, King Rebel.* Los Angeles: Sherbourne Press, 1965. See pp. 35–44.

PEDERSON-KRAG, G. "Detective Stories and the Primal Scene." *Psychoanalytic Quarterly,* vol. 18 (1949). See pp. 203–214.

TOZZI, R., ed. *John Huston, A Pictorial Treasury of His Films.* ("Hollywood's Magic People" series.) New York: Crown Publishers, Inc. (Crescent), 1971. See pp. 32-36.

Casablanca
—If It's So Schmaltzy, Why Am I Weeping?

> Anyway we go, baby, one or the other
> You'll look prettier than me
> When we're laid out in the last scene,
> You in pink or blue with the angels
> Me in the same scar I was born with. . . .
>
> Norman Rosten: *Nobody Dies Like Humphrey Bogart*

Critic after critic has come away from *Casablanca* puzzled, almost vaguely ashamed of enjoying the film as if one should somehow know better. Much has been made of the discrepancy between the picture's aesthetic limitations and the intense gut response it has invariably provoked. Pauline Kael calls *Casablanca*—"the result of the teamwork of talented, highly paid professional hacks"—"a movie that demonstrates how entertaining a bad movie can be. . . ." For Andrew Sarris, *Casablanca* is "the happiest of happy accidents," an inexplicable pop masterpiece that eludes auteurist theory.

Certainly, *Casablanca*'s makers had no pretences that they were worshipping in the temple of high art. The director, Michael Curtiz, was an old reliable of the Warner's stable with an impressive roster of bread-and-butter pictures to his credit (*Adventures of Robin Hood, The Charge of the Light Brigade,* etc.), and no particular cinematic philosophy other than giving his audience one hell of a good time. Howard Koch assumed the mantle of chief writer by default when a shaky collaboration with Philip and Julius Epstein broke down. The brothers Epstein left for greener pastures once they sensed the picture was in trouble (or so Koch claims), forcing him to improvise madly from the sketchiest ideas based upon a play that never made the Broadway boards —*Everyone Came to Rick's.* A tight production schedule constantly threatened to outrace the hapless author's inventive powers—right down to the wire no one was sure who would wind up on the Lisbon flight, as Curtiz, cast members and assorted colleagues and kibitzers assailed Koch's sensibilities with contradictory advice.

Small wonder that—on paper—the screenplay rarely heaves itself above the pedestrian. One must grant Koch a certain pithy irony, still many of his lines read monumentally hokey, or merely graceless— "Victor, please don't go to the underground meeting tonight!"— "Was that cannon fire, or is it my heart pounding?" Improbable device and unlikely coincidence abound, but—"Don't worry what's logical," said the amiable Curtiz, "I make it go so fast, no one notices!"

In the best Hollywood fairy-tale tradition, Koch's uneven scenario underwent a striking metamorphosis before the camera. The lines were now utterly convincing, acted by a superbly polished cast against Max Steiner's lovely, if slightly overripe, score. Bergman and Bogart—the first and last time they played together—lit up the screen. The film went on to garner three Oscars—picture, direction and, incredibly, screenplay. During the three decades since its release, *Casablanca* has acquired an ineluctable shimmer of nostalgia, yet it still speaks powerfully to young people born after World War II who are only marginally acquainted with the politics of its day. "*Casablanca* succeeds as allegory, popular myth, clinical psychology . . . and as a superb romantic melodrama," writes Richard Corliss; the secret of the film's perennial appeal continues to elude easy definition, but to a large measure I believe it is the extraordinary attractiveness of the Bogart hero that has made *Casablanca* into the stuff of legend.

I have already pinpointed the paranoia of Fred C. Dobbs and Sam Spade—blatant paranoia in the former character, latent and better concealed in the latter's case; Dobbs is Spade decompensated, at a more advanced, delusional stage of psychological decay! Throughout his career, Humphrey Bogart was exceptionally successful as the outsider, the dweller in marginal and dangerous milieus, exiled from love. Typically, the Bogart protagonist has thrust closeness away and exercises eternal vigilance to survive in a hostile world. Men savagely compete with him; women seek to ensnare and exploit him. Inevitably, his deepest allegiance must be owed to his own embattled self, if he is to keep his tenuous balance on the precipice.

But if the essence of the Bogart persona were pure paranoia, nothing truer or finer, I do not think we would still be drawn to his mystique. Paranoids are never notable for their endearing qualities. Dobbs and Spade are unpleasant, unadmirable men. In their cold denial of the heart, they resemble the ruthless gangsters of the earlier Bogart films. Yet, it is unlikely we would have been given the later, disillusioned romantics and cynical humanists were it not for these melancholy hoodlums. In Bogie's criminals, taken at their best, the potential for violence could be tempered by an unexpected sadness and softness. One remembers Roy Earle, the inarticulate heister of *High Sierra*, who spent his ill-gotten gain healing a faithless crippled girl, and whose affection for his raggedy mutt brought on his bloody end.

As Bogart grew in stature, the troubled idealist behind the callous facade likewise became more accessible. One discerned an authentic decency shining through the uncaring mask the wounding past had forced upon the protagonist. Surely the prototype of these embittered gentlemen is Rick Blaine, exiled champion of lost causes come to uneasy rest in pro-Vichy Casablanca, owner and sole proprietor of the nightclub wherein the silver screen's headiest blending of patriotic and sexual fantasy is acted out. . . .

Casablanca was filmed while the United States still preserved its ties with the Vichy regime in France and its North African colonies, an allegiance that provoked sharp censure of President Roosevelt by increasingly vocal anti-Fascist Americans. In retrospect, Roosevelt's tangled Vichy policy was never dictated by sympathy for the Nazis or their minions. Rather, his advisors failed to grasp the charisma of Charles DeGaulle, and Roosevelt himself seemed to have a marked antipathy to the ascetic, inflexible Colonel exiled in England and heavily touted by Winston Churchill. Roosevelt sought to woo better-known French military figures thought friendlier to American interests. Unfortunately, some of these were in fact frank collaborators, such as the notoriously corrupt Admiral Jean Darlan, while others owed a divided loyalty—like General Henri Giraud, a personal friend of Pétain, but an avowed anti-Nazi. Roosevelt hoped that Giraud and Darlan could persuade the conservative, Anglophobic colonial French army elite not to resist a combined English-American invasion of North Africa.

Casablanca was released in November, 1942. By then, the reactionary French officers who ruled the colonies with our tacit consent had proven as harsh, repressive and unfriendly to the allies as the Nazis. American troops had been killed by Vichy gunfire on North African soil. Despite his opposition to the Gaullist cause, Roosevelt significantly elected to show *Casablanca* at the White House on New Year's Eve, December 31, 1942. The President, I believe, may very well have been telegraphing a change in strategy, for soon thereafter the controversial connection with Vichy was severed. Two weeks later, January 14, 1943, Roosevelt traveled to Casablanca where he conferred with Churchill, DeGaulle and Giraud. Giraud was discarded not long after the Casablanca conference, and Roosevelt, however unhappily, accepted Charles DeGaulle as unquestioned commander of the Free French. My summary does scant justice to the Byzantine complexity of US-Vichy-Free French-Allied relations; the interested reader is referred to *OSS*, by R. Harris Smith.

Warner Brothers had sounded the alarm over Hitler long before America's formal entry into the European theater. The studio had already produced strong anti-Fascist pictures in the late thirties and early forties—*Confessions of a Nazi Spy, The Great Dictator*, etc. It is not impossible that the makers of *Casablanca* were either ignorant or scornful of Roosevelt's devious games. (Warner's top brass had access to high government sources, but I have been unable to ascertain whether word of Roosevelt's true intentions vis-à-vis his Vichy policy ever "leaked" to the studio.) If not, one may speculate that Rick

Blaine's refusal to take up the sword at a time when Hollywood had become a haven for talented emigrés fleeing Nazi persecution was intended to be symbolic of the Roosevelt administration's vacillation in North Africa. Rick's change of heart at the end would then forcibly point out to our equivocating leaders the path of honor.

At any rate, the cinematic Casablanca does capture the essence of the actual city during those turbulent days, if inevitably perceived through Hollywood's distorting prism. Espionage flourished—one reason Roosevelt insisted upon keeping a legitimate American presence throughout Vichy territory was to facilitate the machinations of an impressive intelligence network. For instance, a dozen "Vice Consuls" dispatched to North Africa to study "social and economic conditions," were actually OSS operatives on the payroll of the famous (or infamous) "Wild Bill" Donovan. They regularly frequented haunts very much like Rick's cafe, sleazy hotbeds of intrigue where "German and Italian officers, spies, double agents, genuine diplomats and elegantly coiffured prostitutes" rubbed elbows.

Thousands of refugees from the Blitzkreig swelled the city's population. Many were Jewish and at least fairly well-to-do. They came by tortuous routes and then, unless they had wealth or influence enough to promote a quick exit, were caught in the corruption and prejudice of the Vichy bureaucracy. Victimized by the pitiless preditors who fattened upon their suffering, their hope and cash dwindling with each passing day, the refugee presence lent Casablanca the air of a bourgeois concentration camp, a kind of festering Brighton.

The film's opening quickly sketches in this frenetic milieu. Columns of the dispossessed trudge wearily forward, superimposed over the revolving globe. The camera pans down from a mosque into the teeming streets of Casablanca; to the ominous strains of *"Deutschland Über Alles"* a police official intones over the radio: "Two German couriers carrying important official documents murdered on train from Oran. . . . Round up all suspicious characters. . . ." A man in the crowd is seized. He breaks away and is shot down before a poster of Marshal Pétain—in his wallet, documents bearing the Cross of Lorraine. Suspects are herded into the station house, under the tarnished motto—*"Liberté, Egalite, Fraternité."*

An airplane drones overhead, followed by the hungry gaze of the refugees. But the plane is not the daily flight to Lisbon, gateway to freedom in the Americas; instead, it shows the swastika, and carries Major Heinrich Strasser (Conrad Veidt, earlier in his career a German matinee idol—and the somnambulist of *The Cabinet of Dr. Caligari*), a Gestapo official complete with monocle, disdainful smile and thoroughly nasty disposition. Strasser is met by the Vichy Prefect of Police, Captain Louis Renault (Claude Rains). The two are perfect foils—Strasser, the apotheosis of the Hollywood Nazi, Renault, a stock company Parisian, urbane, witty, an inveterate womanizer. Renault regards the corrupted world and his own corruption with equally amused detachment. He is outwardly deferential, but his *politesse* has a derisive edge that is mostly lost upon the arrogant Nazi:

> RENAULT: . . . *Unoccupied* France welcomes you . . . you may find the climate of Casablanca a trifle warm, Major.
> STRASSER: Oh, we Germans must get used to all climates, from Russia to the Sahara. . . .

Renault assures Strasser that the couriers' murderer will be taken tonight, at ''Rick's''—''Everyone comes to Rick's!'' Dissolve to the *Café Américain,* at the edge of the airport. A finger of light from the beacon sweeps periodically across the cafe throughout the film, subtly evoking intimations of escape or confinement.

The camera ushers us inside, where the decor is ersatz Moorish, and a jaunty Negro, Sam (Dooley Wilson) entertains a polyglot crowd from his piano. We drift from table to table, through shady deals and the exchange of dubious information in diverse accents: ''Waiting, waiting, waiting . . . I'll never get out of here, I'll die in Casablanca. . . . Sorry, Madam, but diamonds are a drug on the market, everybody sells diamonds . . . the fishing smack *Santiago*. It leaves at one tomorrow night . . . bring fifteen thousand francs, *in cash.*'' The clientele comprises nearly every race and condition; dressed elegantly or humbly, faces reflecting hectic gaiety, furtive greed, blind hope, dumb resignation. Everyone *does* come to Rick's; the club is a ship of fools, a feverish microcosm of Casablanca and the larger world beyond the airstrip, a world in chaos, where tradition and class distinctions have been turned upside down.

In the gaming room, affluent guests ask the genial waiter, Carl, a former higher mathematics professor (S. Z. "Cuddles" Sakall) to invite the owner to their table. Carl refuses—Rick never drinks with the customers. Perhaps, insists a gentleman, if Rick knew he ran the second largest banking house in Amsterdam?

> CARL: . . . That wouldn't interest Rick—the leading banker in Amsterdam is now the pastry chef—and his father is the bellboy!

Close-up: an empty glass, a smoldering cigarette, a hand scribbling across a check—"OK—Rick." The camera pulls back, revealing Richard Blaine staring expressionlessly at a chessboard, the perennial loner in a crowd. Commotion at the door—he rises, peremptorily disposes of a bumptious German trying to bull his way in. An unctuous little exporter of refugees, Ugarte (Peter Lorre) approaches him. He pointedly evades questions about his origins and disparages Ugarte's hypocritical expression of sympathy for the murdered couriers—"They got a break. Yesterday they were just two German clerks. Today, they're the Honored Dead."

Ugarte then insinuates that he killed the couriers to obtain "Letters of Transit, signed by General Weygand. They cannot be rescinded, not even questioned. . . ." * He is going to sell the letters tonight for a fortune, and leave Casablanca. Precisely because he knows Rick despises him, Ugarte thinks the American can be trusted. He hands him the Letters, Rick surreptitiously slips them under the top of Sam's piano to the tune of "Who's Got Trouble?" (Sam's songs cleverly furnish a running commentary on the action throughout the film.)

Señor Ferrari (Sydney Greenstreet), the bloated proprietor of the rival "Blue Parrot" and head of the thriving black market importunes Rick to sell him the cafe—an offer, one senses, that has been tendered many other times and is once more ritually rejected. As Rick passes by his bar, a young woman drunkenly reproaches him:

> YVONNE: Where were you last night?
> RICK: That's so long ago, I don't remember.

---

* General Maxime Weygand, 74-year-old Vichy Governor of North Africa, supposedly was the bastard son of the ill-fated Emperor Maximilian of Mexico. Although the person of Weygand was real, no Letters of Transit, with such absolute irrevocability, could ever have been issued by him.

YVONNE: Will I see you tonight?
RICK: I never make plans that far ahead.

Before she can make a scene, Rick hustles her out and directs his mad Russian bartender, Sascha (Leonid Kinskey) to take her home. "What a fool I was, to fall in love with a man like you!" she cries after him.

Renault, who has observed the scene, joins Rick on the terrace. He wonders wryly if his chances with Yvonne will improve now that Rick has thrown her over. He, too, attempts to probe Rick's past:

> RENAULT: I have often speculated on why you don't return to America. Did you abscond with the church funds? Did you run off with a Senator's wife? I should like to think you killed a man!
> RICK: It was a combination of all three.
> RENAULT: And what in Heaven's name brought you to Casablanca?
> RICK: My health. I came . . . for the waters.
> RENAULT: The waters? We are in the desert!
> RICK: I was misinformed. . . .

When Renault advises him not to interfere in an arrest at the club tonight, Rick counters sharply—"I stick my neck out for nobody!" The film has quickly established him as the morose master of a unique private kingdom. He has indeed come to Casablanca for his health—his spiritual health, on a misguided quest to cure melancholy with solitude. Within the perimeter of the *Café Américain* Rick has reinvented himself. Like Sam Spade, his paramount concern seems to be the preservation of his privacy. Outsiders, whatever their purposes, are treated as unwelcome intruders into his life space—the customers who want him to join them, the obstreperous German, Ugarte, Ferrari, Yvonne, even Louis Renault. Spade enjoyed thwarting intruders, but there is little zest in Rick and much grimness. His waning energies have been consumed in constructing a sanctuary run by a cadre of devoted followers, requiring minimum personal engagement from their boss. Defended against human contact and comfort beyond the ritual camaraderie of his staff, Rick exudes an air of haughty withdrawal that provides enormous drawing power for his fascinated customers. But his attention is inextricably turned inward: depressed and dispirited, he prowls his borders, a brooding enigma cloaked in inviolable sadness. Unlike Dobbs and Spade, Rick does continue to evoke warm responses and concern from others. His paranoia is not yet confirmed, although given time it might prevail.

Of those who seek to penetrate his cover, Rick is most sympathetic towards Louis Renault. Renault wants Rick's friendship, but his questionable politics and competitiveness stand in the way. Renault envies and resents Rick's easy success with women—note his fantasy of taking up with Rick's discarded mistress. Rick shares Renault's mistrust of altruistic motives, but Renault's opportunism is worn gaily, and he is still very much a social being, while Rick has come to serve himself alone out of the extremity of his despair and distrust.

Renault reveals that a famous Czech freedom fighter, Victor Laszlo, has escaped from the Gestapo and come to Casablanca. A mysterious beauty travels with him, and it is rumored he has the cash to purchase the Letters of Transit. Renault observes that Rick is impressed by mention of Laszlo's name, the first he has ever seen him impressed by anyone. Rick bets the Prefect 10,000 francs that Laszlo will succeed, but wonders why Renault thinks he would help the Czech. Renault suspects that the secretive American is a closet idealist: he knows that Rick ran guns in Ethiopia and fought in Spain against Franco. Rick grows obviously uncomfortable, implies that he has always acted purely for profit, but fails to convince the wily policeman.

Meanwhile, Strasser and his party are ushered to a choice table ("I have . . . given him the best," says Carl, "knowing he is German and would take it anyway!") On cue, Renault's men arrest Ugarte at the roulette wheel; he pulls a gun, flees through the club to Rick who coldly refuses to lift a finger as the little man is dragged off screaming for help. "I stick my neck out for nobody!" repeats Rick, to an offended bystander.

Renault introduces Rick to Strasser, and it develops the Gestapo has a file on him, too—"Richard Blaine, age 37—cannot return to his country—the reason is a little vague. . . ." Like Renault, Strasser thinks Rick might help Laszlo, but his interrogation yields only bland evasions and Rick's assurances of absolute neutrality—"You'll excuse me gentlemen, your business is politics, mine is running a saloon!" Strasser's dossier compounds rather than clarifies Rick's mystery.

Noble and base motives are mixed in this "saloonkeeper": he has fought on the right sides but, he would have us believe, always for the worst reasons, strictly as an entrepreneur. Rick is an exile, much is made of this, but the film will never explain why he cannot go home again.

Rick might have been scapegoated for a Red-lover: there were American witch-hunts in the thirties, too. Still, it is unlikely that he would have been exiled for his politics alone. I would rather believe that he has never committed an actual deportable offense. His banishment is symbolic: quite possibly *Casablanca*'s creators meant it as a metaphor for the bitter estrangement of those on the Committed Left from the majority of their fellow countrymen who remained indifferent to the rallying cry against injustice at home and abroad.

But at a deeper level Rick is exiled from *himself*—because of a crime, or, more accurately, because of the disturbing fantasies attendant upon one of the first crimes mortals ever contemplate. Oedipus, King of Thebes, was condemned to wander blindly through alien lands because he slew his father and married his mother. Louis Renault jokes that Rick cannot return to *his* homeland because he is guilty of stealing sacred property (the church funds), absconding with a high official's wife (intriguingly, the *President*'s wife in an earlier script, later amended to a senator's wife), or murdering someone.

Equally in jest, Rick confesses to "a combination" of these three transgressions. The psychoanalyst, accustomed to searching out hidden truth in such banter, would interpret the sacrosanct stolen treasure as the wife of a preeminent older man; her husband is the one murdered—and by the love-thief. Thus, the essence of this "combination" of offenses is the child's original desire to kill his father and possess his mother! Renault, Rick's alter ego, meditates upon the Oedipal struggle in his mock charge against the man he would have as friend. The deadly intent towards the beloved father, so crucial to the remorse and anxiety of the little boy during the Oedipal period, still appears to trouble Rick's adult sensibilities.

Victor Laszlo enters the club, clad in immaculate whites, lean, elegant and self-assured (the underground appears to be taking good care of its own!); on his arm, a woman of extraordinary loveliness, also in white. The couple make an instant cynosure; Sam, looking up from his piano, recognizes the lady with a sense of yearning catastrophe and shortly thereafter launches into "Love for Sale"! Renault goes to their table, and she asks him about "the boy who is playing the piano." Renault tells her that Sam came from Paris with Rick, and Rick— "Rick is, well, Mademoiselle, he is the kind of man that . . . if I were a woman . . . and *I* were not around, I would be in love with Rick!" The Prefect has unwittingly betrayed repressed homosexual longings for the very man he has been competing with. In therapy, one often discovers unconscious sexual attraction towards an idealized and envied rival.

Strasser attempts to speak with Laszlo; when Laszlo is deliberately offensive to him, the iron Major superciliously orders him in for questioning at Renault's office the next morning and stalks off. Laszlo goes to the bar, learns to his dismay from an underground contact that Ugarte has been taken. Meanwhile, the woman in white has bidden Sam and his piano to her side, setting in motion the mainspring of the plot. The Negro is deferential, wary: he well remembers how this Circe can enchant and hurt. We, too, have been moved by the powerful melding of her innocence and sensuality. The camera eye catches Bergman in a series of breathtaking close-ups as she tempts every man who sets his eye upon her, the more enticing for her disarming lack of seductiveness.

She asks Sam to play "some of the old songs;" he tries "Avalon"—it is not what she wants to hear, and he evades her questions about Rick with the assumed imbecility of a black man who dares not confront a white woman head-on with his true feelings. When she persists, he drops the handkerchief-head routine with a gentle admonition—"Leave him alone, Miss Ilsa. You're bad luck to him. . . ." Still she presses him—"Play it once for old time's sake. . . . Play it, Sam. Play—'As Time Goes By'!" Against his better judgment, Sam is swept away by her allure, by their shared nostalgia for happier days. He sings of the timeless rituals of lovers, and Ilsa's eyes brim with tears. Rick tears out of the casino, furious at hearing the forbidden song. The music stops for a few heartbeats as Rick, shocked, gazes at Ilsa across the months of his anguished, now abortive, mourning.

Renault and Laszlo, returning from the bar, come upon them, thus.

Before Renault can introduce them, they greet quietly. Renault tries to present Laszlo, but Ilsa firmly takes over—she *wants* these two to meet, and at her direction! To Renault's surprise, Rick breaks his standing rule and accepts Laszlo's invitation to drink. They exchange compliments. It is evident that Rick considers himself the Czech's inferior:

> LASZLO: This is a very interesting cafe. I congratulate you.
> RICK: And I congratulate you. . . .
> LASZLO: Thank you. I try.
> RICK: We all try. *You* succeed.

At Renault's instigation, Rick and Ilsa speak about their last meeting—in Paris, the day the Germans occupied the city. "I remember every detail," says Rick. "The Germans wore gray. You wore blue." Their recollections skirt the edge of indiscretion. Laszlo, unperturbed, rises to leave and Rick takes his check. "Another precedent broken," Renault exclaims with relish.

Throughout the scene Rick has addressed Ilsa evenly, as if there were nothing between them. After she goes, his poise crumbles. A few hours later we find him hunched numbly over a half-empty bottle as the airport beacon intermittently probes the darkened, empty cafe. Sam tries to cozen Rick into going fishing, drinking or some other worthy masculine pursuit. Rick is obstinate—"I'm waiting for a lady!"—so Sam stays on to keep watch over his employer.

How deeply rooted were our prejudices that in a film of so much liberal pretense, the slighting reference to the "boy at the piano" falls so trippingly from the White Heroine's lips! Sam is on far more equal footing with Rick than most blacks with whites in forties' cinema, but his character is nonetheless warped by racist convention. He has enough native dignity to escape total caricature, but if he is no Steppen Fetchit, there is still a great deal of Uncle Tom in him, in his self-effacing service to "Mister Rick," his humble attitude towards "Miss Ilsa."

Sam's music is the key that unlocks the lovers' longing. Sam himself, like his songs, is finally only a touchstone, lacking substance or sexuality, a gelded servant. He loves Rick, but is not even permitted the limited prerogatives of the less glamorous "sidekick" of the Lily-

White Hero. Note that he is not allowed to fight beside Rick with the Free French at the film's end. Sorrily, one concludes that Sam is a slightly liberalized edition of that old Hollywood favorite, the faithful family retainer of the ante-bellum plantation house, Uncle Remus in *Song of the South,* Mammy in *Gone With the Wind*—the surrogate darky parent who watches anxiously over the fortunes of adoptive white children and respects, indeed treasures, a lower place in the order of things.

"It's December 1941 in Casablanca," Rick muses. "What time is it in New York? . . . I bet they're asleep in New York—I bet they're asleep all over America!—of all the gin joints, in all the towns, in all the world, she walks into mine!" He free-associates America's unwillingness to recognize the rise of Fascism to Ilsa's reappearance; the connection is not accidental. Rick projects upon the remiss homeland his own ideological dereliction, for he has let his commitment to the cause of liberty slumber because of his disastrous affair with her. Now he bids Sam to "play it again," and the camera slips away from his face, bleak with memories stirred by the music, into a flashback. . . .

Paris before the German invasion—Rick and Ilsa meet and fall in love. Presaging the lovers of *Last Tango in Paris,* they promise not to question each's past, but Rick, like Brando, cannot keep to the bargain. Why should he be lucky enough to find someone like her unattached? Even the happier Rick, one notes, is faintly self-minimizing. Ilsa admits there was another man, but he is dead and Rick her only beloved. Cut to newsclips of the *Anschluss.* Now it is not safe for Rick—he has a "record," a Gestapo price on his head, although we are never told why.

At the bar of their favorite bistro, Sam playing in the background, Rick toasts Ilsa with the last of the proprietor's champagne—"Here's looking at you, kid!" Ilsa pleads with him to flee; chuckling at the thought, he suggests they marry on the train from Paris. She does not share his joy, but he is oblivious to her suffering. She promises to go with him later in the day, and asks to be kissed "as though it was the last time." Dissolve to Rick, waiting at the station. Sam brings him word that Ilsa has checked out of her hotel, leaving a cryptic message that she can never see him again. . . . "You must not ask why. Just believe I love you. . . ." Rain blurs the page, Ilsa's cruel farewell seems to dissolve in tears. Rick throws the fatal letter away and stares, devastated, down the platform. . . .

Back to the present. Ilsa stands at the door; she says she would not have come earlier had she realized he was *the* Rick, but this only exacerbates his smouldering resentment. He wants neither her sympathy nor her explanations, only to punish her relentlessly until his pain is driven away. She belatedly tries to tell him something of her history, about a young girl from Oslo, freshly arrived in Paris, who met "a very great and very good man." He opened her eyes to a new world of ideas and ideals—"and she looked up to him, worshipped him, with a feeling she supposed was love."

Rick stops her rudely. He's heard it all before, to the tune of "a tinny piano in the parlor downstairs." Ridden with self-disgust, he nevertheless must plunge on, driven to soil irreparably that which he once held so dear. "Who was it you left me for? Was it Laszlo—or were there others in between? Or—aren't you the kind that tells!" She refuses to honor his spite with an answer, leaves silently. Rick's head slumps forward, and we do not see, but rather sense, his tears.

Degrading her into every man's slut will redeem his loss, he hopes, for if she is a whore, then it is of little consequence to have lost a whore's dubious affections. Yet, listening with the third ear, one hears the strangled screams of rage over his beloved's betrayal of him in the arms of a more desirable rival. The Bogart protagonist rarely speaks openly of these abrasions upon his spirit. Instead, one will more likely encounter the precipitate of his pain, the protective shell of paranoia, flawlessly articulated against the peril of involvement—"Nobody ever takes advantage of Fred C. Dobbs!"

Rick dismisses Ilsa's account of a schoolgirl infatuation with Laszlo as a cheap gloss upon her promiscuity. There is a kernel of psychological truth in his sordid accusation, for Ilsa is not quite the innocent she seems. She has actually been unfaithful to Rick *and* to Laszlo, although the picture will go to great lengths, as we shall see, to rationalize her infidelity. She would have us believe that she would never have come to the cafe had she known Rick was in Casablanca. If the name of the club was not sufficient tip-off, Sam's presence should have been for, knowing *his* fidelity, she must have guessed that whither Rick went, there surely followed Sam. Nevertheless, she compels him to play the song that must bring Rick back into her life, instead of turning on her heel and leaving on the spot.

In the previous chapter I described the ''Madonna-Whore'' syndrome, wherein a man cannot allow one woman to satisfy both his sexual and non-sexual needs because of anxiety over unconscious incestuous feelings toward his mother. The feminine image becomes split, so that woman is viewed either as a ''good'' source of nurture and support, or a ''bad'' object of sexual desire. The typical Madonna-Whore type goes unaroused or impotent with his spouse, for the wife unconsciously represents the forbidden mother. But sex will be highly enjoyable away from the marriage bed, with women who are likely to be chosen from a lower social class, as different from the mental construct of the idealized, non-sexual mother as night from day. The Madonna-Whore syndrome is one of many symptomatic outcomes of the boy's Oedipus complex. If the little girl cannot work through her corresponding Electra complex, she too may suffer a ''good-bad'' split in her unconscious image of man. This frequently occurs when a father has behaved seductively towards his daughter, escalating her normal erotic fantasies about him, intensifying her wish to supplant her mother, and her fear of her mother's punishment for harboring these reprehensible longings.

Such a daughter, in the first flush of youth, may find herself unaccountably drawn to an older man—frequently a widower!—who awakens in her bosom the noblest of sentiments, yet fails to inspire passion, for passion would complete a dreaded equation between suitor and father. Sooner or later, she grows physically attracted to another man, usually younger and, in the more disturbed variations upon this theme, from a baser or frankly debased background (cf., *The Barefoot Contessa*—whose predilection for grimy types is ascribed in the film to her Gypsy origins rather than incestuous anxiety!).

The young lady may opt for marriage to the older man because of his wisdom, kindness or prestige, then keep a troubled relationship afloat by a succession of affairs, but always returning to the father substitute (the ''Contessa'' marries a castrated Count, still can't keep her mitts off the gardener and other assorted louts). She may eventually

work through her neurosis with or without therapy, leave her husband
with the healthy recognition that her marriage is a bloodless fiction, or
discover that she truly loves him and make a decisive commitment.

Ilsa Lund has been incapable of a commitment to one man, neither
to Laszlo, who we will discover is her husband, or to Rick. Her vacillation makes her a teasing riddle to both men, indeed to every man
who comes within her magnetic field and thinks she can be his, for she
is in fact no one's! Laszlo constitutes an idealized asexual father figure. He inspires heroic thoughts, but leaves her frigid below the neck-
line. I suggest that Rick, this mysterious man of questionable background, lacked Laszlo's ethical purpose even before Ilsa left him, his
ideals compromised by self-doubt and more than a tinge of venality.
For Rick, a dethroned and humanized Laszlo, for flawed and fallible
Rick, Ilsa may burn. Relative to the Czech's implacable righteousness,
Rick is made of baser metal, but he is also inherently more attractive,
just as Milton's bloodless God pales in comparison to Lucifer!

At Renault's office the next morning, Strasser offers Laszlo freedom
in return for betraying the underground leaders. Laszlo predictably denounces the Nazi with thunderous eloquence and Renault, ever
amused by any excess of zeal, takes the wind out of his sails with the
news that Ugarte has died during the night, probably from foul play.

Rick goes to the Blue Parrot to allow the police to search the cafe.
Ferrari, suspecting he has the Letters, offers to dispose of them at an
enormous profit, but Rick plays dumb. Laszlo and Ilsa arrive; while
Laszlo goes off to confer with Ferrari, Rick fumbles an apology to
Ilsa. It is her turn to play the rejector. Soon she will quit Casablanca,
never see him again, it is better that way. Rick let his guard down tentatively—now it goes up, instantly. He says she will lie to Laszlo as
she lied to him, and then he will be waiting for her—"up a flight."
Never, she rejoins, Laszlo is her husband, and was at the time of their
affair! Having delivered the *coup de grace,* and incidentally vindicated
his paranoid convictions of her faithlessness, she leaves him speech-
less.

Ferrari has told Laszlo he cannot secure him a visa—even though
"as leader of all illegal activities in Casablanca I am an influential and
respected man." It would be possible to smuggle Ilsa out. But she
stands firm—she will not abandon her husband, just as he has never

abandoned her. Ferrari is transformed, another cynic converted to altruism against his better judgment (the movie is full of them!), and counsels Laszlo to see Rick about the Letters.

Later that evening, the same cast of characters is reassembled at the cafe. Rick gloomily mulls over Ilsa's revelation. A comely Bulgarian refugee, Annina, interrupts his drinking, pleading for guidance. Her husband is trying unsuccessfully to raise money for visas at the tables. Captain Renault has promised to waive his usual bribe if she will give herself to him. Can he be trusted? She asks Rick to grant her absolution in advance of sinning:

> ANNINA: If someone loved you—so that your happiness was the only thing that she wanted in the world . . . and she did a bad thing to make certain of it . . . could you forgive her?
> RICK: Nobody ever loved me that much. . . .

Rick dismisses her as harshly as he did Ilsa last night. Yet, a moment later, after greeting Laszlo and Ilsa courteously, he fixes his own roulette wheel, letting Annina's husband win, to her overwhelming gratitude, his staff's admiration and Renault's chagrin. But when Laszlo asks him, either in the name of the dignity of man, or for several hundred thousand francs to part with the Letters, Rick paradoxically refuses—"I'm not interested in politics. The problems of the world are not in my department. I'm a saloonkeeper." (Note that he positively glories in that title, masochistically relishing his downfall.) He tells Laszlo his wife knows why he will not yield.

Annina's dilemma has struck uncomfortably close to home. Like Ilsa, she seems the soul of innocence, yet she is ready to betray her beloved and sell herself—out of the purest reasons, of course. Pity for her plight and rage at her perfidy struggle for mastery in Rick's bosom. By letting her husband win, Rick affirms his basic decency, but also cheats the Prefect of his prize. We have seen that Renault is more than Rick's competitor—he is an extension of Rick's persona as well. His principles, too, lie in hopeless disrepair. He, too, has excluded himself from the lists of love—he indulges in casual liaisons with women who value his power over his person. Tellingly, he says to Rick: "Why do you interfere with my little romances? When it comes to women, you have charm, I have only visas!" Rick has only the Letters with which to vanquish his rival Laszlo, and win back Ilsa—how shoddy a victory!

Strasser leads his party in a thumping rendition of *"Die Wacht Am Rhine."* Hearing the hated song, Laszlo strides decisively over to the orchestra and demands the *"Marseillaise."* The bandleader looks uncertainly to Rick, who having just stated forcibly his disinterest in crusades, again reverses directions and nods permission. On one side of the cafe, Strasser urges his men into the harmonic fray, while on the other Laszlo shakes his fist at the despoilers of liberty to the stirring beat of the French national anthem, while Ilsa watches admiringly. The scales shift—the majority take up the *"Marseillaise"* with mounting exhilaration as the Nazis subside and sit by, glumly. Tears stream down the cheeks of patriot and erstwhile collaborator. The die is cast. At Rick's behest, a line has been drawn between good and evil in a place where moral ambiguity, also at Rick's behest, has been the order of the day.

The *"Marseillaise"* concludes to wild applause. Outraged, Strasser commands Renault to close down the cafe on any pretext. "I'm shocked!" cries the Prefect, *"shocked* to find that gambling is going on here!" as a croupier hands him his winnings. Strasser threatens Ilsa with Laszlo's death unless both come with him back to occupied France on safe conduct. From his goatish glance, it is clear he would enjoy having her for himself, with Laszlo out of the way.

Back at their hotel. Laszlo tells Ilsa about Rick's intransigence, and asks about her life in Paris while he was interned. She evades the question, her words echoing her last message to Rick—"Victor, whatever I do, will you believe that I. . . ." Aware that he stands on delicate ground, he kisses her tenderly, without much passion, and goes off to an Underground meeting.

Dissolve back to the cafe. Rick enters his apartment to find Ilsa waiting, just as he predicted. She begs him to put aside his jealousy and remember the Cause, but he asserts sardonically that "I'm the only Cause I'm interested in!" She invokes an unshared secret that will explain her apparent betrayal, but he is adamant in his mistrust. She reproaches him for a self-pitying coward, then breaks down sobbing. He is their last hope—without the Letters, Laszlo will die in Casablanca.

RICK: What of it! I'm going to die in Casablanca. It's a good spot for it.

He turns away to light a cigarette and back, to see her level a gun at his heart. With an oddly pleased smile he denies her the Letters again: "If Laszlo and the Cause mean so much to you, you won't stop at anything . . . go ahead and shoot, you'll be doing me a favor. . . ." The gun wavers, drops; she cannot kill him, she has never stopped loving him. Resigned to whatever fate attends upon the surrender of her responsibility to her husband, she comes into his arms.

Later, Ilsa reveals the secret that will exonerate her: shortly after her marriage, Laszlo went to Prague and was arrested. After months of anxious waiting, word came of his death. Then she met Rick. Laszlo had sworn her to silence about the marriage because she knew so much about his work—hence her lack of candor to Rick. (Of course, one may justifiably wonder why the Nazis should be less interested in interrogating a single woman—since they already knew of her relationship with Laszlo—than a married one!) Just as she was resolved to leave the city with Rick, Ilsa found that Laszlo was alive, grievously ill near Paris. She could not tell Rick, because she knew he would have stayed at his peril. Now she cannot ever leave him again, but she lacks the strength to deal with Laszlo—Rick must think for both of them, and arrange her husband's passage out of Casablanca so that he can carry on with his work. Then he will have everything he has lived for. "All except one," Rick says heavily, "he won't have you. . . ."

Here is the psychological fulcrum of the film. Until now, Ilsa has divided her commitment; her splitting of the male image and her predisposition towards infidelity are explained away by the familiar "dream factory" practice of rendering an unacceptable wish acceptable and "legitimizing" psychological conflict by invoking the demands of reality or a twist of fate—Hollywood reality, Hollywood fate. The fortunes of war and the Nazi evil have forced two lovers upon this pitiable woman, not the vagaries of her unconscious. Thus is she kept worthy, pure and guiltless, exciting our admiration rather than our censure!

If Laszlo and Rick are unconscious reflections of Ilsa's father, she in turn appears to *his* unconscious as a mother-surrogate. His anguish since Paris is an updating of the intolerable suffering sustained by the little boy during the Oedipal period, when he realizes that his beloved mother belongs irrevocably to another; that he can never make the same demands upon her affection as his father. Today it is fashionable to mock at Freud as a naive reductionist, but the analyst who breaks down the walls of a patient's repressions still will stand as amazed and discomfited as that wise man of Vienna at the timeless agony of the Oedipal child raging at his "faithless" mother.

Bested by an unknown rival, Rick sinks into boozy depression and rages at Ilsa as a faithless slut. The discovery that his adversary is Laszlo consolidates the Czech patriot's position in Rick's mind as a revered, envied father-substitute, for Laszlo, unswervingly committed to his ideals, represents an ideal towards which Rick once aspired and then fell away. The core of the Oedipal dilemma is the mixture of murderous and loving feelings towards the father. Freud believed this fundamental ambivalence could only be worked through when the little boy ceased competing with his father and instead began to iden-tify with him (a similar resolution hopefully takes place with the little girl vis-à-vis her mother). The child affirms that when he grows up he will be like his father, sharing the father's values, allowed the preroga-tives of manhood, including a sustaining relationship with a woman, just as father had with *his* wife. This process is never as simple as marrying a girl just like the girl who married dear old dad. We spend the rest of our lives forging and reforging the instruments of identity; assimilating what makes sense of parental values, discarding what does not.

The blow that destroyed Rick's trust in a woman's love has also soured his dedication to the "Cause," a dedication that never rested on as firm a foundation as Laszlo's. The film never clarifies whether Rick worked for the Underground in Paris, and leaves more than a shadow of a doubt concerning his motives in Ethiopia and Spain. I make my usual disclaimer: we know little about Rick's past, his fam-ily, childhood or adolescence—still, all signs indicated he was not as whole and centered a personality as Laszlo even before Paris, quite possibly because of his inability to resolve the Oedipal dilemma and identify effectively with his father. When Laszlo pops up with Ilsa in

Casablanca, I submit that Rick's long-repressed Oedipal ambivalence resurfaces with a vengeance. He respects, admires Laszlo, but will send him to most certain death by withholding the Letters, unless he can get Ilsa back, regaining the lost mother and healing the Oedipal trauma.

Ilsa Lund, like Brigid O'Shaughnessy, metamorphoses into the Bogart hero's death, a death Richard Blaine would gladly meet, for he has nothing to lose except his pain if Ilsa pulls the trigger. Her hand falters, the balance shifts back to the side of life. It is an instant of epiphany: Ilsa finds the commitment that has eluded her as she perceives how very deeply she has hurt Rick, how very much she has deluded herself into thinking she loved Laszlo. But Rick, winning the Oedipal victory, holding all the cards, immediately is guilt ridden as he perceives what her loss will mean to the valiant Czech. His remorse demonstrates that his mask of selfish cynicism is dropping away, and his authentic, moral self is now reborn.

Carl returns to the cafe with Laszlo, who has been wounded when the Gestapo broke up the Underground meeting. The original triangle of Paris is recreated. Hearing the commotion, Rick comes out upon the balcony, sees Laszlo below. He asks Carl to join him and, out of Laszlo's line of vision, tells the avuncular waiter—a Jewish Sam, yet!—to take Ilsa home. He goes downstairs and pours Laszlo a drink:

> RICK: Don't you sometimes wonder if it's worth all this?
> LASZLO: Do you know how you sound? . . . like a man trying to convince himself of something he doesn't believe . . . I wonder if you know that you're trying to escape from yourself, and that you'll never succeed. . . .

Laszlo reveals he knows Rick loves Ilsa. Since no one is to blame, he demands no explanation, seeks no revenge. He asks only that Rick use the Letters to save her. Then the police crash in and take him away.

Rick's conscience, already troubled by Ilsa's capitulation, is further burdened when Laszlo nearly catches him *in flagrante delicto*. He discerns Laszlo's unwavering belief in the Cause, his selfless devotion to Ilsa, and his complete lack of vindictiveness towards *his* rival. (Note that the fortunes of war also defuse the competition, allowing Laszlo to disavow any anger towards the man who stole his wife while he languished in a concentration camp, just as Ilsa was allowed to take two lovers!) Rick is forcibly reminded that where he has been inconstant, selfish and spiteful, the Czech has proven almost inhumanly virtuous.

I have said that the Oedipal crisis passes as the boy gives up his claim upon his mother and identifies with his father. After Laszlo is seized, it would have been only too easy for Rick to let the Nazis execute his own murderous designs and keep Ilsa for himself. But no child ever really wants to win the Oedipal struggle: he would rather go down fighting, secure in the knowledge that the bond between his parents will be preserved against his manipulations. Now certain that Ilsa loves him, Rick chooses to renounce her and take up the cherished Cause, vindicating Laszlo's faith in him, consolidating his identification with Laszlo. Rich has found that cure he sought in the spiritual wasteland of Casablanca.

His apathy dissipates, and he commences shuffling and baffling his adversaries as adroitly as Sam Spade, but without Spade's narrow ends of protecting a threatened, suspicious ego. At police headquarters, Rick persuades Renault to free Laszlo by appealing to the Frenchman's greed, his need to placate Strasser and his delight in scandal. He admits he has the Letters, and intends to use them this evening; he wants to take Ilsa with him out of Casablanca, without Gestapo interference. He proposes to trap Laszlo by handing over the Letters to him at the *Café Américain*. Renault will then arrest Laszlo on the spot as an accessory to the couriers' deaths, a crime weighty enough to send the Czech back to concentration camp. Rick and Ilsa will depart unimpeded, Renault will profit by Strasser's goodwill and the 10,000-franc bet. Plotwise, Rick's plan has about the same credibility as the Letters of Transit, but Curtiz, true to his promise, accelerates the last scenes to such a clip that the leaking premises of the scenario are hardly noticed, especially since our attention is now riveted to the issue of who will wind up with the lady.

Rick sells his business to Senor Ferrari, securing the lion's share of the profits for Sam and leaving the rest of his staff liberally provided for. Back at the cafe, he conceals Renault and greets Ilsa and Laszlo.

Ilsa is worried because Laszlo still thinks he is leaving with her. Rick promises her to tell him at the airport—"the less time to think, the easier for all of us!"

Rick brushes aside Laszlo's gratitude, refuses to take any payment. As he hands him the Letters, Renault steps in, pistol drawn—exactly what would have happened had Rick decided to finesse his rival. But instead Rick turns his gun on Renault and forces him to phone the airport that two passengers will be coming aboard for the Lisbon flight. Renault relays Rick's instructions—directly to Strasser, who calls out the troops.

Cut to the airport, shrouded in mist and rain, *Casablanca*'s characteristic weather for conflicted departures. While Laszlo puts the luggage aboard, Rick commands Renault to fill out the Letters in the name of—*Mr. and Mrs. Victor Laszlo!* Rick thus announces to the world that Ilsa is wedded to another, and overrides Ilsa's tearful protests, a hypnotic urgency rising in his voice as the theme song plays for the last time:

> RICK: You said I was to do the thinking for both of us. . . . Well, I've done a lot of it since then, and it all adds up to one thing. You're getting on that plane with Victor, where you belong. . . . Inside of us we both know you belong with Victor. You're part of his work . . . the thing that keeps him going. We'll always have Paris. We didn't have . . . we'd lost it until you came back to Casablanca. We got it back last night.
> ILSA (*ruefully*): And I said I would never leave you!
> RICK: And you never will. I've got a job to do . . . where I'm going, you can't follow. What I've got to do, you can't be any part of (*touching her chin*). . . . Here's looking at you, kid. . . .

Over Laszlo's objections, Rick says that Ilsa visited him last night, but only for the Letters. She tried to convince him that she still loved him—"but that was long ago." Laszlo welcomes Rick back—"This time I know our side will win!"

"Good-bye, Rick—God bless you!" Ilsa murmurs. Numb, drained, she turns away and walks toward the plane with her husband. Laszlo regards her with a quizzical, sympathetic expression. From their vantage point, Rick is framed, standing alone. He has foresworn and affirmed his love. Giving Ilsa back to Laszlo, he has metaphorically returned his mother to his father, yet enshrined Ilsa in his memory as a perpetual reassurance of his dignity. His last speech is meant to undo the competition with Laszlo and to exonerate Ilsa from adulterous taint. Rick would have the Czech believe Ilsa came to him to protect her marriage, rather than to destroy it.

The reality, of course, is exactly the opposite. But Laszlo remains, as usual, remarkably tolerant, totally accepts Rick's explanation which is tendered to alleviate Rick's still unquiet conscience as much as to assuage Laszlo about Ilsa's fidelity. Laszlo implicitly commends Rick's sacrifice like a benevolent father, who welcomes his prodigal son back to the fold.

I have always believed that Ilsa gets short shrift while the menfolk are busy solving their problems, and the film seems to hint obliquely that she deserves what she gets. Rick's arguments cannot hold much validity for her. Why can she not go where he must go, in some capacity, since she has repeatedly followed Laszlo into the very jaws of death? When all is said and done, she goes with her husband out of her love for Rick!

Having designated Rick as her final choice, he turns the tables on her, recapitulating in reverse his abandonment at the Paris train station as he hustles her forever out of his life, back into an unfulfilled marriage wherein nobility serves as a tepid substitute for sex. Rick disposes of Ilsa with something of the fierce purpose of Sam Spade "sending over" the chronically treacherous Brigid O'Shaughnessy. Bergman's blasted appearance as she boards the plane is uncannily reminiscent of Astor's blank mask as the elevator descends at the end of *The Maltese Falcon*. Rick *sends over* Ilsa to an analogous imprisonment, to make peace with the Oedipal father, and to disentangle himself from the possibility of future trauma at the hands of a woman he can never completely trust again.

Rick's murderous impulses towards Laszlo find an acceptable displacement in the person of Major Strasser. We have marked Laszlo's striking absence of ill will towards Rick. Strasser, on the other hand, is perfectly cast for the part of the baleful avenger, the very embodiment of retribution who deserves to die (note that the film has implied that Strasser, too, wants Ilsa for more than her politics!). When the

Gestapo chief arrives, tries to call the control tower to halt the flight, Rick coldly guns him down.

Renault has witnessed everything, correctly gauging that Ilsa left unwillingly. In the face of Rick's recommitment, the Prefect's gibes ring hollowly in his own ears, and he can no longer maintain his ironic detachment at the price of honor. Ever Rick's mirror, Renault suddenly executes an ideological about-face, recovering his lost self-respect, and orders his men to "round up the usual suspects" rather than arrest Rick. He drops a bottle of Vichy water into the wastebasket, kicks it away distastefully. They gaze up at the Lisbon flight climbing to freedom. Renault suggests he can be induced to arrange passage for Rick to the Free French garrison in Brazzaville, and Rick reminds him of their bet.

> RENAULT: . . . that ten-thousand francs should pay our expenses.
> RICK: *Our* expenses—Louis, I think this is the beginning of a beautiful friendship!

The camera pans over them, as they turn and walk into the mist bordering the airstrip, to the triumphant strains of the *"Marseillaise."* The union of these patriots *manqué* brings *Casablanca* to a smashing finale—it's hard to look upon this felicitous conclusion without a moist eye or a fast pulse. Rick's newly cemented friendship with Renault follows hard upon his relinquishment of Ilsa, and a camp interpretation would have us believe that it is fitting that Rick and Renault should stride together into the night, because it is Renault who Rick has secretly loved.

The idea that Rick has been a closet queen all along is lunatic (and, to members of the Bogart cult, heretical). But his rejection of Ilsa in favor of a friendship that will thrive in the sacrifice of combat is certainly informed by Rick's fear of women and his corollary misogyny. In many Bogart classics, indeed in many adventure epics throughout the history of cinema, one repeatedly discovers the chauvinism and the strong anti-feminine bias characteristic of the typical gang of preadolescent boys. In war, in the mining camp, or the detection of crime, men seem to function at their natural best without feminine intrusion. If a woman does invade the male community, her sexuality renders her suspect unless she proves herself as loyal and as tough as a reliable buddy. Howard Hawks has always been a director particularly partisan to the spartan virtues of male-bonding, and Lauren Bacall's part in Hawks' *To Have and Have Not* is an admirable example of the feminine "buddy." In this regard, Sam Spade's remark to his secretary— "You're a good man, sister!" is perhaps the ultimate compliment bestowed upon a woman by the hard-boiled hero.

I have inferred that Rick is exquisitely sensitized to Ilsa's potential for further harm. Far better to fight on, in the fellowship of comrades, sustained by the remembrance of Paris, before the fall of innocence. It is a fate less lonely than Spade's, who ends the dirty business of the Falcon with neither friend nor love, in fact or in memory. Rick purchases his redemption at a poignant price, a price urged upon him by the limitations of his character, for we may speculate that the intimacy of an extended relationship with a woman would ultimately be unendurable to him. And yet, the victory and the tragedy attendant upon his renunciation continue to move us profoundly, for in losing his beloved he has won back the better part of himself.

Postscript

Woody Allen's *Play It Again, Sam* provides an amusing commentary on the central Oedipal situation of *Casablanca*. Allen's *nebbish* hero bolsters a sagging ego by hallucinating Humphrey Bogart as sexual mentor. With Bogie's assistance, he seduces his best friend's wife. The friend is everything Allen is not—rich, attractive, supremely self-confident, like Laszlo. The wife turns to Allen because her husband is more interested in his business affairs, echoing Laszlo's political involvement at the expense of his marriage. Having vindicated his desirability, Allen persuades the wife to return to her man in a rather lovely airport scene lifted directly from the source.

Other sound interpretations of *Casablanca* which, in my obviously biased opinion, still suffer from the failure to account for the Oedipal theme, have been offered by Barbara Deming and Richard Corliss— see Bibliography.

Bibliography

All quotations from the film are from *Casablanca—Script and Legend.* New York: Overlook Press, 1973. Quote from Howard Koch, ibid., p. 24; Richard Corliss' essay, ibid., p. 198.

DEMING, BARBARA. *Running Away from Myself.* New York: Grossman Publishers, 1969. See Chapter II.

HYAMS, JOE. *Bogie.* New York: The New American Library, Inc., 1966.

KAEL, PAULINE. *Kiss, Kiss, Bang Bang.* New York: Bantam Books, Inc., 1969. See p. 303.

ROSTEN, NORMAN. "Nobody Dies Like Humphrey Bogart" in *Humphrey Bogart, The Man and His Films,* edited by Paul Michael. New York: Bobbs-Merrill, 1965. See p. 5.

SARRIS, ANDREW. *The American Cinema.* New York: E. P. Dutton & Co., Inc., 1968. See p. 176.

SENNETT, TED. *Warner Brothers Presents.* New York: Arlington House, Inc., 1971. See Chapter X.

SMITH, R. HARRIS, *OSS.* Berkeley: University of California Press, 1972. See p. 39.

ZINMAN, DAVID. *Fifty Classic Motion Pictures.* New York: Crown Publishers, Inc., 1971. See Chapter X.

VI

Psycho
—The Apes at the Windows

> . . . The price of progress in civilization is paid in
> forfeiting happiness through the heightening of the
> sense of guilt.
>
> Freud: *Civilization and Its Discontents*

> . . . My love of film is far more important to me
> than any considerations of morality.
>
> Alfred Hitchcock (*to François Truffaut*)

Enter Harold, punctual to the minute, in his usual uniform. The gray twill slacks, blue shirt and brown oxfords have gone through as many re-editions as *Valley of the Dolls;* mother bought his herringbone jacket twelve years ago for his college graduation; he hated it then, hates it now, but has never taken it off. I observed yesterday that change upsets him, so today he is wearing his other necktie, after agonies of indecision before the mirror this morning: was he putting it on as a concession to me, or to prove I was wrong? Either way, I've made a dent in his defenses, and the proof of my influence frightens and angers him. He quick-marches to the couch, not looking at me—for that would further acknowledge my impact—lies down, every button securely buttoned against my further assaults on his integrity. His hands are folded stiffly upon his breast, his legs locked in a painful parody of relaxation. He gives a fair imitation of a man on his way to an embalming, and even his voice is distant and sepulchral:

> "This morning, I awoke at 7:30 A.M., and, after dressing, ate breakfast. I was running a bit late, hence only had time for a single cup of coffee. Whilst riding the subway, several thoughts supervened. (1) It occurred to me I might ask out Edna again for next Saturday. However, I'm not entirely sure I want to see her so soon . . . I'll have to give the matter more thought. (2) A great deal of paperwork has accumulated; I hoped to clean it up before coming here. (3) I worried, therefore, that I might be late, and you would think I was anxious because you said I don't like having my routines disrupted . . . well, I thought about *that* a great deal. Although there is some merit in your formulation, I basically disagree . . ."

Harold drones on, processing the precious stuff of experience into a homogeneous gruel lacking zest or flavor. I keep awake by reminding myself he's trying to bore me asleep. He embarks on a long disquisition about his defective shortwave radio. I gently chide him that he's still trying to keep the status quo status quo. He objects testily, explores each crevice and quiddity of my wrongness, then, one minute to go, tells a dream he had last night.

> *He is at his desk, absorbed in his everlasting paperwork; he looks up, to see a band of apes romping outside the windows.* How could they get here, *he thinks,* I'm on the fiftieth floor! *They pound against the glass, their toothy simian grins unutterably obscene. In a moment the windows will shatter, they will swarm in.* He awakens in a cold sweat . . .

The psychoanalyst spends a goodly part of his days suffering along with people like Harold. The treatment of the obsessive-compulsive personality is likely to be demanding, frustrating and lengthy. In Freud's day, obsessionals at least presented him with symptoms; perverse thoughts—*Fuck God! Let Mother Die!!*—descended from nowhere upon these most upright of citizens, and had to be redeemed by obscure rituals, repetitive hand-washings and touching of doorknobs, arranging the pillows just so before retiring. These strange obsessions and compulsions are, however, only the tip of the iceberg, pathological spin-offs from an underlying system of coping with stress by imposing rigid rules and restraints upon the self. When the system becomes overloaded beyond its limits, florid symptoms erupt into consciousness.

No one knows why, but today's obsessional usually presents the system entire, rather than the symptoms, to the therapist. If there has been a serious episode of compulsiveness, it will often have occurred many years ago, during childhood or adolescence, and then have sealed over spontaneously. The adult patient is mildly depressed, vaguely unhappy and lonely, but is frequently unaware of how desperately the obsessional style has diminished the quality of life.

But do not automatically assume that to be obsessional is, per se, always to be "ill"—at least in the medical sense. The obsessional adaptation is simply another way of being in the world, one accorded high survival value in cultures like ours that still reward the puritan virtues. While the obsessional character may yield up confining rituals, these afflict only the small minority; the remainder live on, unsymptomatic, some perhaps *more* trapped by their inability to suffer consciously!

Typically, an obsessional individual is industrious, clean, orderly, thrifty, cautious and doubting. Note that Harold's prolix speech is shot through with references to his thoughts. Indeed, he thinks so inordinately about his thinking, there is little room for him to feel. Feelings are risky commodities, unquantifiable and uncontrollable, and if there is one illusion treasured by the obsessional, it is the possibility of absolute control over everyone and everything. The self is experienced as a computer programmed to reduce the mysterious wholeness of existence into myriad petty duties and details that must be cleared up with relentless efficiency. But feelings intrude; since the mechanism can never be brought to a state of perfection, breakdown always seems imminent. The obsessional dreads the clamor of his instincts, protecting himself by developing a passion for the mundane. When I interpreted Harold's fear of change, I became a harbinger of change, and set the apes to dance around his defenses of intellectualization and isolation.

Intriguingly, it is these timorous souls who make us most cognizant of the cleavage between "civilized" morality and the netherworld of chaotic, primitive desire. Monsters from the Id continually assail the obsessional: unacceptable needs and wishes constantly threaten homeostasis, the more so because the psychic repository of morality and conscience—the Superego—tends to be so unremittingly harsh. For the obsessional, an evil thought is as reprehensible as an evil deed. Being is pervaded by doubt whether to follow the lascivious promptings of the Id, or the implacable sanctions of the tyrannical Superego.

How comes this misery to prevail? Some experts tout heredity, since obsessionalism frequently runs in families. Others believe a parent indoctrinated in the obsessional style during childhood inflicts it upon the next unwitting generation. Freud thought that obsessionals were "anal erotics" by nurture or nature, that is, they are "fixated" in coping strategies that originate out of the amalgam of pain and pleasure during the second year of life, when the child delights in its own excrement, and learns the impact upon its parents of defecating and urinating at the right place and time (or the wrong place and time!). The psychological issues of the anal stage extend beyond the potty. Erik Erikson writes:

> ". . . The anal zone lends itself more than any other to the display of stubborn adherence to contradictory impulse because . . . it is the modal zone for two conflicting modes of approach, namely, retention and elimination . . . the sphincters are only part of the muscle system with its general duality of rigidity and relaxation. The development of the muscle system gives the child much greater power over the environment, in the ability to reach out and hold on, to throw and push away, to appropriate things and keep them at a distance."

The two-year-old anal-ist should be handled with a mixture of firmness and respect more easily described than achieved by parents driven to distraction by the bewildering contradictions of the age. The child must be protected from intoxicating excesses of stubborn hostility, yet the yearning for autonomy that informs the infuriating nay-saying of the "terrible twos" must also be cherished. Toilet training can unfortunately be metaphoric of global attempts to leash in the child's natural exuberance, the archetype of catastrophic shaming experiences that raise primordial doubts about one's dignity and worth; the self is then perceived as a container of filth to be cleansed periodically upon demand. Erikson warns that:

> ". . . If denied the gradual, well-guided experience of free choice, the child will turn against himself all his urge to discriminate and to manipulate. He will overmanipulate himself . . . develop a precocious conscience . . . he will become obsessed with his own repetitiveness . . . he then learns to repossess the environment and to gain power by stubborn and minute control, where he could not find large-scale mutual regulation. Such hollow victory is the infantile model for a compulsion neurosis. . . ."

Parents act for their society and themselves: the kindness or abrasiveness of their interventions will be intimately related to the stringency of cultural prerogatives. In his early career, Freud discovered that neurosis often attended the taming of the child's passions during its difficult passage towards maturity. In a work written during the last decade of his life—*Civilization and Its Discontents,* Freud theorized that society evolves with equally repressive effects upon its membership, likening acculturation to the induction of an artificial obsessional state. If men are to live together without tearing each other apart, the strictest order must be set over the unruly instincts:

> "Order is a kind of repetition compulsion, by which it is ordained, once and for all, when and how a thing shall be done, so that on every similar occasion, doubt and hesitation shall be avoided."

Civilization requires that man transcend his native messiness, his anality and carnality. As the baser drives give way to the sway of intellect, as man acquires the ability to sublimate, so is he cleansed of angry ape, but is also compelled by an increasingly oppressive morality to feel ever more guilty at incitements from the Id. The escalating harshness of the culture's collective Superego takes a heavy toll in emotional suffering; war is yet another signet of that fearful price, an organized, legitimized release of aggression that always threatens to destroy that which it was designed to protect. Freud was pessimistic about the possibility of liberating society from its obsessional tendencies. A single patient might learn to live less neurotically, but the conventions of a neurotic world would never cease to hem him in, must even be respected!

We must remember that Freud was a model of bourgeois propriety; the placid domesticity of his life reflected the modest rewards of one who, at least outwardly, accepted the status quo. Although he sowed the seeds of several revolutions, there was a strong conservative, yes, even obsessional streak in him. It is likely he never personally intended that his theories should be used as a strident call to arms against the manifold injustices society perpetrates in the name of its perpetuation. That call was sounded by wilder spirits like Wilhelm Reich, who Freud disavowed, as I rather think he would have disowned and abominated the Freudian Left today.

I have framed the personal and cultural manifestations of obsessionalism at some length, because the cinema of Alfred Hitchcock has been marked so persistently by his very obvious obsessional concerns, above all by his insistence upon the preservation of a prudent, carefully ordered existence, lest the sanctions of culture be overthrown, the very substance of reality be rent asunder by the monsters from the Id, or lest the imperfect, sinning self be crushed by the pitiless avengers of the Superego.

The roots of Hitchcock's obsessionalism can only be dimly surmised. His private life is as unremarkable as was Freud's. He has been happily married for many years, keeps carefully apart from the glitter and scandal associated with screen luminaries. He admits to being exceptionally neat and fussy in his personal habits, to growing uncomfortable when his routines are disturbed:

> "I'm full of fears and I do my best to avoid complications . . . I get a feeling of inner peace from a well organized desk. When I take a bath, I put everything back neatly in place. You wouldn't even know I'd been in the bathroom."

His penchant for rigorous control in his work is well-known. He maps out his films in the office in meticulous detail; his *oeuvre* has essentially been accomplished upon a mental sound stage, and it is in the setting of intense communion with the wellsprings of private fantasy that he finds the greatest pleasure as a "director." Shooting itself could almost be an afterthought—his editing is minimal. He scorns looking through the camera on set since he has already composed the *mise-en-scène* with a formidable mind's eye.

In public—and he has always been the shrewdest publicist for his endeavors—Hitchcock teases us with impishly disarming references to the foulest evils. He beguiles with his avuncular presence, thus many still conceive of him as an entertaining bogeyman who, for pleasure and profit, jangles our nerves with easily cast-off nightmares. In serious reportage, he discusses technique with alacrity, but seems to regard the searchers after "deeper" meaning in his work with a mixture of disbelief and amusement. When pressed, he says he prefers to let his pictures speak for themselves.

He will give only the most perfunctory details of his autobiography—his fear of the Jesuits who schooled him, his repugnance for the police, which, in an oft repeated tale, he ascribes to being sent by his father to the station house at age five, with a note that directed the constables to lock him up for being "naughty." This is quite likely a "screen memory," one that distills volumes of life experience into a single traumatic recollection, quite possibly emblematic of other episodes of disastrous shaming Erikson describes in the history of obsessionals.

However, it would be impertinent on the basis of such limited data to infer the extent of Hitchcock's "neurosis," nor does it matter much for our purposes if in fact he were "neurotic" at all. Whatever the status of his mental health, Hitchcock is first and foremost an artist, a poet of ambiguity who has, under the aegis of light entertainment, made us witness the disturbing dilemmas of the obsessional viewpoint at first hand, made us cognizant of our own obsessionalism with a power denied to the clinician restricted by rational interest in the "rules" of diagnostics and therapeutics. In this chapter, I have chosen *Psycho* as a touchstone, for it represents the extremity of Hitchcock's black vision of human vulnerability and corruptibility. Themes elsewhere latent are blatant in this most shocking of his films, the nightmare from which there is no easy awakening for a commercial break!

The credits of *Psycho* are presented to frantic, pulsing music * over an abstract pattern of horizontal and vertical lines that arbitrarily mesh, separate, and recombine, then ascend and coalesce into a dazzling cityscape. The camera hovers breathtakingly above new skyscrapers, and descends to travel over a shabbier neighborhood, then, in a series of dissolves, zeroes in on one building, one wall of windows, a single window with drawn shade. As in a TV newscast, titles converge at bottom frame: PHOENIX, ARIZONA . . . FRIDAY, DECEMBER 11 . . . TWO FORTY-THREE PM.

The opening implies random selection: we could just as easily, as indifferently, move to the left or right, to another block, another building, another time of day—and another story. Hitchcock's first perspective dwarfs the unseen characters and their unknown entanglements, rendering them supremely unimportant in a schema that cuts the city itself down to toy-size. Still, a choice has been offered; the director has borne us away from the glamorous center of the metropolis into seedier territory. The camera hesitates, then slides furtively under the half-open window, into a drably furnished room where a semi-nude couple fitfully embrace and pick over the bones of an ungratifying midday tryst. She is Marion Crane (Janet Leigh), an attractive Phoenix secretary slightly past her prime, still single. Her lover, Sam Loomis (John Gavin) toils in a small-town hardware store to pay off his father's debts and his alimony. Marion hankers after marriage, Sam refuses on the grounds he won't have her live in poverty. It is an old and unresolved argument between them.

Loomis' divorce, his father's malfeasance (never explained) have dislocated the basic complacency of the man. He has shouldered an enormous burden of meaningless responsibility, to slog on until stability is restored and his virtue proven to the distant fates: "I've been sweating for people who aren't there . . . I sweat to pay off my father's debts and he's in his grave . . . I sweat to pay my ex-wife's alimony, and she's living on the other side of the world. . . ." Sam relishes his martyrdom, since it earns him the good opinion of his

---

* Bernard Herrmann's impressive score was written for unaccompanied strings; Herrmann's skill is the more evident for the absence of instruments traditionally—and all too often artificially—employed to heighten suspense.

neighbors and the right to wallow in self-pity. After the curious fashion of obsessionals, Sam thinks he's earned the right to a little pleasure, but too much, too soon would be unallowable. Perhaps some day, when his dues are sufficiently paid to the masochist club, he will "deserve" marriage; until then, he keeps Marion at a distance and, having struck a bargain with his conscience, enjoys the sleazy side of their affair.

But Marion has come to resent the disorder in her life, and the taint of whoredom. She is hurt by Sam's secret delight in their illicitness, and now insists on respectability and chastity. Sam will dine at the apartment she shares with her sister, as an approved suitor—"with my mother's picture on the mantle. . . ."

> SAM: And after the steak? Send sister to the movies, turn Mama's picture to the wall. . . .
> MARION: . . . they also pay who meet in hotel rooms . . . I haven't been married once, yet.
> SAM: Yeah . . . but when you do, you'll *sweat*—live with me in a storeroom behind a hardware store . . . I'll tell you what, when I send my ex-wife her alimony, you can lick the stamps.

He grudgingly agrees to upgrade their affair short of marriage, and betrays an unpleasant mean streak in the comfort he takes at the thought of Marion's daydreams being ground down as she "sweats" in the coils of respectability. He makes an unenviable hero—but then, Marion is not a particularly appealing heroine, not at first, aside from her physical attractiveness: small people hassling over small ends, seeking a modicum of approval in a dull, judgmental world.

Down through the years, Hitchcock has zealously assaulted the sensibilities of just such conventional protagonists with deadly intrusions into their respectable lives. His people are usually of the bourgeoisie—lower through upper (rarely, a protagonist assumes the mantle of bourgeois respectability to repair or conceal a disorderly life-style—like John Robie, the ex-cat burglar of *To Catch a Thief* or the prissy kleptomaniac heroine of *Marnie*). His male characters in particular tend to be weak or vacillating, even if they invariably surprise themselves with new-found courage.

The most terrifying disruptions of the status quo occur in the most prosaic settings. In *North by Northwest,* a Madison Avenue ad-exec is attacked by a crop-dusting plane in a Midwestern wheat field. In an amusement park, the unimaginative tennis player of *Strangers on a Train* wrestles for his life with a psychotic killer, beneath a carousel spinning madly out of control. The more commonplace the hero and setting, the greater our anxiety, as the apparently diamond-hard surface of obsessional reality is fractured by the Apes at the Windows, the Monsters from the Id.

Hitchcock has increasingly ordered his *mise-en-scène* with the priorities of a surrealist painter—one thinks principally of René Magritte. Everyday objects, and people, "objectified," are grouped with startling clarity, transmuted into dreamlike configurations that articulate with the unconscious fantasy and questionable motivation of the characters. *Psycho* has little of the frenetic pacing of "adventure" films like *North by Northwest;* its actual violence lasts only a few heartbeats. Yet, despite the sharply etched familiarity of the surroundings, things are subtly out of joint from the beginning, the visuals infused with an ineluctable strangeness, more laden with eery presentiment than any other Hitchcock picture. The dialogue has an unnerving Pinteresque quality—shut your eyes for a moment next time you see the film, you'll easily discover what I mean. The most trivial statements seem pregnant with meaning and menace. People do not speak, so much as their words collide, bounce off at a tangent, creating even in the act of love a pervasive tone of tension and alienation.

Sex has always been a supreme challenge to Hitchcock's obsessional order, the spur for unsettling experiences of archaic aggression and fear. Sex opens the Pandora's box of the unconscious, unleashing the mindless primitive—and lovers are never far from becoming murderers (e.g., *Dial M for Murder, Suspicion*). The director frequently dwells upon "heavy petting," adolescent gropings on the verge of embarrassing interruption. The essence of sexuality is prolonged tumescence—*vide* the interminable Bergman-Grant kiss of *Notorious.* Hitchcock has filmed one definitive orgasm—in *Frenzy,* wherein an engaging sexual psychopath rapes the frigid directress of a matrimonial agency upon her desk while the poor lady mutters her prayers. Afterwards, he strangles her with at least equal pleasure!

The sexuality of *Psycho* is particularly colored by Hitchcock's peculiar blend of puritanism and lubricity. Sam and Marion's lovemaking defies small-town convention. Although they meet in Phoenix, the big city, where morals traditionally become unglued, it is the harsh ethic of Fairvale, Loomis' hometown, that shapes their anxiety over losing face. *Psycho* begins with an invasion of privacy. The audience— especially the man in the audience—is placed in the uncomfortable dual role of voyeur, panting after a better look at Leigh's luscious bosom, and moral watchdog, implicitly identified with Marion's dead mother, peering out disapprovingly from her picture frame.

Sam and Marion upbraid each other over the legal sanctions for their love, while the promise of genuine intimacy without a care for the neighbors goes a-begging. Their furtive copulation is bracketed by his financial worries and her fear of being accounted a spinster or a fallen woman. Still, the affair has been integrated into the status quo, granting them a release from routine without destroying routine. Marion disturbs routine by trying to alter her circumstances, denying Sam her body. Her decision registers on destiny's seismograph, and an infernal retribution machine winds itself up, for the gods of Hitchcock's universe have decreed that her punishment is paramount to the preservation of order.

Back at her office, Marion endures the smug chatter of a recently married coworker, Carolyn, about her husband's proprietary attitude and her mother's nosiness. Lowry, the boss, enters with a drunken oilman, Cassady, who has just purchased a house for a soon-to-be-wed daughter. He leers goatishly at Marion:

> CASSADY: Tomorrow's the day my sweet little girl—oh, not *you*— tomorrow she stands her sweet self up there and gets married away from me . . . eighteen years old, and she never had an unhappy day. . . . You know what I do about unhappiness? I buy it off. Are you unhappy?

He brandishes $40,000 in cold, undeclared cash. Lowry hustles him out, gives Marion the money to put into safe deposit over the weekend. Carolyn observes forlornly that Cassady didn't flirt with her: "I guess he must have noticed my wedding ring." On a sudden impulse, Marion goes into Lowry's office, sidesteps a crude proposition from

Cassady, pleads a headache and asks to be excused for the rest of the day after going to the bank.

Marion has returned from her troubled assignation to contend with petty vulgarians who goad her with reminders of her unmarried condition. Of course Carolyn and Cassady are hardly content; neither Cassady's money or inebriation salves his pain, and there is a great deal of desperation underpinning Carolyn's prattle. But Marion is too immersed in her deprivation to be objective. Should these pampered dollies—Carolyn and Cassady's daughter—have respectability without a second thought as their natural due, while she must sweat on her back in a dingy hotel room for lack of funding? No, let her be a winner once! Besides, Cassady will not miss the money, he came by it illegally, Lowry probably will keep it undeclared, too. Let her turn the tables, show Cassady what it's like to be "taken." One discerns an odd complementarity between Marion and Cassady, a curious blurring between their two disparate personae, a crossing of circumstances and motivation common in Hitchcock—like the proposed exchange of murders in *Strangers on a Train*. Cassady would have used his illicit gain to ease the pangs of loneliness, keeping a presence in his daughter's house. Marion is tempted to steal, and thereby transforms Cassady's purpose, forcing Sam into making the commitment that will protect her from the loneliness of her spinsterhood. We have been seduced into applauding the theft, surrendering our scruples and assenting to Marion's criminality.

She does not go to the bank. We discover her alone, again half-nude, in her apartment. An envelope containing the money lies on the bed. As she dresses and packs, the camera insistently cuts back to the envelope, until in distorted close-up it fills the screen temptingly. The money evokes mingled resonances of desire and apprehension, security and sinfulness. Behind her, we see the bathroom door with a glimpse of the shower. She stares hard at herself in the mirror, snaps the suitcase shut, slips the envelope into her purse. The die is cast: in questing for an elusive respectability, Marion surrenders herself to the shameful accusations she feared!

From now on, she will be untied from the familiar, cut off and cast away from any deliverance. Her sister, in Tucson for the weekend, thinks she is spending a quiet weekend at home, as does Sam, for she has not told him she is coming with a pilfered deliverance. Her last touch with Phoenix reality is unnerving. At the wheel of her car, her mind invents Sam's startled reaction to her appearance: his voice betrays her unease—already she half-realizes that his hypertrophied conscience will not let him use the money, must make him view her in a new and unfavorable light. As she stops, Lowry and Cassady pass directly in front of her. She smiles nervously, waves, Lowry looks back with a puzzled frown and she pulls away. . . .

Next morning, she sleeps inside her car near the highway. A patrol car pulls up, an officer raps on the window. She wakens with a start, automatically tries to leave. He restrains her; she emanates an almost tangible aura of guilt:

> POLICEMAN: There are plenty of motels in this area . . . you should've . . . I mean, just to be safe. . . .
> MARION: I didn't intend to sleep all night . . . have I broken any laws?
> POLICEMAN: No, Ma'am.
> MARION: Then I'm free to go?
> POLICEMAN: Is anything wrong?
> MARION: Of course not. Am I acting as if there's something wrong?
> POLICEMAN: Frankly, yes.

Pure Pinter! The cop is really worried about her, but in one fantastic shot we see him through Marion's eyes: an enormous, goggled face towering over the car window as she desperately tries to hide her purse from his omniscient gaze. He is the Cop of the Mind, the eternal vigilante every obsessional fears. He lets her go—she turns off the freeway, into a gaudy used car lot, picks up a newspaper from a vending machine, scans it for mention of the theft. There is none, but the cop has returned, standing tall behind his vehicle, watching her intently. She sees him with a shock, and in an ironic role reversal, high pressures a fast-talking salesman into an exchange of cars before he gets his spiel off the ground. His bogus joviality undercut, the salesman, too, grows wary: "You *are* in a hurry! Somebody chasin' ya? I take it you can prove that car is yours???"

In the washroom Marion extracts $700 over a grimy sink; the camera is angled above her, so she appears pressed in as by the walls of a prison cell. As she completes the purchase, the patrolman quietly eases his car into the lot. She panics, almost driving off without her luggage. From the angle of her departure, it is evident the cop has gotten a full view of her license plate. In one of Hitchcock's matchless compositions, an attendant, the salesman and the cop, aligned in a portentous diagonal, stare after her. . . .

During my Army hitch I treated several cases of a rare syndrome called "travel psychosis." The patients were psychologically marginal men who disintegrated during bus rides taking them from customary surroundings to a new post halfway across the country. Over long hours of monotony, their vision turned inwards, with disastrous results. Marion undergoes an analogous decompensation—hermetically sealed in her car, enmeshed in the flow of vapid scenery, a species of sensory deprivation erodes her contact with reality. Day fades, the lights of oncoming traffic strike her full face, creating the ambience of an interrogation chamber. She has converted those along her way into extensions of her punitive Superego, and now her uneasy conscience rises up to torment her.

While Hitchcock has allied us with her, made us hope she will escape out of the gray frame of obsessional reality, he has also shown that she will never escape, for she *wants* to be caught. Had her near abandonment of her suitcase (an intriguing Freudian slip) been successful, she would have been left only with the clothes on her back, the prototypical fugitive. The money at this point possesses no significance beyond establishing her guilt. As she drives on, she plunges deeper into the darkness of the fugitive mentality, restlessly rehearsing the events leading up to her almost certain arrest. We hear the patrolman agree with the salesman that she acted like "a wrong one . . . I better have a look at those papers, Charlie."; Lowry's sudden recollection, when she fails to show up at work, of seeing her in her car; Cassady's demand for revenge—"I ain't about to kiss off forty thousand dollars, I'll replace it with her fine soft flesh!" These are her forecasts, but also her *fantasies:* Cassady's threat is conjured up as much out of her masochism as her intuition: she *needs* to be punished sadistically!

Hitchcock shows a Shakespearean flair for setting the natural world reverberating with the prevailing emotional climate. Lear's rage at his daughters evokes the howling tempest; in *Marnie,* lightning flashes punctuate the heroine's descent into traumatizing memory, and in *Psycho,* Marion's orgy of self-condemnation hurls down a savage rainstorm, clouding her vision, emphasizing her lost spiritual state. Morally derailed, she drives around for hours through the deluge until she spies a sign glowing through the blurred windshield—BATES MOTEL . . . VACANCY. The frenetic music fades on a long-held note, leaving the soothing patter of the rain, and the slap-slap of the wiper blades.

She dashes out of her car into the motel. The office is empty; from the porch she sees, perched on the hill above, the very model of the dark old house integral to the iconography of gothic tale and horror film. The figure of a spare old woman is silhouetted against one of two lit windows. One almost smiles at the banality of it all—surely Hitchcock has more imagination! But the Bates house is ominous beyond satirizing itself, a bizarre incongruity counterbalanced against the nondescript motel below, and the other lackluster environments Marion has passed through during her abortive flight.

At the sound of her horn, a gangly young man, Norman Bates (Tony Perkins), bounds out of the house. Marion has heard only the imaginary voices of her accusers since the debacle at the used-car lot, so Norman's homely welcome comes as a benefice. The motel is completely vacant—the only guests strays from the beaten path:

> NORMAN: They moved away the highway—but there's no sense dwelling on our losses, we just keep lighting the lights, and following the formalities. (*sic!*)

While Marion registers under a false identity, he reaches for a key to the third cabin, and with a furtive sideways glance, instead picks the key to the adjoining unit. He takes her to the cabin, and in showing her around points to the bathroom, but can't bring himself to name it. Pathetically attracted to her, he is every inch an upright, uptight all-American obsessional Mama's boy, yet withal so ingratiating that one is inclined to overlook his eccentricity. He asks her to supper and leaves. Marion unpacks, wraps the money in her newspaper. As she places it on the bed, she hears the indistinct voices of Norman and an old lady quarreling.

> MRS. BATES: And *then* what, after supper—music, whispers? . . .
> Go on, go tell her, she'll not be feeding her ugly appetites with my
> food or my son!!
> NORMAN: Shut up!! Shut up!!

He returns, crestfallen, with a tray of sandwiches and milk. He's too nervous to eat in her cabin, so they go into the parlor behind the office. The meal is overseen by an enormous stuffed owl mounted high on one wall. Norman, it seems, practices avian taxidermy to relieve the tedium of a stultifying existence—"A hobby's supposed to pass the time, not fill it. . . ." His father died when he was a child; he had mother all to himself until several years ago, when she fell in love with a man who convinced her to sink her life's savings into the motel. When it failed, he died under mysterious circumstances, and Mrs. Bates' sanity snapped, making the mother an invalid child and the son her nurse.

> NORMAN: You know what I think? . . . we're all in our private
> traps, clamped in them, and none of us can ever get out. We scratch
> and claw, but only at the air, only at each other.
> MARION: Sometimes we deliberately step into those traps.
> NORMAN: I was born in mine. I don't mind it anymore.

Like many seriously troubled people Norman possesses an unhealing insight, but his duty appears unassailable and he accepts it passively. Marion is moved, with us, to sympathize with this odd fellow; she takes his side against his deranged mother, and commits a fatal error in judgment. When she suggests that mother be committed. Norman becomes furious:

> NORMAN: An institution . . . a—madhouse? . . . have you ever
> seen the inside of one of those places? . . . the laughing and the
> tears . . . the cruel eyes watching you?
> MARION: I only felt . . . it seems she's hurt you . . . I meant well.
> NORMAN: People always mean well. (*bitterly*) They cluck their thick
> tongues and shake their heads and suggest, oh so delicately . . .

(*suddenly affable again*) of course, I've suggested it myself . . . but
I hate to even think about it. She needs me . . . it's not as if she
was a maniac . . . she just goes a little mad sometimes. We all go a
little mad sometimes . . . haven't you?
MARION (*firmly*): Sometimes just one time can be enough. Thank
you.

Hitchcock has engineered another crossing: he underscores the
equivalency between Marion and Norman while she is registering;
they face each other across the counter, and by adroit camera work
and lighting their profiles seem mirror images as their plights mirror
each other. They are both caught in draining, parasitic relationships:
Norman ministers to his sick, minimizing mother, Marion to her
weak, degrading lover. As they talk in the parlor, Norman's agreeable
mask slips away, and we sense his madness. *Mutatis mutandis,*
Marion's grip on reality slipped after the theft but, in comprehending
Norman's awful resignation, she is able to pull together and renounce
her fugitive identity. She tells Norman she will return to Phoenix next
morning—"I stepped into a private trap back there. I'd like to go back
and try to pull myself out of it, before it's too late for me, too. . . ."

She leaves; Norman stands in the darkness, surrounded by his repel-
lant trophies, the owl perched menacingly over him as if about to
strike. His expression hardens. He removes a picture from the wall—
of a pneumatic nude being assaulted by two satyric gentlemen. He
peers through a rough peephole at Marion undressing near her open
bathroom door. Just as she removes her slip, the camera cuts away to
Norman's unblinking eye, filling the screen in sideview, then back to
Marion, donning her robe. Norman replaces the picture, his jaw
twitching with frustration. He, and we, have been deprived of her
nakedness—another unconsummated sexual act, and this time unmistakably perverse. Norman glares accusingly up at the decaying old
house, then bounds up the hill.

Marion checks her bankbook to see what will be left after she pays
for the getaway car. She tears up her jottings, flushes them down the
toilet, eases off her robe, displaying her shapely back. A close-up of
her bare legs as she steps into the tub. She draws the curtain, turns on
the shower—close-up of the showerhead—she offers herself up lux-
uriously to the cleansing water, closing her eyes and stretching out her

long delicate neck. We have been subliminally primed for this moment, teased by repeated shots of her, half-nude, covering and uncovering herself. The motel bathroom has been evoked by the previous marginal awareness of the bathroom in Marion's apartment and the filthy lavatory of the used-car lot. The painting of the ebullient rape covering Norman's peephole gave a tiny intimation of the horror about to occur. Through the translucent curtain, we see the bathroom door open, and a tall, indistinct shape slips in. Then, to the agonized ululation of the strings, the curtain is torn aside, revealing a shadowy old woman—we see only her eyes, her hair drawn into a tight bun, and, indelibly engraved upon the riveted consciousness, an enormous upraised knife.

Hitchcock's skill at montage—"putting little bits of film together"—reached an extraordinary summit in the shower murder sequence. As James Naremore notes, we are actually shown very little intrinsic violence, yet such is the rhythm established by the elegant shuffling of sixty separate camera set-ups, that one reels with the impression of an unparalleled savagery which seems to sustain itself past its bloody termination, echoing down the corridors of the mind like the shrieking violins. Hitchcock intercuts between Marion's petal-like screaming lips, the knife rising and falling; an ejaculatory spurt of blood soils the gleaming white bathtub, the knife makes a tiny bloodless belly puncture, overhead views show Marion trying to turn away as she shields her breasts. . . .

The old woman rushes out as quickly as she entered. Close-up of Marion's upper torso and face—miraculously spared—slowly sliding down the wall, as the eyes fix, glaze over; her blindly outstretched hand clutches the curtain, ripping it away from the frame hook by hook as she pitches forward onto the floor. The music descends in a series of deep minor-key groans, then ceases, leaving only the patter of the shower, strikingly reminiscent of the unaccompanied rainfall when she entered the imagined haven of the Bates Motel. Her blood mingles with the bathwater, gurgling down the drain in a small clockwise whirlpool—and, in a masterstroke of aesthetic balance, the camera spirals back counterclockwise from a freezeframe of Marion's staring eye, to show drops of water gleaming on her cheek—are they real tears, or gratuitous?—and her dead face pressed awkwardly against the floor. As the water continues to stream down, the camera drifts leisurely across her bathrobe into the bedroom, pausing significantly at the newspaper still on the bed, then passes over to the window, and Norman cries from the hill—*"Mother, Oh God! Mother!! Blood!!!"*

Obsessionals suffer under a general interdiction of sexual pleasure, but they are particularly haunted by guilt over their childhood voyeuristic and exhibitionistic fantasies. The wish to observe the sexual activity of others, initially one's parents, and the need to display oneself as a sexual object are normal components of the child's instinctual heritage, smoothly integrated, if all goes well, into later sexual activity (one takes delight in drinking-in the sight of the beloved, and in being similarly admired). But if these wishes to see and be seen are ringed about with the scathing humiliation so prevalent in the early history of obsessionals, it is likely they will later become highly conflicted gratifications, stamped with a peculiar confluence of fear, shame and secret longing, and may easily verge over into frank perversion.

Hitchcock's films are filled with voyeurs, with heroes or villains watching others unobserved, for sinister or worthy purposes. One recalls the famous scene at the tennis match in *Strangers on a Train:* the heads of the audience swivel, obedient to the flight of the ball, while the villain stares unmovingly through the crowd at his victim playing below. *Rear Window* is an extended essay on repressed voyeurism. The hero is a professional "watcher," a news photographer laid up with a broken leg, alleviating his boredom by spying on his neighbors across the courtyard. This visual eavesdropping nearly precipitates his end at the hands of a murderer he has discovered. More than meets the conscious eye is stirred by Hitchcock's clandestine surveillances, because he has so artfully tapped the unconscious sexual basis of our desire to watch, unknown, out of the darkness.

As a rule, Hitchcock presents such sexual disorder and perverse longing through a glass darkly, concealed in the cloak of criminality. The frigid heroine of *Marnie* acts out her rape fantasies in reverse, by plundering her employers after winning their confidence. Bruno Antony's homosexual yen for Guy Haines in *Strangers on a Train* is hidden in the emphasis placed upon an exchange of murders for profit instead of lovers' vows. But in *Psycho,* Hitchcock has for once dropped the pretence of concealment. Norman Bates is an unregenerate peeping Tom, and we are manipulated with exceptional cunning into participating in his dirty business. In fact, we are placed precisely in the position of the obsessional's ego—wooed by the forbidden delights of the Id, then trampled by the punishment of the Superego.

Psycho began with a voyeuristic invasion of privacy, to which we assented without question. We have been interminably tempted by Janet Leigh's spectacular body, until the director pointedly makes Norman's eye our own, his frustration our own, and compels us to watch Norman watching Marion, the better that we may appreciate the depth of our complicity. Then we are repaid in full, forced to attend the ultimate invasion of privacy: we gag upon our voyeurism as Marion expires in a frenzy of bloody eroticism, and we are left spent and obscurely guilty, like an adolescent who has masturbated into the toilet bowl.

We identify with Norman-the-watcher, but also empathize with Marion, unwitting exhibitor and focus of desire. We wince when the knife pierces her vulnerable flesh. Hitchcock's attitude towards his women has always been frankly ambivalent. They are snares or helpmeets, keepers of the hearth or treacherous Jezebels; often, like Sam Spade, the hero must puzzle out the heroine's good or evil intentions to save himself: it is only at the end of *North by Northwest* that Roger Thornhill realizes Eve Kendall wants to marry rather than murder him. Although personally uxorious, Hitchcock emerges in his pictures as a lady-killer. He has been exterminating the supposedly weaker sex since his earliest silent work (*The Lodger*). His latest film, *Frenzy,* contains much latent misogyny: A Scotland Yard inspector tracks down a modern-day Jack the Ripper, and at home his loving wife serves up repugnant dishes from her course in *haute cuisine;* while domestic bliss prevails, she could almost be poisoning him!

Hitchcock's perceptions of Marion veer back and forth between sympathy and dispassionate distate. To Cassady and Mrs. Bates, her putative executioner, she is a malevolent seductress; Sam resents her for withholding her favors, Norman grows furious when she turns her body away from his avid eye. Hitchcock betrays his own buried resentment towards woman as perennial tantalizer, but he also feelingly shows Marion as an abused sex-object (her resemblance to Marilyn Monroe, on this score, is rather remarkable). Sam has leeched the life from her, Cassady longs to butcher her, Norman's sensitivity gives way to sordid lust at the peephole, the meanest manipulation of her yet, before she steps into the shower to consolidate her victim identity forever.

But Hitchcock's sympathy is never absolute: it is tempered by a coldly objective awareness of Marion's masochism. He implies that something damaged in her sought out the role of chronic loser before the theft, allying her unprofitably with Loomis. During her flight she masochistically provokes unpleasant treatment from total strangers, a well-meaning cop (who could have saved her), and the used-car salesman, whose worst offer she took without a thought.

But, even granted her self-destructiveness, one must still be struck by the unfairness, the cruel algebra of her death. She alone, however wrongfully, has striven to break the fetters of obsessionalism that bind Sam and Norman to their thankless duties; she alone has tried to flee out of the thankless rituals of obsessional reality. "They also pay who meet in hotel rooms," she said in Phoenix; now the circle has come full round in the Bates Motel room. At the liberating moment of insight into her "private trap," she pays an exorbitant price for disturbing the status quo. I always like to think she would have given back the money, quit her dreary job and booted Sam out of her life, but we shall never know. The frozen tear on her dead cheek renders poignant testimony to all her lost possibilities . . . .

Even after repeated exposures, the shower scene still leaves one numb with disbelief. It is incomprehensible that Janet Leigh should simply cease to be. Never before had a star of such magnitude, a female sex goddess, been so utterly expunged in midstream. Thus Hitchcock drives home the incontrovertibility, the awesome finality of death. Our yen for sanctioned sex and sadism has been dreadfully surfeited by Marion's crucifixion. With Leigh gone, the comfortable conventions of the Hollywood suspense vehicle have been totally violated. *Psycho,* half completed, dangles in midair, apparently deprived of its center.

Hitchcock alleviates our disequilibration with a typical obsessional device—the big cleanup. Norman rushes into the bathroom, fights back a wave of nausea, then grabs a mop and pail and sets about putting everything methodically to rights like the automaton housewife in a TV detergent commercial, scouring down the bloody tiles, bundling the corpse in the shower curtain. His relentless ritual cleansing is punctuated by fragments of Marion's nudity, heaping necrophilia upon voyeurism as yet another perverse impulse of which we stand guilty, if we are pricked by the queasy desire to view the remains a little closer.

Norman stuffs the body in the trunk of her car, with her pitiful belongings, then pitches in the folded newspaper. Marion's crime, so momentous within her frame of reference, has been reduced to an addendum of concealment, as she herself has been negated. Norman drives to a swamp-hole conveniently bordering on the Bates property, and pushes the car into the morass. The previous shots of filthy sinks, gurgling drains and flushing toilets coalesce into one magnificent, appalling anal image. Down, down into the muck goes lovely Marion, her white car, and the $40,000—dust unto dust, dirt unto dirt.

But the car sinks only halfway, then stops. Norman gnaws his thumb: we are instinctively with him, hoping it will not stick. After a few anxious seconds, it vanishes irrevocably. He flashes a mirthless little grin, a quick study in obsessional satisfaction—all done, all gone—my, that felt good! He joins a long and impressive roster of Hitchcock's sympathetic villains, engaging messengers from the Id we are encouraged to root for against our civilized judgment. These attractive monsters woo sedate citizens with their charming plausibility; their evil frequently comes within a hairsbreadth of eluding detection. Hitchcock clearly empathizes with them, and part of him, I suspect, dearly wants them to get off. In *Suspicion,* for instance, his producers insisted he rewrite the original ending, in which Cary Grant did in his mousy wife. The new denouement, with Grant properly repentant and his marriage rehabilitated, is singularly unconvincing.

Dissolve to Sam Loomis' hardware store in Fairvale; Sam is visited by Marion's sister, Lila (Vera Miles), who blames him for Marion's disappearance. They are confronted by Milton Arbogast (Martin Balsam), a private investigator hired by Marion's employer. Arbogast comes on as strong as Marion's patrolman, but we will find that, like the cop, he truly wants to help. Thus the "watcher" is either a decent sort or an agent of the persecuting Superego, depending upon one's guilt level and need for punishment.

Arbogast infers that Sam may have plotted the robbery with Marion, possibly with Lila's collusion. He canvasses the motels in the vicinity; at the Bates', Norman denies knowing Marion, but his boyish insouciance fragments under the detective's skillful probing. Caught in uncomfortable contradictions, he stammers and twitches—now his perimeter suffers unfriendly intrusion. Arbogast elicits that Marion did indeed stay overnight at the motel, dined with Norman, and infers she "met" Norman's mother. When Arbogast suggests Norman might still be hiding Marion in return for sex, he becomes angry, refuses to let the mother be interviewed, and orders Arbogast out.

Arbogast telephones Lila that Sam is innocent, and that he is going back to the motel to check out Norman's story. He enters the dark old house, slowly climbs the steep staircase. As he gains the top, the camera swoops upwards to give a bird's-eye view of a door opening off to one side. The strings emit a shrill shriek, as the old lady dashes around the corner and strikes Arbogast full in the face; he stumbles backwards, his hands and feet flailing for balance, down the stairs; Mrs. Bates flings herself upon him, the gigantic knife upraised as the scene darkens. . . .

When Arbogast fails to return, Sam procrastinates for hours, until Lila demands that he go to the motel. He finds only the silhouette of the old woman in the window. Norman has handily swamped the shamus. Sam and Lila contact Chambers, the Fairvale sheriff, a crusty old country type who tries to dispose of the affair with plain horse sense, concluding that Arbogast got a hot lead from Norman, immobilized them with his call and then took off alone after the money. Norman is phoned and supports the sheriff's theory. But one item does not yield so conveniently: Sam and Arbogast both claim they saw Norman's mother, yet the sheriff reveals that Mrs. Bates died ten years ago by her own hand, after poisoning her unfaithful lover! "If the woman up there is Mrs. Bates", the sheriff asks, "who's that woman buried in Greenlawn cemetery?" The odor of sanctity emanating from Norman's martyrdom has suddenly changed to a whiff of brimstone.

Back at the Bates' house, Norman enters his mother's room. From behind the closed door, we hear her cackling: "No, I will *not* hide in the fruit cellar, ah hah, you think I'm fruity? I'm staying right here in my room, and no one will drive me out of it, least of all my big bold son!!!" The obscene vigor of the raucous old voice, the maniacal attacks, do not sort with the frail, still figure Norman carries down the stairs, into the cellar.

The sequence is marvelous, vintage Hitchcock, amusing and terrifying. The camera pivots from that same staggering height from which we watched Arbogast's fall. The sheriff said that Norma Bates lay in her grave, but we have just heard her arguing with her son. Norman bears her like a paralytic, yet we have had horrific evidence of her mobility. The mind reels, verging upon scarifying revelations: we are left suspended over a metaphysical void. Hitchcock frequently employs vertigo as a visual metaphor for the state of emotional imbalance he builds carefully in his characters and audience. Naremore comments that Hitchcock's epiphanies at the abyss (e.g., the Mount Rushmore and Statue of Liberty finales in *North by Northwest* and *Saboteur* respectively), more than mere devices to arouse suspense, are "poetic figures, perfect expressions for the chaos which disrupts the lives of his protagonists. . . ." *Vertigo,* like *Psycho,* is an extended contemplation of this theme, and hinges upon the hero's actual fear of heights. Patients often grow vertiginous when some dark corner of the psyche is illuminated, and the intuition of the familiar is fractured by the resurfacing of buried wish or memory. I have treated several cases where dizziness arose *de novo* while a deeply repressed fear of death was being analyzed. Arbogast, one recalls, died fighting for balance, his commonplace explanations for Marion's disappearance shattered by the demoniacal apparition of Norma Bates . . . .

We cut from Norman's descent into the fruit cellar to a view of the Fairvale church spire rising against a crisp Sunday sky. Hitchcock artfully balances the "below" of psychotic disorder against the false reassurances of order and morality promised "above" in return for obsessional faith in a small-town deity. On the church steps, the sheriff tells Sam and Lila that he visited Norman earlier that morning and found him completely alone: perhaps Sam is a victim of "illusions"! For once, Loomis rises above his engrained compulsiveness and is unconvinced by appeals to reason. He and Lila drive to the motel, register as man and wife. While Sam draws out Norman in the office, Lila steals away to explore the house.

Sam and Norman are photographed in profile as they talk across the desk, echoing the earlier "doubling" of Marion and Norman. Beyond an uncanny physical resemblance (Sam is a more robust, "filled out" version of Norman), both are basically timid, unassertive men unaccustomed to abrasive confrontation. But a competitive, almost sexual tension hangs over their pleasantries, as if Sam intended to rape Norman rather than expose his misdeeds. Lila makes a parallel assault upon Norman's privacy. In a series of eery tracking shots, the house seems to rise and float towards her, instead of her climbing towards it.

The atmosphere within is heavy with solitude; the cluttered Victoriana, aside from its inherent strangeness, belongs almost palpably to others—*None of your business—Private, keep out!*—the old house seems to flash, yet as in a nightmare Lila is compelled onwards, her anxious progress intercut with Sam's penetration of Norman's defenses below. Mrs. Bates' room is immaculately preserved, its appointments precise reflections of Mother's obsessive, anhedonic nature: a sterile washbasin, an armoire with a prim row of highnecked dresses, a sculpture of lace-cuffed hands clasped in prayer. The large double bed contains strange, deep indentations that nag at the edge of awareness.

Meanwhile Sam presses Norman to confess that he would grab at the chance to escape the poverty of the motel. (Both the amateur and professional sleuths have harnessed their bourgeois imaginations to the $40,000 and cannot conceive a motive other than profit to explain Marion's absence.) "This place happens to be my only world!" Norman cries, "I grew up in that house. . . . My mother and I were more than happy!!" Despite his iniquity, we are moved by his pathetic illusions about the past that saw his spirit broken upon the rack of his mother's inflexible will. His room is filled with the artifacts of childhood—toys, schoolbooks, a stuffed teddy bear—a small, squalid space enclosing vast emptiness.

Suddenly realizing that Lila is gone, Norman knocks out Sam and hurls himself up the hill. Lila ducks into the basement, tiptoes into the fruit cellar, where a silent old woman sits, her back turned. Lila touches her shoulder tentatively—"Mrs. Bates? . . . Mrs. Bates?" The chair swivels . . . *and here is Norman's mummified Mum, her wizened flesh stretched over the ancient skull, her leathery lips pulled back into a charnelhouse grin!* The violins take up Lila's scream: bewigged Norman stands at the door in matronly drag, a sheep in wolf's clothing, the knife brandished and ready to pounce, as Sam comes up behind him, seizes him by the throat. Norman's body convulses into an intolerable arc, his face spasms into a hideous grimace—his wig flies off, his dress rips and he collapses in a ruined heap. The pendulum-swing of a bare bulb creates the horrid illusion of movement in Mrs. Bates' empty sockets, and it seems that she has been resurrected by her son's dissolution, the final, dreadful "crossing" of the film.

Dissolve to the county courthouse. An officious psychiatrist reports the results of his interview with the entity that calls itself Norman's mother. From "her" story, he constructs for Sheriff Chambers, Sam and Lila and a few bystanders the "scientific" explanation for the horrors at the Bates Motel. Mrs. Bates was a "clinging, demanding woman." For years, she and her disturbed son had lived "as if there were no one else in the world." Then she took a lover, and Norman killed them both. Afterwards, overcome with remorse, he dug up and preserved her corpse, to erase the consciousness of his crime, playacting her presence as a defense against "danger and desire." The masquerade escalated to the point where "Mother" became as real as himself, then more real: "He was never all Norman, but he was often only Mother, and because he was so pathologically jealous of her, he assumed she was as jealous of him. . . ." Pretty young women aroused "Mother" to insane vengeance, while "Norman" would wink out of existence, to awaken later horrified at "Mother's" crimes. Marion was at least "her" third victim, Norman was the first and last, for he has simply ceased to be. . . .

Psycho's psychiatrist speaks inexactly to the basis for Norman's madness, his twisted solidarity with his mother. There is always a dialectic of pleasure between mother and child. Out of a complex matrix of shared satisfaction—the nursing situation is paradigmatic—evolves basic trust: the self is tacitly acknowledged as worthy of care. As once she ministered to her child's helplessness, a healthy mother will demonstrate her affection by encouraging the growing child's efforts to obtain mastery over its environment.

Unfortunately, a troubled mother instead may encourage the child's overweening dependency because of her own unresolved neurotic difficulties—for instance, in caring for her baby, she may be caring for the still-ungratified infant within herself, and paradoxically may feel abandoned if she must relinquish that care. Unwittingly she invades the child's developing autonomy, implying that without her comforting presence, the child will be unable to function, or will fall prey to dire catastrophe in a hostile world.

The child of such a mother is frequently "adultified" as well as "infantilized," forced to fulfill needs that should be met from another quarter. ("A son is a poor substitute for a husband," says Norman to Marion.) One discovers a continuum of psychic disorder roughly corresponding to the extent of the mother's unnecessary intrusions into her child's life space. At the most pathological extreme is the malignant symbiosis fostered by an eccentric, egocentric woman like Norma Bates.* In this stultifying partnership, Norman came to find existence equally impossible with or without his mother, hated her for dominating him, loathed himself for his crippling dependency. And it is not unlikely that Mrs. Bates also came to resent Norman's intrusions into her life, sought to remedy this burden by taking a lover during Norman's adolescence. Norman had, in a sense, won the Oedipal victory, he gained exclusive possession of Mother when his father died. There is no doubting his rage when Mother turned away from him to another; adolescents have been known to kill under these circumstances.

But let us not be too quick to buy the psychiatrist's convenient explanation. Every critique of *Psycho* has simply assumed that Norman murdered Mom and her lover simply because "Mother" said so to the doctor. Paranoids like Mrs. Bates do not admit to being or doing wrong, so one must at least ponder an alternate possibility: *Norman is guiltless of his mother's death. Mrs. Bates killed her unfaithful, swindling lover and took her own life. The "Mother" who thereafter became institutionalized in Norman's skull accuses him to exculpate herself!*—entirely consistent with what can be gleaned of her manipulative, malevolent character.

But even if Norman was guilty, he did not exhume Mother out of

* See ch. 11—"The Fatal Urge to Merge" for a lengthier discussion of the ramifications of symbiosis.

remorse, as the psychiatrist urges, but primarily out of *loneliness,* to recreate the demeaning protections of the symbiosis and maintain the nursery illusion of eternal sustenance if only Mrs. Bates could be preserved—how many nights has he lain on that indented bed, clutching her corpse? As the years passed, "Mother" grew more crazily oppressive and possessive, as she would have had she remained alive and uninvolved with anyone else but her son. The young women who stumbled upon the motel and aroused Norman "Mother" ruthlessly eliminated to keep the precious union intact. Norman executed Marion and the other girls in an altered state of consciousness: each murder was a symbolic rape-revenge against his seductive, rejecting mother, as well as an abortive, brutal disengagement from her for which she, not he, would take the blame. Lila and Sam carried out the threat for which Arbogast died, exposed Mrs. Bates' decaying mortality, and Norman, rather than face the reality of his utter aloneness, took flight backwards into the womb of time, returning from whence he came, leaving "Mother" to rule in triumph over the husk of his body.

Norman's macabre hobby was pitched at redeeming his mother's shrivelled ruin. His stuffed birds are also mute representations of the negated ego, the damaged self certain latent psychotics experience as a dead hollowness enclosed within an obsessional envelope.* Mummy looks like Norman's dummy, but in fact he has always been *hers,* despite token resistance. With the terminal submersion of his personality, his dummyhood becomes absolute and unassailable.

One is irritated—I think by design—at the presumptuousness with which the pompous psychiatrist disposes of Norman as if he were a bizarre insect to be pinned and duly catalogued. Hitchcock's strong attraction towards Freudian psychoanalysis has always been curiously diffident, even slapdash, in its undiguised manifestations. He is least satisfying a Freudian when trying hardest to be one, and does his best

---

* The birds of *Psycho,* as Naremore observes, are overdetermined images, admitting of many other interpretations. They are the silent "watchers," expressive of passive victimization or predatory attack. Marion, that perennial victim, "eats like a bird" according to Norman. Mother's depredations are accompanied by bird-like keening. Hitchcock's next film, *The Birds,* depicted an avian onslaught upon a California seaside town like Fairvale, mysteriously related to the anger of a jealous mother when her bachelor son brings home an attractive young woman!

when Freudian themes are woven unobtrusively into the films. Contrast the bogus dream sequences of *Spellbound,* the arm-chair psychologizing of *Marnie* and *Psycho,* with *Psycho's* authentic ambience of the dream—as during Lila's excursion through the Bates house; with its wealth of visual free association, appreciated only in multiple viewings; with its subtle insistence on the influence of childhood pain upon adult destiny, and with its evocation of sexual aberration with a minimum of garish cues. Hitchcock would probably agree that one must be terribly wary of the blandishments of psychology, lest one deny the mystery of what can never be known about other people. At one level, "scientific" speculations constitute only another obsessional peg from which to hang one's faith in rational order, while the Id writhes and the Superego hovers, contemptuous of puny reason.

We are fetched away from the psychiatrist's facile testimony by "Norman's" request for a blanket—"He feels a little chill," says a guard with unconscious irony. We see Norman's shell sitting still as death in a bare cell, and the sight defies all rationalizing. "Mother's" voice speaks off-camera:

> MRS. BATES: It's sad when a mother has to speak the words that will condemn her own son . . . they'll put him away now, as I should have years ago. He was always *bad* . . . and in the end, he attempted to tell them I killed those girls and that man . . . as if I could do anything but sit and stare, like one of his stuffed birds . . . they're probably watching me . . . well, let them, let them see what kind of a person I am . . . (*the mad eyes dart down to a fly crawling on its wrist*) . . . I'm not even going to swat that fly . . . they'll see, and they'll know—and they'll say . . . why—*she wouldn't even hurt a fly!*

It peers cannily straight at us, its lips firm into a tiny, knowing smile; for a fraction of an instant we register Mrs. Bates' rictus behind her son's skin, then an actual skull, then dissolve to Marion's car, winched out of the fecal swamp.

With this grim deliverance, we have touched psychic ground zero, reached an ending beyond "The End" of a mere "thriller," and encountered as subversive, as nihilistic a vision of man's insignificance and inhumanity as any called up by Lear in his ravings or in the barren recognitions of Samuel Beckett. Endgame indeed!

Exploitation is the core experience of relatedness in *Psycho* and elsewhere in Hitchcock's universe. The film unfolds as an articulating chain of abuse: we are, the director tells us, destined to be each other's victims or victimizers, and sometimes both. Sam Loomis is victimized by his dead, failed father; he abuses Marion's love, Marion cheats her employer, turns the tables on Cassady who sought his pound of flesh even before the robbery. Norman seduces Marion into trusting him, then murders her, but he is a zombie, the marrow of his ego sucked dry by the same mother he has (possibly) slaughtered, gutted and stuffed. Caring and closeness have everywhere degenerated into prying and preying. The past preys upon the present; the parent preys upon its helpless child. (Mothers most of all, the basis, I suspect, for Hitchcock's lady-killing!) and God, who wears Hitchcock's inscrutable features, shits us into the world to shit us out again.

Andre Bazin and Eric Rohmer postulate that Hitchcock's God is Catholic, more specifically Jansenist. For Raymond Durgnat, He is cruel, capricious and Calvinist. To the analyst, Hitchcock's Deity seems the essence of the obsessional's cruel, sanctimonious conscience. However we name Him, from whatever premise, He emerges as His maker, an omnipotent sadistic Santa Claus who always knows if you've been bad or good, renders few gifts and mocks the mixed motive. He created the abominations of Norman and Mother, for which He holds both equally to blame. He sends Marion Crane into the swamp, resurrecting her carcass to her irredeemable defamation. Since no one will ever know her change of heart in Norman's parlor, she will be remembered as the sexy girl who stole all that money and got herself killed. Poetic justice! Served her right, with those tight sweaters!

In *Lear,* the blinded Gloucester cries: "As flies to wanton boys are we to the Gods—they kill us for their sport!" In Sam's store, after Marion's murder, one of Hitchcock's wacky old ladies searches for a painless insecticide. She is the Lord of the Flies, and we are ruled by a similar providence. The best one hopes for in this life of pain is a numb extinguishment by the imponderable forces cooly regarding us from afar, as we claw and struggle within our private traps.

Norman Bates has lived at the antipodes of estrangement from the vital center that afflicts normals like Marion and Sam in their pursuit of respectability as proof against the rule of Chaos. Freud, despite his obsessionalism, was at least able to offer us some surcease from the torment of the blaming Superego, asserting that knowledge of the past and of one's disavowed natural instincts might yet create a more tolerant view of the embattled self, allowing a less rigid adaptation to authoritarian culture. Hitchcock, for all his genius, can give no better prescription for the alienation he portrays so tellingly in *Psycho,* and the greater balance of his mature work, than the obsessional's credo: there is little that can be done to stave off madness or retribution, the Apes at the Windows or the Cop of the Mind, except to keep one's eye squarely on the task at hand, mind one's business, do one's duty, and never hope for too much pleasure or freedom—except, of course, at the movies!

Several otherwise admirable studies of *Psycho* have been marred by assuming that Hitchcock intended something more therapeutic than this affirmation of obsessionalism. Leo Braudy believes that the director is challenging the complacency with which we thirst vicariously after evil in the theater's darkness. *Psycho* makes "the irresponsible audience" acknowledge "the rooted violence and perverse sexuality that may be in our motives." For James Naremore, *Psycho* is a monstrous joke—"some viewers have been offended—but if we could not laugh, we would go mad." Robin Wood, chief apostle of Hitchcock as "therapist," also finds balm in *Psycho's* sardonic humor—"it enables the film to contemplate the ultimate horrors without hysteria, with a poised, almost serene detachment."

Unfortunately, audience response does not betoken healing or mastery of the "ultimate horror"—our entrenched fear of death. Who, especially a woman, has been able to step into a motel shower with equanimity since *Psycho* was loosed upon its unsuspecting public? At best we laughed a little, screamed more, were only too happy to thrust *Psycho* out of consciousness thereafter. At worst, a few marginal souls (I have interviewed two) suffered brief psychotic episodes during the film. No, the serene detachment Wood applauds is not ours, but very particularly Hitchcock's.

If the director is challenging us with our darker desires, I submit that it is with the moral force of a *tu quoque* argument. *Psycho* after all had its inception in *his* imagination, in his overweening interest in "rooted violence and perverse sexuality;" by making us responsive and responsible for his preoccupations, he has exonerated himself and spread the blame, reaping enormous material profit in the process. The imputation of "irresponsibility" should be aimed squarely where it belongs, at Hitchcock himself, especially since *Psycho's* box office triumph spawned a plethora of execrable imitations that debased cinema. Hitchcock has issued pious pronunciamentos about the callousness and brutality of our age, yet he must stand implicated for much of the ubiquitous violence in the movies today. And if *Psycho* is a joke, the joke has surely been played on us, at our expense literally and figuratively, since we have paid admission to be degraded and dragged through the mire of Hitchcock's contempt, like *Psycho's* characters!

Bibliography

BLOCH, ROBERT. *Psycho*. New York: Simon & Schuster, Inc., 1959. (The source for Joseph DiStefano's screenplay; Hitchcock often chose second-rate potboilers with a germ of a first-rate idea; Bloch's novel is no exception.)

FREUD, SIGMUND. *Civilization and Its Discontents*. 6th ed. London: International Psycho-Analytical Library, Hogarth Press, Ltd., 1953.

LA VALLEY, A. J., ed. *Focus on Hitchcock*. Englewood Cliffs, N.J.: Prentice-Hall, Inc., 1972. (Series of thoughtful and generally excellent essays, some more specifically noted below.)
LaValley, A.J. "Introduction." See pp. 1–17.
Bazin, Andre. "Hitchcock Versus Hitchcock." See pp. 60–69.
Durgnat, Raymond. "The Strange Case of Alfred Hitchcock, Part 3" and "Inside Norman Bates." See pp. 91–96 and pp. 127–138. (Durgnat is my favorite critic of *Psycho*.)
Braudy, Leo. "Hitchcock, Truffaut, and the Irresponsible Audience." See pp. 116–126.

NAREMORE, JAMES. *Filmguide to Psycho*. Bloomington/London: Indiana University Press, 1973. (Longest and most detailed work on the film.)

WOOD, ROBIN. *Hitchcock's Films*. New York: A. S. Barnes & Co., Inc., 1965. See pp. 112–123.

VII

8½—The Declensions of Silence

> As for the directors, an investigation should be made to
> find out why they, too, even the "greatest," usually
> collapse after three or four good films, and again fall
> into banal conformity, or wild ostentation.
>
> Federico Fellini

At first glance, *8½* seems to offer unparalleled opportunities for the
psychoanalytic critic. All the familiar touchstones are there: dreams—
both sleeping and waking, troubling memories of childhood, exuberant
free associations. But if our craft is invoked too easily, Fellini will
surely elude our grasp, for he is a mercurial phantast, an inspired liar.
No base libel is intended—for he has said as much: "The virtue of the
spontaneous lie is that it distorts truth, to render it strange, significant,
and enchanting. . . ."

No two histories of the great *auteur* have ever coincided; the confusion has multiplied because Fellini really *believes* his own confabulations. The only definitive autobiography—his entire *oeuvre*—has produced wildly divergent critical reaction and interpretation. The
film-director hero of *8½*, Guido Anselmi, shares the elusiveness of his
maker. If one proposes venturing into the inner world of this intriguing

138

wreck, one must not be taken in by facile clues Fellini strews so liberally about that serve sometimes as signpost, sometimes as subterfuge. One then discovers at the heart of the film the seeds of a monumental emptiness that has pervaded Fellini's work since 8½. But that is the end of the story. . . .

In the beginning: Guido (Marcello Mastroianni) stalled in a monstrous traffic jam. His car fills with noxious vapor, he struggles impotently to escape while the occupants of nearby cars stare unsympathetically as if he were some lower life form displayed under glass. He manages to clamber out and soar into the clouds, high over strange girdered towers, to the edge of the sea. Far below, a horseman gallops down the beach, arousing a man who holds a coil of rope attached to Guido's foot. His captor yanks the rope, tumbling Guido headlong into the waves. . . .

He awakes with a scream, to find himself in a suite at a health spa. A doctor prescribes mineral water and mudbaths for "a touch of liver trouble. . . ." Enter Daumier, a noted writer Guido has enlisted for his new picture. Daumier murmurs ominously that they must have a very *long* talk about the project, and leaves. Guido peers into the mirror; his face, deeply lined with fatigue and misery, stares back.

Dissolve to the outside. In the opening sequence, the automobiles and clothing were contemporary, but the fashionable ambience of the spa is inexplicably Gatsbyish or more likely mid-thirtyish, straight out of the "white telephone" era of Italian cinema. Pampered women wave coyly, a nurse giggles, turns away. Guido is obviously well-known and sought after. He joins a line of fellow sufferers inching towards the fountain where young girls are dispensing the healing waters. Sudden stillness—a breathtakingly lovely brunette in virginal white, Guido's fantasied Muse, holds out a glass—then she disappears, replaced by the real serving girl.

Later on: Daumier and Guido in conference; the writer lacerates the director with a formidable, desiccated intellectualism; Guido's script is a total failure, lacking "poetic inspiration, philosophical conscience, artistic seriousness." Why does Guido even bother asking for his help? Guido's mind is elsewhere, but he assures Daumier he values his opinion, he truly needs to make this film, he has only been delaying because . . . because. . . . Then Guido drops Daumier cold as he catches sight of his old friend Mario Mezzabotta (Mario Pisu), a handsome, vaguely dissipated man of middle age who names Guido for the first time and actually resembles him. Mario tells Guido he has ditched his wife of thirty-one years and is waiting for an annulment at the spa with his "fiancée," a vapid beauty half his age.

Dissolve to the railway station. A train pulls in and Guido is obviously disappointed when his mistress, Carla (Sandra Milo), alights and greets him fulsomely. Pneumatic, resplendently vulgar, her mind is resolutely empty save for thoughts of creature comforts—dresses, food and comic books. On the thinnest pretext, Guido lodges her in a hotel near the station. She tells him a dream in her room: her husband caught them making love and murdered them both with a broomstick. Guido has her dress up like a prostitute, persuades her to go out and reenter as if she were a stranger. His interest quickens for the first time when she asks if he would be jealous if she really did "things like this." After sexual relations, Guido dreams:

His mother, a handsome woman in widow's weeds, draws him into a devastated landscape. He wears a schoolboy's cape. "Ah, the tears I've shed, the tears!!" she sobs. His father, a dignified old gentleman, walks away as Guido pleads in vain for him to wait. They enter a mausoleum, the father complains the ceiling is too low, asks Guido to fix it. Two more elderly men, who we shall later identify as Pace, Guido's producer and Conocchia, his chief assistant, enter the crypt and consult gravely with father over "this son of mine." Conocchia warns Pace not to let the father play on his sympathies, and the producer, with an eloquent Latin gesture, indicates that affairs stand very poorly indeed. Pace and Conocchia exit. Father sighs—he has failed miserably, turns his back on Guido and walks away once more. Guido weeps—*"what place is this, why are you here?"* No answer. He hands the father down into a freshly dug grave. His mother complains she does the best she can, what more can she do? She kisses him lightly, then with a sudden, alarming passion. He struggles against her embrace to discover his mother has changed into his wife, Luisa (Anouk Aimee). . . .

8½ begins *in medias res.* In his first dream, Guido is brought to the brink of death, hemmed in by an audience indifferent to his agony. He escapes, only to descend with shuddering fall, and awakens to intimations of mortality. He is forty-three years old, there is a film he cannot make, and his time is running out.

Daumier sickens him—why has he hired on this perturbatious fellow? The writer is a Devil's advocate, the projection of Guido's doubts, a metaphor of the aridity that reigns over the artist's imagination when the muse has fled; intriguingly, Daumier directs his most withering scorn at Guido's Muse, the beauty in white who gave Guido his curative cup in his fantasy, and who is supposed to be a principal character in the new script.

Mario Mezzabotta is Guido *in extremis,* the debris of a gay blade, pathetically trying to retrieve the lost vigor of youth through an empty liaison with a fatuous glamor girl. It isn't far from Mario and his chippie to Guido and Carla, just over the tracks! Having appropriately installed his mistress in the Hotel Terminal (!), Guido whips his faltering libido by having her act the whore, while the threat of her husband's retaliation hangs over their tryst.

Guido's second dream is a product of their sex, of the occurrences since his awakening at the spa, and of obscure recent and past trauma. The atmosphere is unrelievedly gloomy. Dressed as a child, Guido is blamed by his mother as a major cause of unspecified woe. It is an oft-repeated ritual of accusation and exculpation on her part, usually designed unconsciously by such a mother to rationalize her awesome selfishness and indifference. The paternal image is distributed between the real—dead—father, Pace the producer, and Conocchia, Guido's factotum. The father is genially unavailable, moving away at a tangent to his son's distress. Pace, distant and ungiving, mutely testifies to Guido's desperate condition. Conocchia's injunction to Pace not to be "taken in" is an oblique reference to the game of cat-and-mouse Guido has been playing with his backers over the stymied picture. Also, in the manner of dreams, the different characters represent different sides of Guido himself; from this viewpoint, one speculates that Guido has been gulling himself, *taking himself in* by leaving vital personal issues unexamined.

He seeks guidance from male authorities who offer him only veiled criticism or the silence of the tomb. Was the real father distant, minimizing, unable or unwilling to provide the signets of a viable masculine identity? Is Guido, still mourning his death, sunken into paralyzing depression? Like Rick Blaine, Guido meditates on Oedipal shenanigans—in Carla's dream, Guido the interloper is murdered by *her* husband. Hearing her dream, Guido dreams of helping his father into his grave, leaving *him* in *his* mother's arms! But having gotten rid of Dad, he confronts his impossible Mom—self-pitying, guilt-provoking, more unsupportive than the father, and bewilderingly, frighteningly sexual. Watching him pinioned by her lust, one recalls the repeated references to fatal entrapments: suffocation in the locked car, the father's complaints about the constrictions of his mausoleum. Claustrophobia may have its root in the fear of engulfment by a mother like Guido's, who presents a confusing mixture of overstimulation, seductivity and hostile, blaming rejection to her little boy.

Mother changes into Luisa at the instant of her passion. Is there a dreaded identification between the two that has sent Guido into the arms of the blowsy nitwit Carla? Fellini provides more questions than answers, but it is certain that Guido is terrified of growing old. The loss of his creative voice looms as a premonition of death. . . .

Guido returns to his hotel, where a horde of movie people descend upon him. The pace is frenetic, everyone wants undivided attention. An audience has been arranged for Guido with the Cardinal staying at the spa. Conocchia—the real one—has a great idea for "the spaceship." Carla phones that she doesn't like her room. A vulgar journalist demands details of Guido's love life. He fobs most of them off with elliptical courtesy, but is unforgivably rude to Conocchia and three old men auditioning for the father's part—is he shooting science fiction, autobiography, or what? Pace arrives with his entourage, more confusion, Guido makes a mock *salaam* and reassures him unconvincingly.

Dissolve: evening, an impromptu cabaret. Guido sits abstracted, while the others continue to plague him with inane questions about politics, aesthetics, religion. A lithe unearthly figure, Maurice, bounds onto the stage, announces a mind reading act. He places his hand above a woman's head, and his assistant speaks the subject's deepest wish—to live another hundred years (surely Guido's wish as well!). Afterwards the mentalist greets Guido, who he knows fondly from less fortunate times. It is Guido's only authentic moment of engagement so far in *8½*. How does the act work, he asks?

MAURICE: Part of it's a trick, and part of it is real. *I don't really know how it works, but it does!*

He then transmits Guido's thought—the assistant, puzzled, chalks on a blackboard: ASI NISI MASA. . . .

Dissolve to the kitchen of an old farmhouse in northern Italy. It is a custom to immerse boys in wine lees every year to ensure their strength and virility. Ample peasant women chatter affably as they carry dazzling white linen to and fro. Robust men lift the youngsters high and plunge them into the wine. Little Guido, protesting vigorously, is caught and dunked, the women swaddle him lovingly, carry him upstairs to a room filled with children. A girl urges him not to sleep, to stare instead at the picture of a bearded man:

GIRL: Tonight the man in the picture will move his eyes . . . whichever way he moves his eyes, that's where the treasure will be . . . say the magic words: *asa nisi masa . . . asa nisi masa. . . .*

Guido conjures up this luminous memory in response to Maurice and his assistant's "act." In an earlier version, Guido was taught a "secret language" by a friend: the vowel of every syllable of a word was repeated, preceded by "s." ASA NISI MASA thus "translates" as ANIMA—soul, spirit, life. Maurice the magician transmits a telepathic impulse to his female assistant as the seed is passed from man to woman for the deeper necromancy of insemination. Child-Guido partakes of the ancient rite of immersion and rebirth; basking in the affection of generous women, he is granted the power to "animate"—to breathe life into the unliving, as the grown-up Guido makes his celluloid pictures move!

Later in the evening Guido telephones his wife Luisa in Rome, says he is lonely, asks her to join him. The invitation is grossly inappropriate, not to say inflammatory, since it is inevitable that wife and mistress must meet, but Guido's childhood memory is working potently upon his subconscious, making him throw caution to the winds. He is a man who needs women, many women, but always one special woman. Carla and the other ladies of the spa who have importuned him cannot make the pictures move again, so he turns to Luisa, the wife-mother for the resuscitation of his faltering powers.

He visits his production crew; the devoted executors of his fantasies labor late into the dawn, sewing costumes, tallying accounts, planning sets, unaware that their master is leading them down the blind alleys of his flawed imagination. Only Conocchia realizes Guido's plight, but when he tries to help, Guido angrily calls him an old idiot:

> CONOCCHIA (*weeping*): Old—now it comes out . . . I'm in your way, that's all there is to it . . . I'm quitting the picture tomorrow morning, you need younger people, but be careful, watch out— you're not the man you used to be either!

Conocchia *is* Guido's older self, fearful of replacement by the indifferent young. Usually the soul of European tact, Guido has lashed out twice at this venerable adviser, attacking in Conocchia the projection of his own anxieties.

Back in his room, Guido has a momentary inspiration; his heroine will be the daughter of the local museum's curator, raised amidst classical beauty. The supremely lovely muse of the springs materializes, leafs through his manuscript and laughs at this sophomoric invention. She lies down next to him, whispering—*"I've come here never to leave . . . I shall create order . . . scrub and clean. . . ."* He awakens to the rude jangle of the telephone: Carla is feverish, begs him to join her. At her hotel, he orders her to call home; she moans that her husband will take her away (exactly what Guido wants), and she'll never get to wear her pretty dresses. Why does he stay with her, why, why? He cannot answer.

Dissolve to Guido's audience with the Cardinal, next morning. Guido tells the prelate's secretary that his hero's Catholic background has created "certain complexes . . . a Cardinal appears as an oracle of a truth he can no longer accept . . . nevertheless . . . he looks to the Cardinal for help, perhaps for a revelation." The Cardinal is discovered reading under the trees. He inquires after Guido's age, if he is married and has children. To the last, Guido quickly answers yes, then corrects himself—no, he has none. The Cardinal bids him listen to the mournful song of the Diomedes bird, which, after the death of its namesake saint, sang a funeral chorus, according to legend. Does the bird's cry not sound like sobbing? Like the father in the second dream, the Cardinal eludes contact, refuses comfort, calling up imagery of barrenness and death. Discomfited, Guido spies a heavy barelegged woman going down a path, and drifts off again into his past. . . .

Schoolboys gather at a ramshackle hut by the sea to offer money to an enormous whore, "La Saraghina." Her hair in Medusa-like disrepair, her wide mouth lipsticked garishly, her dress in tatters and her huge legs bare, she is the awesome apotheosis of preadolescent sexual hopes and fears. She hitches her bodice down, her skirts up, and launches into a ghastly, joyous rhumba. As she dances with little Guido, two priests burst upon the scene. Guido's companions scamper off, leaving him to his fate; after a Chaplinesque chase down the beach, he is collared and dragged back to school, hailed before the tribunal. Led by the Father Superior, castigated for his iniquity and commanded to look upon his mother. She is elegantly dressed and coiffed; on cue, she buries her face in her hands—"Stop, oh, Lord, the shame, the shame!!"—then peeps furtively through her fingers to see if her mortification is being duly appreciated! Dissolve to the school refectory at mealtime; Guido, wearing a dunce cap, is forced to kneel on peas while a reader intones the life of the virtuous saint who so abhorred the sight of women he fled the presence of his mother! Dissolve back to little Guido praying before the loathsome remains of an embalmed female saint. A confessor reproves him: "Didn't you know Saraghina is the Devil?" Outside the confessional, he looks up to an alabaster-white Madonna, then the serene image is superimposed over Saraghina's hut. Despite threats of perdition, Guido has come back to her; she sits humming to herself, gazing out at the sparkling sea. The very air shimmers with promise; everything grotesque about her is transformed into a precarious beauty. She smiles invitingly . . . and waves—"*Ciao!*"

There is more in these sequences than a single-minded attack upon clerical misogyny and puritanism, nor are Guido's priest-prosecutors simply masculine authority figures. The priests are played by *women*, a brilliant invention that merits consideration on other grounds than sheer cinematic effect. This entire chain of recollections encapsulates Guido's splitting of the feminine image, a familiar splitting I have already commented upon in *The Maltese Falcon* and Hitchcock's work. Embodied variously by Saraghina, the tribunal of disguised matrons, the rotting saint, the madonna and finally by his blaming and corrupt mother, woman is both pure and sullied, enticer and accuser. One flees her in inchoate fear as from the demon, or yearns after her at the precipice, vertiginous with desire. Despite censure and scorn, Guido returns to Saraghina, the bounteous and degraded Saraghina, her image melding with the Madonna, the *Ur*-Mother—who is ambiguously equated with the forces of repression and renascence.

Fellini, still brooding upon Hell, now turns the spa into a parody of Dante; pilgrims of the healing establishment, clad in sepulchral sheets, ascend and descend a long staircase, their progress to mudbath and massage directed by half-naked minions. Guido, going down, forever down (there are innumerable descents in the film) with Pace, pays no attention, as usual, to his producer's prodding. Amidst clouds of infernal steam, Guido sits next to Mezzabotta, whose dissipated visage seems nearly moribund. A preternatural silence envelops them, and the voice of an airline stewardess announces that His Eminence waits upon Guido—the projected audience of his script.

Guido is ushered into a low oppressive room, reminiscent of the father's mausoleum. The Cardinal is nude, his back turned, his ancient body shrunken. Attendants wrap him in a winding sheet, while the mud for his bath is kneaded, falling in repellent lumps from the masseur's hands. The ambience reeks of mortality. *I am not happy,* complains Guido. *That is not the task in life,* rebukes the Cardinal. *No one has said we are on earth only to be happy. Remember Origines: There is no salvation outside of the Church.* A window closes over the strange visitation with utter finality. The Cardinal is even more categorical in his refusal to guide Guido than in their real meeting under the trees. A complex symbol of failed paternal authority and inadequate maternal sustenance, he urges upon Guido a salvation the director no longer can accept. Whatever faith Guido held for rescue from his despair by the sheltering Church of his youth has been voided by the Cardinal's implacable coldness. There are no further ecclesiastic adventures in *8½*.

At twilight, Guido strolls through the town, spies his wife in the crowd, dressed in white. At first he seems genuinely happy to be with her. They are joined by Pace, Luisa's sister—obviously no friend of Guido's, and Rosella, an amateur spiritualist and close friend to the couple. Pace invites the company to visit the site of Guido's mysterious "spaceship." Cars are called. Luisa, who has been off-camera for a moment, reappears; her manner towards her husband changes to frosty indifference. Dissolve to the launchpad. Two enormous towers are illuminated against the night sky—one realizes they are the strange structures Guido flew over in the opening dream. Pace says the towers rest on sand—no contractor wanted to build them. He leads the party up a winding stairway, relating Guido's "plot":

> PACE: A shot of the world ravaged by thermonuclear war . . . in the middle of desolation and death stands the new Noah's Ark, our spaceship . . . hoping to escape atomic death, the survivors of the world try to get to another planet. . . .

Guido has externalized his distress into a trite, sci-fi world destruction and rebirth fantasy, while the movie he really wants to make about his personal apocalypse reveals itself in disconnected fragments, its coherence eluding him while he wrestles with the chimeras of depression. He confides to Rosella that his new picture was meant to purge the past so he could begin again. Instead, he's horribly confused, fearful he has nothing to say—"but I want to say it anyway!" What do the spirits advise?

> ROSELLA: Always the same thing . . . you are free, you must make a choice . . . and you don't have much time before you!

Back at the hotel Guido is lying alone in bed. Luisa enters; he pretends sleep. She laughs brusquely, calls him a transparent liar. A hot quarrel ensues: Luisa echoes Carla's protests. They have been at a dead end for years. What does he want from her? Why does he torment her? Like Carla, she has been seduced here, then exposed to the cutting edge of his indifference. Guido really believes that Luisa—like Carla—makes terrible demands upon him while he remains totally oblivious to his own maddening evasiveness! Next day, Guido sits on the terrace with Luisa and Rosella. Guido sees Carla and slumps down to avoid recognition. Luisa informs him caustically that she discovered his mistress last night, but he nevertheless continues his outrageous confabulations. He didn't know Carla was down here, besides, it was all over three years ago. Luisa explodes—is it possible he's become so expert at lying that he doesn't know the difference between truth and falsehood anymore? Guido regards her reflectively, then Carla, smiles, murmurs—"And yet . . ."—setting in motion the film's most elaborate, famous fantasy:

Carla bursts into rapturous song, Luisa links arms with her and they skip off. Dissolve back to the old farmhouse. Guido comes in out of a blizzard, distributing gifts to an omnium-gatherum of his ladies, past, present and possible: Luisa, clad in peasant garb, the angry sister-in-law ("who became a wonderful girl after she learned to like me!"), Saraghina, Carla, Mario's fiancée, the buxom nurses of childhood, a mysterious beauty from the hotel he's lusted after *en passant* ("It doesn't matter what my name is, I'm happy to be here, that's enough . . ."), a Danish stewardess, Rosella ("like Pinocchio's conscience—so you finally got your harem, eh?")—and many, many others.

The women immerse Guido in the winebath and swaddle him, extravagantly praising his charms. But a discordant note threatens the festivities—a weeping chorus girl, Jacqueline Bonbon, emerges from the cellar, pleading with Guido not to be sent "upstairs—with the old ones"—she is only twenty-six, twenty-six years old "on the fourth of July, 1938!" Guido is adamant, but the aging chorine gathers partisans. Ripples of discontent spread, then open revolt breaks out:

> WOMEN: It's unfair . . . a real man could love a woman regardless of her age . . . down with the tyrant!—what makes him think he's still young . . . he's a lousy lover . . . talk and kisses, that's his speed, then he goes to sleep!

They bare their teeth like beasts, Saraghina in the forefront. (In the earlier version, Guido was a lion tamer, caged with snarling women.) He beats them back with a bullwhip; Jacqueline pleads with Luisa in vain:

> LUISA: No—my husband does exactly as he pleases . . . that's one of the house rules!

Jacqueline finally agrees to go "upstairs" in return for a pathetic farewell dance. Cut to Guido at the head of a long table, addressing the assembly gloomily:

GUIDO: I thought it was going to be such an amusing scene . . . hidden here from the world . . . but what went wrong? Why all this sadness?

MYSTERY WOMAN: Ah, we've made him feel guilty, poor darling!

They vanish. Luisa is alone, scrubbing down the stone floors.

LUISA: Ah, it's nice being all together—at first I didn't understand . . . but now you see how good I am . . . I don't bother you anymore, I don't ask you for anything . . . twenty years to understand!

This rhapsody to male chauvinism is sparked by Luisa's anger at Guido's infidelity. The Luisa of his vision presides over his harem without complaint. The last sight of her is where he wants her—down on her knees. Having finally grasped the lesson he has been covertly teaching, she has fused with the subservient nurses of his youth. (The real Luisa, astringent, coolly intelligent, of course, is an unlikely candidate for the role of forbearing earth-mother Guido yearns after.)

The Janus-like aspect of woman resurfaces with a vengeance in the harem sequence. Either Guido is immersed in lavish care or savagely menaced. Either woman feeds him into a state of blissful satiety or devours him. He must be her absolute master or she will turn on him and tear him apart. While his harem fantasy is partly determined by the competitive compulsion to own every man's woman, at a deeper level the harem is a function of Guido's fear of closeness with his horrific mother and the attendant desire to tempt and degrade all women: evasive retaliation is his standing battle plan.

But as I have noted, he must eternally return to his idealized, sentimentalized and damaging image of woman for his revival: there is a powerful articulation between his Muse, the nurses of childhood, and the Luisa of the mind—pure, docile, adoring, they are the harbingers of calm and order. To be looked at and worshipped is a crucial ingredient of Guido's libidinal life. His films are extensions of his exhibitionism, elaborations into art of the firm body and straight legs extravagantly praised by the peasant women. He is a vain, handsome man who worries that his aging physique will be found repulsive, and fears that his audience will be equally unaccepting of his cinematic exhibitions.

Guido is marginally aware of his shabby treatment of women; in his fantasy they revolt after he rejects the used-up chorine, although from his point of view she has been collected greedily, and will live on "upstairs," forever young, as a memory of conquest. He cannot tolerate older women, Jacqueline or his wife, because they remind him of his own declining charms. As he sits at the table, he has a surge of remorse, dimly recognizing how destructive he can be to the woman who wishes to be prized as a whole person, with separate needs of her own. But this uneasy self-appraisal is transient—the dream-Luisa reappears, and her comforts are ominous, for Guido is retreating further into himself, further away from the rewards and problems of loving in the real world. His paramount desire is to be left alone: appropriate demands by his women, his friends or his colleagues are distorted into merciless depredations.

Now time—real time—is indeed running out. Pace hires the town cinema to screen Guido's rushes so that final casting decisions can be made. Guido sits dejectedly in the empty theater, while Daumier delivers his last judgment: the script is foul, beyond redemption. Guido raises a finger in wordless command and two assistants hang the writer from the rafters. For once his incessant carping is stopped, a ludicrous and chilling moment: the hostile forces stirring within Guido are breaking into consciousness.

Back in reality Daumier still lives; Pace, Luisa, Rosella and the others take their seats. The theater is darkened, and a succession of actors and actresses parade across the screen, auditioning for the *dramatis personae* of Guido's life. Carla—or someone inside Carla's clothes, another Carla, closer to her physically, but the intonation is wrong. Luisa's double speaks lines that continue last night's quarrel: "I don't care what you do—why can't you be honest—if you don't lie, that would be enough—don't you think I'm alone right now?— What good am I to you?"

Offstage, Guido prompts her to be "more aggressive, more—*bitter!*" Enraged, the real Luisa rises. Guido, innocent as a newborn babe, tries to quiet her, after all, it's only a movie! She detests his despicable "honesty," and has made up her mind to leave him. The tangle of the real and the illusory waxes more impenetrable. Shadows of Guido's people, Carla, Saraghina, the Cardinal, cascade across the screen, uncanny near-likenesses or grotesque parodies, themselves yet not so, an eery, hallucinatory procession. And one realizes with a start that Fellini himself stands behind his camera, shooting a film about a director who cannot make a film, trying to make a film about a director who cannot make a film. As in the surfaces of two interposed mirrors, Guido's cracked vision reflects endlessly backwards and forwards. The mind boggles.

Luisa flees. Pace demands angrily for some—any—decision. Guido is rescued from the inquisition of his own devising by the arrival of Claudia (Claudia Cardinale). She has already appeared as the girl of the springs, and Guido wants her to play the same role both in his film and in his life. He drives away with her and asks: "Could you choose one thing . . . and stay faithful to it? Could you make it the thing that gives meaning to your life, that connects everything? . . . The character I'm thinking about couldn't. He wants to possess and devour everything . . . he changes direction all the time because he's afraid he'll lose the right one. He feels drained, dying—then he meets the girl of the springs . . . it's obvious she could save him. . . ."

They stop at an empty piazza, near the springs. In his mind's eye, Guido sees the fantasy-Claudia spreading a table for him in the square. The real Claudia challenges Guido's tale: his hero doesn't deserve sympathy, he doesn't know the meaning of love, so he cannot expect love in return. The very quality Guido prized, her simplicity, pierces to the core of his egotism. Fearful of closeness and commitment, he invents a romance of which he is the sole and perpetual beneficiary, but she will have none of it. In disgust, he exclaims: "You're just as much of a pest as the others!" He thrusts her away, like Luisa. In his terms, she has failed him, become only another drain on his overtaxed energies because she sought more than the surface charisma with which he has danced his way through life. Deeply dispirited, he breaks off his oblique proposal. He is tired of lying and of filming lies: "There isn't any film, there's nothing, the whole thing is finished!" Pace's car roars into the square; the producer has decided unilaterally to call a press conference at the spaceship, launching Guido's derelict project once and for all.

Next day: Guido unwillingly dragged to the spaceship towers. An ill wind whips pennants strung from the gantries. Guido joins Pace and

Conocchia on the dais. A horde of journalists assault his sensibilities
with impertinent questions. He can or will not answer, and they turn
vicious as starved dogs, the women worst of all:

> LADY JOURNALISTS: You're nothing but a failure . . . what could
> you say that would interest the public . . . He's lost! (*laughing*)
> . . . He has nothing to say!!!

Pace threatens to ruin him, and Conocchia weeps openly.

> GUIDO (*to himself*): Conocchia, forgive me, you're the very best
> . . . Claudia, where are you? . . . Where are your spirits, Rosella
> . . . Luisa, do you want me to believe you're going to get a separa-
> tion?

Luisa appears, in her wedding gown.

> LUISA: What should I do, leave? Disappear? Won't I be your wife?
> Won't you ever *really* marry me?

She fades into the crowd. Amidst a swelling tide of mockery, he
ducks under the table, takes out a revolver and presses it to his temple.
The camera swoops away from his mother, crying after him—"Guido,
Guido, where are you running now, you wretched boy?"—and a shot
rings out. Even at this penultimate moment, she rises out of his unconscious to harry him.

But death is only another illusion. Dissolve to the launch site at
twilight, the mob dispersed. Workmen disassemble the towers. Guido
sadly waves farewell to his crew, goes to his car and gets in next to
Daumier.

> DAUMIER: Bravo! Today is a great day for you . . . it's always bet-
> ter to destroy than to create what is inessential . . . we are being
> suffocated by words, by images that have no reason to exist . . .
> any man who is really worthy to be called an artist should swear one
> oath. . . . *Dedication to Silence!*

Suddenly Maurice materializes, dressed for his "act."

> MAURICE: Wait, Guido, wait! We're ready to begin!!!

Daumier drones on. Guido sees, in a series of luminous snapshots:

—Child Guido, held by a peasant nurse.

—Saraghina.

—Mother and Father.

—Claudia, walking solemnly away from him.

Then, all the figures who have crowded his real and imaginary stage, dressed in refulgent white, moving towards him with the same measured steps, and onto the towers. He whispers: "What is this sudden feeling of happiness . . . gentle creatures, forgive me, I did not understand! It's so right to accept you, to love you . . . Luisa, I suddenly feel free . . . everything is just as it was before . . . but this confusion *is* me!"

His wife stands apart, forlorn and vulnerable. At Maurice's bidding, great banks of light switch on, holding back the night. Guido addresses Luisa tenderly: "I'm not afraid of telling the truth, of admitting that I don't know what I seek, and that I have not found it . . . only this way can I feel alive, can I look into your faithful eyes without shame. Life is a holiday, let's enjoy it together. . . . This, Luisa, is all I can say to you and to the others: *accept me as I am.* . . . It's the only way we have to really find ourselves. . . ."

An improbable band of clowns marches in, brought up by little Guido wearing his schoolboy uniform (in white), tootling on a flute, followed by a raggedy mutt. Maurice leads everyone past a circus ring, through a curtain covering the entrance to the rocket tower. Guido steps out of the car, takes up his megaphone. Child-Guido takes up his place by the drawn curtain, and his grown-up self shouts: "Everyone come down! *Come down! Talk to each other!!*"

The boy pulls open the curtain—they all descend, Mama, Papa, Pace, the Cardinal, Mario Mezzabotta, his fiancée, Saraghina, the harem girls, priests, others we have never seen, surging down the stairs, laughing, arguing, a benevolent torrent of humanity. They mount the edge of the ring, link hands and dance to the lilting music of the clowns. Guido greets them as they stream past. He calls after his mother—she gives a humorous shrug, turns back to her husband who leads her into the dance, as if to say "What else can I do?" Carla says: "I understand . . . you mean you can't do without us. When will you call me?" Guido graciously waves her away, then stretches out his hand to Luisa. After a moment's hesitation she joins him, circling the ring. The music softens and all depart, save for the clowns and the boy who conducts them offstage with imperious little gestures. The lights wink out, the child is spotlighted alone, piping into the darkness. Then he, too, marches off.

Guido has risen again, phoenix-like, from his own ashes. Maurice is his metaphor, old friend and artificer, who starts the pictures moving without really knowing how the magic works. The director has re-engaged the hurtful, redemptive images of childhood, to draw forth new vigor. He triumphs over his psychic chaos by objectifying it into consummate art—"This confusion is me"—welding the past, present and conditional tenses into one tight love knot. His Muse slips gracefully away before his miraculous rejuvenation. Perhaps she is no longer needed, once his inspiration is rekindled. Fellini would have us believe she is a snare, a dangerous delusion—"the most disturbing sign of Guido's impotence, his desire for an ideal woman who would tell him, both as man and artist, what to do . . . his nostalgia, his childish desire for protection. . . ."

It is impossible to look unmoved upon the dance of life that ends 8½, yet from all we have intuited about Guido, it is obvious that the rapturous harmony of this felicitous conclusion obscures—*must* obscure—his still desperate frame of mind. He severs his connection with Luisa, rejects Claudia and, feeling abandoned and worthless, relinquishes his precious project, rushing headlong to embrace the very death he fears. Daumier, grim alter ego, with as much enthusiasm as that withered soul will ever command, praises the artist's Dedication to Silence. At once, Guido soars into the realm of purest fantasy, and his lady Muse, the Claudia of dreams, quits the scene forever.

In psychoanalytic terms, Guido has sustained an overwhelming rupture of his tie to the nurturing material image and inevitably to the entire world. The brave reconciliation of the ending, from this perspective, bears the mark of an abortive attempt at restitution. Guido asks us to accept him as he is, in return for his pathetic entertainments. In exchange for the privilege of being permitted to exhibit his damaged, exhausted self and shaking his tattered cap and bells, he will continue to prevaricate, manipulate and treat others—especially on the distaff side—as dumb providers of his pleasure.

There is, of course, absolutely no evidence that anyone will be more disposed to accept him following his indulgent pseudo-insight than before. But at this juncture, Guido is no longer particularly concerned with reality. Symbolism of confinement and release, death and rebirth, inform *8½* from the beginning, when Guido delivers himself from the deadly enclosure of the traffic jam, only to be jerked downward by the fatal umbilical that connects him to the spa and his unborn film. As a child, he is delivered out of the wine bath, in the fullness of his nurses' love is granted the power of *animation,* a benefice he tries to regain through his harem fantasy. In actuality, he divorces himself, one by one, from every person who might help him weather this time of travail. Women, as we have seen, are special targets for revenge and angry withdrawal, because of their identification with his Harpy-Mother.

His worst fears are realized at the press conference. He exhibits himself and is derided by the lady critics for a puny, impotent fellow. Again he fantasizes death and transfiguration: with no real attachment left, he tragically transcends the need for human contact by invoking the "love affair with the world" which Phyllis Greenacre has suggested is the special provenance of the artist in health or neurosis. All wounding is undone by a singular act of omnipotent fructification, as Child-Guido draws open the womb of time and gives birth to the cast of his life cycle, inutterably vivid, pristine in white raiment, beheld through the distorting prism of art and illness.

His mother's refusal to heed his call as she goes with father to the dance recreates the original rejection of the Oedipal configuration. But pain and longing vanish with mother's doleful shrug, making light of this profound trauma. Indeed, *every* pang of pain is swept away in a tidal wave of manic grace. Mama, Papa, Luisa, Carla, are all magnificently blended together, everything forgiven, everything possible. Here, then, is the ultimate fusion of subject and object, the infant artist forever fulfilled at the unfailing maternal breast. Then, as tragic residue, we are left with the poignant picture of the lonely child, fluting into the night. . . .

If this remarkable finale is merely an exuberant facade erected like, Guido's towers, on insubstantial ground, the psychoanalyst may predict that the troubled director's future will be gloomy indeed. Guido is destined to sink into a morass of narcissistic preoccupations; his facade must inevitably crumble, and a monumental depression reach malignant fruition.

Guido is, however, only his master's creation; his autobiography ends with "The End." Cinematically, 8½ stands, fulfilled and complete on its own considerable intrinsic merits. No subsequent Guido Anselmi production could ever be unveiled, but Fellini has gone on to make seven more films. Let us now investigate how the circumstances of *his* career articulate with the revelations of Guido's life. . . .

Federico Fellini was born in 1920 at Rimini, a seaside resort on the Adriatic coast of Italy, into a provincial middle-class family. He has little to say about his childhood or his parents. His father, dead in the early nineteen fifties, was a traveling salesman in groceries and confectionery, regarded as a "reliable man . . . with a certain touching simplicity." His personality reflected "Italian provincial sanity, its traditional common sense, modest desires, and steadfast moral conscience," qualities Fellini is said to admire, but not to emulate. According to those who knew him, the father is quite accurately depicted in *La Dolce Vita* and 8½ (the same actor took the role in both films). Fellini's references to his mother, still alive in Rome, are as allusive as Guido's memories of his mother—"A good housewife who has had much cause to worry over me. . . ." (*"I've done my best, what more could I do. . . . Ah, the shame of it, the shame!!"*) Fellini has a younger brother and sister; Guido is presented as an only child, which may well attest to Fellini's early wishes on that score.

One of the director's earliest memories is constructing a toy theater; even as a boy he was intrigued by magic, the occult and science fiction. He quickly revealed a capacity for inventive fantasy that often turned into downright lying. He was a consistently poor student except in drawing. He spent several years at a dreary Catholic boarding school, suffering the same privations and punishments as Guido. His agonies of boredom were relieved by summer vacations at his grandmother's country home; probably the ASI NISI MASA sequence springs from those happy holidays.

Fellini claims he ran away to join a traveling circus as a child (denied by his mother). He places the "Saraghina" episode in his eighth year, when he visited the beach hut of a giant prostitute who exposed herself for a few coins. (She was named "La Saraghina"—the "sardine lady"—because she also serviced Rimini's fishermen.) The experience left an indelible impression upon his mind: voluptuous giantesses perenially romp through his films. In his teens he fell in love with a girl named Bianchina—"little white one"—and records a chaste, unsuccessful elopement with his Ideal. She admits their relationship, but says the elopement was his fabrication.

During his adolescence Fellini hung around with a pack of idle scroungers (*Vitelloni* in local slang), sponged off his parents, caricatured tourists at the town cafes and drew posters for the local cinema in return for admission. He eventually shook the dust of Rimini from his heels, leaving without a word of explanation for Florence, where he worked as a comic strip artist. He then traveled to Rome "with a large blonde," continued drawing and writing for satirical magazines, evaded military service by registering in law school without ever attending classes (his father wanted him to be a lawyer).

His fortunes improved when he began writing for a well-known avant-garde weekly; soon he branched out into radio and cinema scripting. In 1943 he saw a photo of the actress Giulietta Masina, who was playing in one of his shows, and fell in love with her on the spot. He invited her out, and when he failed to impress her with his charm, told her he was disgusted with life and showed her scars on his wrist from a suicide attempt (actually sustained during a drinking bout). Masina warmed to this pathetic tale and agreed to see him again. They were eventually married, and their relationship still endures despite many tribulations. Fellini maintains she rescued him from a "Vitellonian" existence and credits her as the principal source of his inspiration—shades of Guido's Muse and the Luisa of his fantasy!

Masina gave birth to a boy in 1944; the child died shortly after birth, a terrible blow to the couple. There were no other children, so in the truest sense Fellini's films are his offspring. Guido's slip of the tongue during the Cardinal's audience bears eloquent testimony to Fellini's ongoing grief and the persistence of this injury to his narcissism. During the Occupation, he set up a chain of lucrative "Funny Face" shops where American GI's were caricatured. A hectic, seedy milieu quite reminiscent of the *mise-en-scène* of many of his films soon thrived, and it was to one of these establishments that the great director Roberto Rossellini came, seeking help from Fellini with the scenario of *Open City*. They later toured post-war Italy, and out of that journey came the second landmark of neo-realist cinema, *Paisan*. Thereafter, Fellini devoted himself exclusively to film, as writer, assistant director and—unfortunately—only once as an actor, performing brilliantly in Rossellini's *The Miracle*. In 1950 he began directing his own films: *Variety Lights* (with some assistance from A. Lattuada); thereafter came *The White Sheik* (1952); *I Vitelloni* (1953); *The Marriage Broker* (one of five episodes of *Love in the City*—1953); *La Strada* (1954); *Il Bidone* (1955); *The Nights of Cabiria* (1956); *La Dolce Vita* (1959); *The Temptations of Dr. Antonio* (his contribution to *Boccaccio 70*—1961).

Fellini's forbearance and compassion for the dispossessed, the lowly, indeed for every actor in the human comedy, are hallmarks of these movies, although he is equally capable of scathing satire. Surreal and fantastic elements have always played a part in his pictures, but prior to *8½* they were strictly controlled, relegated to a decorative role in favor of the poignant documentation of the disaffected people he has known so well—the "Vitellonian" youths of Rimini, third-rate actors and circus performers, con men, prostitutes as well as the *illuminati* of show-biz and high society.

Repeatedly in Fellini's earlier work one recognizes the figure of a messenger of grace who appears, often by chance, to a character so sunken in alienation and moral squalor that only the most ambiguous response is possible. Fellini's inarticulate and seemingly insensitive heroes (e.g., Augusto, the master swindler of *Il Bidone*, or Zampano, the strongman bully of *La Strada*) are especially prone to questionable epiphanies spurred by innocent young women, ethereal creatures who may be the reincarnations of Bianchina, the director's adolescent love.

At the end of *La Dolce Vita*, the last major work before *8½*, Paola, a lovely teenager, beckons across the beach to Marcello, press-agent, huckster, journalist *manqué;* Marcello cannot hear her wind-tossed words, and one knows that here is Fellini of Rimini, as lost and purposeless in the empty chic of the great world as he was loafing about the cafes of his youth. The personal and artistic crisis foreshadowed by *La Dolce Vita* erupts into public view with *8½*; its roots in the director's life are obscure. Alberto Solmi says euphemistically that "one of those inevitable matrimonial quarrels with Giulietta Masina [came] to light, to the actress' dismay,'' adding that afterwards she forgave her errant husband. To what extent this turmoil was already resolved in Fellini's mind prior to *8½* we shall probably never know, but the evidence points to Fellini's use of cinematic creation in itself as a crucial ingredient in the working through the mastery of conflict, internal and external.

The basic conception of *8½* supposedly came to Fellini as early as 1960, after he visited several health spas for treatment of a ''liver disorder'' (like Guido, whose malady was obviously psychiatric rather than hepatic). Shooting did not begin until the spring of 1962 and extended into the following winter. The title signified that Fellini had previously directed seven feature films and portions of two others (accounting, one gathers, for the ''½'').

Work on the picture proceeded in the carnival atmosphere so well depicted in *8½*. Fellini adroitly escalated public curiosity to fever pitch; he advertised for fat women to play Carla, and after being deluged by offers from thousands of elephantine ladies announced his choice of Sandra Milo—who he had already picked privately before the advertisement was published. He traveled to London to discuss the starring role with Laurence Olivier (who he never met) although he knew at the very time he went that Mastroianni would get the lead. He chose bit players and extras from the raffish crowd of hangers-on that inevitably collect around his work. Except for him and his writers no one, including the actors, knew the story line beyond the limits of personal participation. Predatory journalists trying to break Fellini's rule of silence were fed contradictory releases and came away with wildly different impressions like the seven blind men in the fable.

As filming progressed, Fellini left no doubt of his autobiographical intent, instructing Mastroianni in his own mannerisms, and dress, removing his scarf and draping it around the actor during a take. Like Guido, his mien appeared by turns cheerful, calm, courteous, or disconcertingly haggard and desperate. He suffered a dental abscess and, near the end, an attack of ''sciatica.'' He kept the pot boiling by giving out enigmatic interviews hinting at *his* inability to get his head together and finish the movie. Actually, he had a coherent script from the first—but, as has always been his wont, improvised extensively around it. One sees in all these manipulations the work of a master prestidigitator interpenetrating the reality around him with that of his emerging creation.

The results of this legerdemain are, to my mind, incontrovertibly superb, despite contrary sentiments of a few Daumier-like critics. Guido's people are inalterably *there,* their wholeness instant and intense. To give but one example—Rosella appears on screen for only a few moments, yet one's "recognition" of the character—with her perceptive wit, her genuine concern for her friends, her lighthearted communion with her "spirits"—goes very deep. This solidest of realities is counterbalanced by extravagant and surreal visuals; *8½* recapitulates the important images and motifs of the previous films, but tossed about as in a mad whirlwind. Salachas lists:

—the contemporary world with its false prophets and its folklore perceived as a stifling furnace in which, nonetheless, it is still necessary to live . . .

—the reactionary clergy . . . senile, traumatizing or ridiculous.

—the obsession with decadent spectacles and equivocal festivities.

—the sea, always beginning again . . . modestly present . . .

—the worldliness and the conscientious ennui of the rich . . .

—the extravagant wardrobes, the collection of improbable hats.

—the presence of delectable women of too generous form.

—the telepathic magicians and their troubling powers.

—the return to memories of childhood . . . cruel . . . soothing . . .

—parasites and hangers-on . . . who never stop stirring the wind . . .

—a conscience in disorder, looking for some calming lucidity . . .

—the circus, the farandole. . . .

To which, let me add:

—grotesque visages, in uncomfortable close-up.

—clouded nocturnal revelations in empty piazzas.

—the accidental as prime mover in human affairs.

—the biting edge of satire, blunted by sympathy for the object of derision.

—spectacular mobility of mood, contributing to an unnerving, exciting ambience of permanent flux and disequilibrium.

Fellini's characteristic compassion and tolerance dissipate as Guido's attentiveness wanes. The messenger of grace, his Muse, Claudia, reappears, but she is quickly cast away. The fleeting remorse Salachas suggests is "perhaps the furthest moral development a Fellini hero can make" is replaced by the euphoria of the ending, curiously the most positive termination of any Fellini film, precisely because it occurs strictly within the hero's deluded imagination.

Let us now briefly study Fellini's films subsequent to *8½*:

Juliet of the Spirits (1964–1965). *Juliet* was meant to be the companion piece of *8½*. Fellini sought to liberate his heroine from the coils of an impoverished marriage, restoring her inalienable dignity, and theoretically releasing Luisa from Guido's treachery. If we are to believe Fellini, both will now go on to live free of the trappings of unprofitable convention, still somehow maintaining their faithfulness to one another. Solmi suggests that *Juliet* is the director's atonement to *his* wife for the exposure of their private affairs.

Juliet lives in a luxurious suburban villa. She is visited by friends and relatives while her philandering husband neglects her. When she proves his infidelity, her elegant and protected world crumbles. She is tormented by increasingly bizarre hallucinations. She watches herself as a child in a Catholic school pageant, playing a saint being roasted on a grill. The grown-up Juliet finally unties her child self, the apparitions vanish, and as she walks towards the woods distant voices— "true friends, true friends"—pledge their eternal loyalty.

The visual thrust of *8½* is extended in *Juliet of the Spirits* by Fellini's use of gorgeous color (every film since *8½* has been in color). The narrative flow has become even more fragmented and dreamlike than in *8½*, with past, present and fantasy worlds virtually coterminous. Fluid associational links are provided by sight and sound rather than word. Juliet's privatism and self-absorption exponentially exceeds Guido's. A note of perversity and sadism persistently intrudes in the visions of Nazi officers and barbarian cavalry, in the assignation with Bhisma, a hermaphroditic false prophet who urges sexual excess as the panacea for Juliet's ills, and in the orgiastic entertainments of a lascivious neighbor.

Toby Dammit (1967), Fellini's contribution to *Histoires Extraordinaires*—released in the U.S. as *Spirits of the Damned*. Fellini translates Poe's droll tale, "Never Bet the Devil Your Head," into a macabre vignette. Toby, a famous actor and advanced alcoholic, is brought to Italy as the lead in "the first Catholic Western." He has one overriding ambition—owning a Ferrari. He is drawn to the enticing apparition of a little girl in white, her nails and lips painted blood-red, bouncing a ball. He steals a Ferrari from his producer, takes it on a terrifying joyride, stops at a blasted bridge. On the other side the girl waves at him. He roars across the chasm, and is decapitated by a low-strung wire. The devil-child skips away, smiling malevolently, Toby's head dangling from her hand.

Toby is Guido's burnt-out heir. In his boozy delirium, the denizens of movieland—the pesty agents, seductive actresses, homosexual toadies—are more repulsive than in Guido's worst moments. Narrower in dimension than *Juliet,* the film strikes one with the force of a succinct bad dream.

Satyricon (1968–1969). Fellini's version of the Petronius Arbiter classic was conceived and executed "under the sign of estrangement." The characters live in a kind of moral prehistory, before the invention of conscience or guilt. Encolpius and Ascyltus, two bisexual young men, pursue debauchery in a dying Rome. Encolpius loses his vaunted potency when he cannot copulate in a public fertility ritual. His virility is restored by intercourse with a giant sorceress while his friend, standing guard outside, is murdered. Eumolpus, a poet-philosopher who once preached the virtues of material renunciation, dies after becoming the wealthy sybarite he was accustomed to condemn. He wills that his heirs must devour him to claim his fortune. Encolpius turns away from this ultimate blasphemy with an odd, accepting smile and, without friend or lover, sails off in search of further adventures. . . . In *Satyricon* Fellini strove by his own testament to purge himself of the need to identify with his characters sentimentally and ideologically. The audience is encouraged to experience ancient Rome as a civilization of monsters on another planet; its inhabitants are completely interchangeable in their self-seeking callousness.

Clowns (1970); Roma (1972); Amarcord (1974). The genial trivialities of these three are almost welcome after the abominations of *Satyricon;* each affects a rambling, semidocumentary style. *Clowns* records Fellini's ambivalent recollections of the circus fantastics who frightened and amused him as a child, implicitly comparing them with the grotesques of Rimini. The director interviews contemporary circus notables and, after wryly concluding, "The Clown is dead!", resurrects him in a riotous funeral. Aside from some slim merits as circus biography, the film's chief attraction lies in its evocation of the earliest impingement of the surreal upon Fellini's *petit bourgeois* upbringing. The recreation of the great clowns' routines and the hilarious funeral sequence are entertaining, but hardly memorable. In *Roma* Fellini even more discursively weaves together his past and present impressions of the city. Rimini's folk once more make token, ludicrous appearances, and there are several sequences obviously based on Fellini's arrival as an ingenuous youth in the Italian capital. I find only one remarkable—indeed signatory—episode in the film: during excavations for a new subway, archeologists are called in when a sunken ancient Roman villa is discovered; its walls are broached, disclosing marvelous frescoes that instantly deliquesce in the putrescent modern air. . . .

Reviewers found *Clowns* and *Roma* generally disappointing, but *Amarcord* ("I Remember") has been almost universally hailed as Fellini's best film in years, indisputable proof of the resurrection of his genius. It covers the passing of one year (during Mussolini's rise to power) in a small seaside resort town—evidently Rimini, intertwining vignettes from the noisy life of a typical lower middle-class provincial family with the comings and goings of various Rimini "types"—the pompous headmaster, officious priest, pomaded gigolo, the town beauty, the town idiot and the inevitable gang of adolescent loafers. The action is liberally sprinkled with surrealistic fantasies. Fellini has been here before, most notably in *I Vitelloni*, but authentically engaged with his people. In *Amarcord,* his involvement has cooled, his viewpoint is distanced and at times quite cruel so that the reworking of familiar Fellinian material and motifs seems merely gratuitous and mechanical. There is a wistful hint of the "old" Fellini in one touching scene: the blustering paterfamilias returns home thoroughly humiliated after a grilling by the Fascist police, and his shrewish wife bathes him, clucking with concern. Otherwise, despite a certain degree of visual expertise one expects from this master *auteur,* the film possesses a curious attenuated quality; although more tightly organized than *Clowns* and *Roma,* it is still—like them—as unsatisfying as the meagre leftovers from a banquet.*

Juliet, finally alone with the dubious solace of her spirit voices; Toby Dammit, drowning in alcohol, his only attachment to his glistering machine; the savage, indifferent isolates of *Satyricon*—exist along a continuum of alienation and despair. The airy messenger of grace no longer holds out the salvation of innocence. Paola, Claudia— the child-women in white—mutate into the death-child who seduces Toby to a grisly doom. The enticing ponderous Saraghina, with her fragile moment of loveliness, has also metamorphosed; in *Amarcord,* she is an enormous virago of a shopkeeper who nearly strangles the fumbling adolescent hero between her huge breasts, then rudely rejects him when he proves an inept lover.

In the earlier films, no matter how formidable the armoring against trust, it was always possible for a Fellini hero to be touched, if only briefly, by some intimation of hope that would illuminate his disordered moral state. With *La Dolce Vita,* these precious moments are less probable, and by *Satyricon* they have virtually disappeared, like the faded frescoes of *Roma.* In *La Dolce Vita,* Marcello's quest for peace is shattered by the suicide of his best friend, Steiner, a "committed" intellectual. Nevertheless, in the final glimpse of Paola across

---

* In view of the raves the Academy Award winning *Amarcord* has received from most of the critics, including some highly respected cineasts, I draw some comfort from the analysis of another dissenter, John Simon, with whom I totally concur: *"Amarcord* is even considered by some misguided souls to make a deep comment on Fascists, by showing them as nothing more than petty, spiteful, and ludicrous; but since just about everyone else in the film is mean and risible, the Fascists end up no different from the good guys. Because both *I Vitelloni* and *Amarcord* deal with the provincial life of Rimini, where Fellini grew up, some reviewers have sacrilegiously bracketed the two films. Yet they are as different as bread and mudpies, the early film dealing sympathetically with human beings, however fallible, and allowing the funny-sad life of the town to emerge through their stories, while the recent movie starts with some abstract notion of "the Town" and . . . slaps together some warmed-over autobiography and a few burlesque set pieces into a stillborn self-parody. . . . Yet the worst thing about *Amarcord* and its immediate predecessors is that the chief joke is human ugliness . . . the humor is either . . . puerilely scatological, or virtually nonexistent. . . .''

the sands, a potential for repair is still held out to him. In *Satyricon* there is no such potential. The only characters capable of unselfish love are a patrician couple who kill each other when the old regime fails, rather than face the barbarous future. Their corpses are hardly cold when Ascyltus and Encolpius stumble upon their villa and, in mocking requiem, bed down a frightened slave girl.

As the troubled self hurtles away from its damaging entanglements, there is an escalating obsession with the decadent, the ugly, and the perverse. Fellini passes from Guido's impotence in *8½* through the sadomasochistic rape fantasies in *Juliet,* to the obscene anhedonic sexuality of *Satyricon.* The metamorphosis in Fellini's style and presentation has already been analyzed: a heightened sense of unreality or "surreality," a facile disregard for the exigencies of time and space, elements the analyst customarily interprets as signatory of more archaic mental activity, experienced nightly in dreams, but often daily by the emotionally disturbed. The intrusion of such perceptions into the conscious thinking processes of a patient, if sufficiently persistent and global, would raise the spectre of an impending psychosis—or at least would warrant one's sharpened concern.

If the conflicts of *8½* never reached favorable resolution for the film's creator, what then follows may well be the bitter fruits of Fellini's crisis in middle life; the disillusion and dissoluteness of the later pictures may betoken his mounting hopelessness and disintegration. The historical parameters of this disaster are ill-defined, clouded by his predilection for hand-tailoring his autobiography to the occasion. Fellini has tread the thin line between art and imposture his entire life, delighting in masquerade, disguise, and travesty, in weaving the substance of his entertainments out of pretence and thin air. Guido is another of his many masks, but closer to his authentic persona than any other hero.

And, Guido *is* a close cousin to the impostor! Phyllis Greenacre, in a classic study, indicates that there are varying degrees of imposture, and many intriguing similarities between the artist and the impostor. The making of movies affords Guido an extraordinarily heightened sense of reality that the impostor obtains through his inveterate bamboozling. The impostor's father, like Guido's, is distant and unsupportive. Like the impostor, Guido's Oedipal problems are superimposed upon more serious earlier traumas at the mother's hands. By exhibiting himself and his products, Guido tries to "gain or to retain the mother's attention and indulgence, which in actuality may have been excessive, or conversely eternally and teasingly promised, but never really experienced." In Guido's case, the splitting of the mother's unconscious image has been facilitated by the contrast between her provocative, blaming behavior and the generosity of her substitutes, such as the peasant nurses. Like the impostor, Guido has a glaring inability to acknowledge the autonomy, the separate needs of others and manipulates shamelessly to gain his selfish ends. Greenacre also noted that many impostors were impotent, and showed an increasing disposition in their later years towards perverse sexuality.

Many of these speculations will inevitably raise serious objections on both aesthetic and psychoanalytic grounds. Little is known of Fellini's past beyond his fabrications, still less about his more recent history. One hears dark rumors of illness and sexual failure, fed by his invitations to the scandelmongers to dare interpret him. Treating his films as if they were his dreams, pure grist for the analytic mill, will never totally unravel the mystery and motivation of this complex man. And even if Fellini has deteriorated along the same lines as Guido Anselmi, the relationship between his sickness and his creativity must remain problematic, given our ultimate ignorance of his mental life.

And—how often have the titans of art completed their most monumental work in the throes of utmost spiritual agony! If the traumatized artist relinquishes hope in friends and lovers, the chronicle of his despair may still be a masterpiece. While optimism about the human condition is surely a noble virtue, no artist ever signed a contract with his audience requiring it as a precondition for the actualization of his talent.

The shifts towards more primitive psychic elements that I have delineated in Fellini's later work might just as well signify *breakthrough* as *breakdown:* these changes—both in patients and men of genius—may appear regressive, but are often necessary in the ultimate achievement of higher planes of synthesis, whether within the analysand's personality or a work of art. Furthermore, while "regression" in art can correlate directly with personal symptomatology, it may also be completely split off from an ego that continues to deal well with reality. Even when true pathological regression occurs in the artist's personality, breakdown may be coterminous with breakthrough! The precipitates in terms of art may still be as valid, or even more impressive, than the products of a healthier mind—as in Van Gogh's final pictures.

The connection between the artist's triumphs or disasters in his creative life or his mundane affairs is incompletely understood at this stage of psychoanalytic theory. But granted the necessary reservations about our methodology and the limitations imposed by ignorance as to the actual condition of Fellini's psyche, if the fundamental issue is simply the state of *his* art, then it is painfully clear with regard to this particular man of genius that the terrible relinquishments and false insights of his film autobiography have been succeeded by empty displays of exceptional technique that ring increasingly inferior and hollow at base. Fellini's last three films, I believe, offer no renascence. At best, one hopes they may be holding actions against the eventual recovery of his artistic aim—especially *Amarcord*. But at this point one senses the exhausted magician is still mostly reaching into his worn-out bag of tricks to run through his act numbly, by rote.

In *La Strada,* the Jesus-like tightrope walker, Il Matto ("The Mad One"), speaks to Gelsomina, an innocent waif:

> IL MATTO: Yet everything in the world is good for . . . for something . . . Take this stone . . . .
> GELSOMINA: Which one?
> IL MATTO: This one . . . it doesn't matter which. So this one, too, has a purpose, even this little pebble . . . .
> GELSOMINA: What's it good for?
> IL MATTO: Well, it's good for . . . how do I know? If I knew, you know who I would be? . . . God the Father. . . . He who knows all. When you are born . . . when you die as well! Who can possibly tell? I don't know what it's good for, this pebble, but it certainly has its use! If it were useless, then everything else would also be useless . . . even the stars! That's the way things are . . . you, too, have a reason for being here . . . .

Words on the printed page do scant justice to the loveliness of this scene. One need only contrast it with the horrifying cannabilization of

Eumolpus, the degraded poet, that ends *Satyricon*—surely the ultimate ferocious assault of the audience-mother upon the artist, to realize how far the master has fallen. Daedalus is dashed down; Orpheus torn asunder; Prometheus devoured. Since the fatal moment Daumier applauded Guido near the ruin of his hopes, Fellini himself has essentially been *dedicated to silence!* After the spurious joy that concludes *8½*, the great director has given us only the barren declensions of that fearful stillness of the heart.

Bibliography

All quotations from the film art taken from an English-dubbed print from Embassy Pictures, 1301 Avenue of the Americas, New York, N.Y. 10019.

BOYER, D. *The Two Hundred Days of 8½*. New York: Macmillan Co., 1964.

BUDGEN, S. *Fellini*. United Kingdom: McCorquodale Press, 1966.

Fellini's Satyricon. New York: Ballantine Books, 1970. See p. 10.

GREENACRE, P. "The Family Romance of the Artist" in *Psychoanalytic Study of the Child,* vol. 13. New York: International Universities Press, 1958. See pp. 9–36.

———. "The Imposter," *ibid*. See pp. 359–382.

———. "The Relationship of the Imposter to the Artist," *ibid*. See pp. 521–540.

Juliet of the Spirits. The script and an interview with T. Kezich. New York: Ballantine Books, 1966.

SALACHAS, G. *Federico Fellini: An Investigation into His Films and Philosophy*. New York: Crown Publishers, Inc., 1969. See pp. 31, 69, 86–87, 104.

SAMUELS, C. T. "Fellini on Fellini," *Atlantic Monthly,* April, 1972. See p. 91.

SIMON, JOHN. "The Tragic Deterioration of Fellini's Genius," *New York Times* (November 24, 1974), p. 17, "Arts and Leisure" section.

SOLMI, A. *Fellini*. New York: Humanities Press, 1967. See pp. 59, 60, 61, 171.

VIII

The Rags of Time—
Ingmar Bergman's
Wild Strawberries

> KNIGHT: My life has been a futile pursuit, a wandering,
> a great deal of talk without meaning. I feel no
> bitterness or self-reproach, because the lives of most
> people are very much like this. But I will use my
> reprieve for one meaningful deed.
> DEATH: Is that why you are playing chess with Death?
>
> Ingmar Bergman: *The Seventh Seal*

The angst of adolescence and the mid-life blues are favorite themes of novelists and moviemakers, but with a few notable exceptions the crisis of aging has been neglected in print or on the screen. It is a hardly novel observation by now that America is a frenetically youth oriented culture; we rush our elderly into sordid or serene enclaves of the superannuated, the better to defend ourselves from excessive meditation upon our necessary end.

Psychoanalysts, too, have frequently been guilty of shunning the aged; being no less mortal than anyone else, we do not like to be reminded of our mortality. Some practitioners believe old people lack the flexibility of character to profit from treatment, but this is by no means universally true if one can adjust one's sights to the unique position of the aging in therapy. An analyst's disparaging view of the older patient's prognosis may reflect his impatient ambition, for the rewards attendant upon liberating a young person from neurotic suffering may loom infinitely more promising than the chancy intervention in the nearly completed life cycle of someone who lacks world enough and time to put therapeutic insight into practice. Nevertheless, precisely because time *is* short, the aging often strive that much harder, in and out of treatment, to find enlightenment before the final darkness. The prospect of dying, to paraphrase Dr. Johnson, marvelously concentrates the mind.

Within the past century, we have been given three exceptional studies of old men who on the verge of death undergo cataclysmic emotional upheaval and growth: Tolstoy's *The Death of Ivan Ilyich,* Mann's *Death in Venice* (disastrously rendered into high-gloss homosexual porn in Luchino Visconti's epicine version) and *Wild Strawberries,* an original screenplay by the great Swedish *auteur,* Ingmar Bergman.

Wild Strawberries unfolds during one day in the life—and in another sense within the entire life—of Dr. Isak Borg, a retired Professor of Medicine. On the "real" day, he is to receive the signal honor of Jubilee Doctor for over half a century of distinguished achievements in practice and research. As the film opens, we discover Borg sitting in his study, writing down "a true account of the events, dreams, and thoughts" connected with this memorable occasion. His voice tells us that he is a widower, living alone save for a housekeeper. His only son of his unhappy marriage is also a physician, and childless. He is grateful for his work, but "I have found myself rather alone in my old age. This is not a regret, but a statement of fact." He is "an old pedant, at times quite trying, both to myself and to the people who have to be around me. I detest emotional outbursts, women's tears, and the crying of children." He is seventy-six years old.

The titles are presented against a neutral background, to the accompaniment of a poignant theme for strings. Then, we are plunged into the world of nightmare.

Borg walks through an empty city, enveloped in silence so absolute as to be almost palpable. He comes to a watchmaker's shop, and looks up at its sign—an enormous clock, and a great pair of *pince-nez*. The hands of the clock are gone, the lenses of the eyeglasses smashed. Reflexively Borg checks his own watch—its hands are missing, too! We hear the crescendo pounding of Borg's heart—ceasing abruptly as he spies the figure of a man in black. Oddly reassured, Borg touches the man's shoulder, and he turns to reveal a horribly withered face, the eyes and mouth compressed into pencil-thin lines. (In the shooting script, the man is faceless. He is very nearly so in the film.)

The figure collapses, a foul fluid oozes from its empty clothing. Bells toll mournfully, and a driverless hearse thunders by. Its rear wheel catches up against a lamppost, the horses back and pull, until the wheel drops off and rolls down the street, narrowly missing Borg and crashing to pieces against a stone wall. The hearse sways, tilts and the coffin tumbles out, cracking apart. Released from their burden, the horses thunder off.

Borg approaches the broken coffin. A hand protrudes from beneath the dislodged cover. As he leans over, it stirs, seizes his arm in an iron grip and drags him inexorably down. To his horror, Borg sees that the corpse is *himself,* a mocking grin on his face, and awakens bolt upright. This remarkable vision is the culmination of several months of "evil and frightening dreams." By juxtaposing it against the calm beginning, with Borg's spare self-appraisal, Bergman has adroitly established his hero's obsessional facade and the shattering depression it conceals.

This dream is dreamt on the eve of unparalleled advancement, yet its imagery speaks unrelentingly of futility and decay. The empty city is a powerful metaphor of the hero's impoverished emotional state (borg means "city" in Swedish . . .). The dashed hearse wheel, the broken coffin, the clock minus its hands, the crushed eyeglasses, are multiple reflections of an ego on the edge of dissolution. Anxiety mounts as Borg discovers that *his* watch is handless, his time can no longer be kept. He turns for comfort to a man who crumbles away at his touch. The recognition of mortality grows ever more undisguised, until the dreamer places himself squarely in his coffin, dragging himself into the dust. Freud believed that the primary purpose of the "dream work" was to keep the dreamer asleep, to facilitate some poorly understood process of psychological repair. The workings of Borg's dream cannot bind this moment of supreme terror. Typical of a depressive, Borg awakens fearfully and early. It is three A.M. on a Scandinavian summer's morning, and pale sunlight already streams through the curtain.

Borg rouses his housekeeper, Miss Agda (she is as old as he). He's decided not to fly to Lund, where his son, Evald, lives and he is to receive his award. Instead, he wants to go by car, at once, and without her. Her feelings are understandably hurt; when he stands firm she accuses him of meanness and egocentricity, and refuses to attend the ceremony. Borg tries unsuccessfully to soothe her while she packs his clothes. Her attitude puzzles him, for he is blind to how he can wound with his chronic self-absorption.

Borg's daughter-in-law, Marianne, a lovely blonde in her mid-thirties, is awakened by the bickering of the old people. She has separated from her husband, and has been living with Borg for the past month. She now asks to be taken back to Lund and Evald. Borg wonders at her decision, the suddenness of which curiously parallels his own. So begin two journeys for this venerable physician, one that takes him to his greatest material reward, another far more painful inner voyage that will search out his deepest personal failures. Throughout both, Marianne's fate will be intertwined with his, and she shall play an odd sort of Beatrice to his Dante, a sympathetic—if not always comforting—voice of uncompromising honesty.

In the car, Borg automatically assumes a patronizing air and commands her not to smoke:

> ISAK: . . . There should be a law against women smoking . . . now take the cigar. Cigars are an expression of the fundamental idea of smoking. A stimulant and a relaxation. A manly vice.
> MARIANNE: And what vices may a woman have?
> ISAK: Crying, bearing children, and gossiping about the neighbors.

When she refuses to tell him why she wants to go home, he grows manifestly uncomfortable beneath his sexist gibing. Evald and he are alike in their unswerving adherence to principle. "You don't have to tell me," she says rather caustically. He loaned Evald money to complete his studies, and it is a matter of honor that he be repaid.

Marianne replies that the restrictions imposed by their indebtedness to him are absurd, since he is a wealthy man.

> ISAK: A bargain is a bargain, my dear Marianne. And I know that Evald understands and respects me.
> MARIANNE: (*flatly*) That may be true, but he also hates you.

Caught in close-up, Borg's expression is one of total horror. He then tries to pull himself together and preserve a semblance of his previous imperturbability. She has never liked him, what does she really have against him?

> MARIANNE: You are an old egotist, Father . . . completely inconsiderate. All this is well hidden beneath your mask of old-fashioned charm . . . but you are as hard as nails, even though everyone depicts you as a great humanitarian. . . .

When she first tried to tell him about her floundering marriage, he rejected her plea for understanding out of hand, advising her to try psychoanalysis or religion "if you need spiritual masturbation." Even when she confronts him with his indifference, he is still not moved to apologize, but he unbends enough to admit grudgingly that she is a fine young woman whose company he enjoys. He mentions his dream of the morning, but she does not want to hear. Once more, he has ignored her suffering to involve her in *his* dreams, *his* depression. Marianne cannot see beyond her rancor, but he has set aside his engrained privatism and is haltingly reaching out to her, a vastly new experience in his life.

Impulsively, he drives off the highway and comes to a boarded-up house. Here he summered with his parents and nine brothers and sisters for the first twenty years of his life. Marianne goes off to swim, and Borg sits down near a patch of wild strawberries. As the taste of tea-sweetened *madeleine* sent Proust's hero searching down the corridors of memory, the taste of the fruit spurs Borg to recapture his past, and he slips into another dream. . . .

The house rings with the sounds of music and children's laughter. A lively young girl sits next to him, unaware of his presence: his cousin Sara, to whom he was secretly betrothed in his teens. While he watches, a handsome youth strolls by and commences flirting with her: this is Sigfrid, Borg's next-oldest brother. He speaks contemptuously of Isak, Sara defends him, berates Sigfrid for smoking cigars * and loose conduct with local girls.

Sigfrid embraces her impetuously. She responds, then pushes him away, weeping at her betrayal of Isak.

A dinner bell rings, there is a general rush to the house. Everyone shouts for Isak—Borg cannot answer—then his twin sisters say that he is out fishing with his father. He feels a "secret and completely inexplicable happiness," and goes inside. From the shadows, he watches a bustling birthday party for deaf, foolish Uncle Aron, presided over by a buxom, imperious aunt:

> AUNT: Sigbritt, pass the porridge to Angelica and give the twins their portions. Your fingernails are coal-black. Pass me the bread, Hagbart. Who taught you to spread so much butter on the bread? . . . Charlotta, the saltshaker is stopped up . . . the twins should hold their tongues and eat . . . Benjamin must not bite his nails. Don't sit and jump on the chair, Anna!

The festive spirit is broken when the obstreperous twins taunt Sara and Sigfrid about their indiscreet romance. Sara runs into the hall and Charlotta comes out to comfort her. Sara blurts out her misgivings about young Isak, while old Isak listens unseen:

> SARA: [Isak] is so refined. He is so enormously refined and moral and sensitive, and he wants us to read poetry together and he talks about the afterlife . . . and he likes to kiss only in the dark and he talks about sinfulness. I think he is extremely intellectual . . . and I feel so worthless . . . but sometimes I get the feeling that I'm much older . . . and then I think he's a child even if we are the same age, and then Sigfrid is so fresh and exciting . . . poor little Isak, he is so kind to me.

They go back inside and the meal ends with cheers for Uncle Aron (so does the filmed dream). In the original script, one of Isak's sisters

---

* Sigfrid rejoins—"that's a man's smell!", recalling Borg's earlier allusion to the "manly vice." Like Hitchcock's birds, the act of smoking is an highly overdetermined symbol. Borg's statement about smoking reveals his categorical ideas about masculinity. Smoking is also equated with the relaxation of sexual repression and social restrictions. Borg's puritanical mother, whom we will meet later, cannot tolerate smoking in her presence. Needless to say, she is the source of many of his inhibitions.

says she can see their father returning from the lake. Sara leaves, Borg follows her out of the house and loses sight of her, to stand desolate beside the wild strawberry patch. He is awakened by the voice of a young girl. . . .

The geography of Borg's first dream was stark and devoid of life. The second dream teems with humanity. The relationships within this giant family are tumultuous, abrasive, but a binding warmth pervades the house from which Borg is excluded. He is both within and without the action of the dream, and as its creator he is also its observer. He looks on helplessly while his brother seduces his love, then he is forced to eavesdrop upon Sara's humiliating comparison of him with Sigfrid: she marks him as a typical adolescent obsessional, his character already warped by repression, asceticism and detachment. (Marianne's denunciation in the car probably provides one stimulus for Sara's criticisms.)

Borg's parents are also curiously absent from the dream. By placing him in sole possession of his father at the lake, the dream attempts to heal some secret, central desolation that evidently overshadowed his formative years. But the repair is unsuccessful. Having lost Sara at the beginning of the dream, he is abandoned by her again at its ending. . . .

He awakens to regain her by a coincidence which in the hands of a lesser artist would be too marvelous to be acceptable. The girl beside him, also named Sara (the same actress plays both roles), is a student hitchhiking to Italy. They engage in light-hearted banter, Sara obviously taken with his gentle irony.

> SARA: Is this your shack?
> ISAK: No, it isn't . . . I lived here once, two hundred years ago. . . .
> SARA: My name is Sara. Silly name, isn't it?
> ISAK: My name is Isak. Rather silly, too.
> SARA: Weren't they married?
> ISAK: Unfortunately not. It was Abraham and Sara.

He invites her to accompany him with a rare spontaneity that has characterized his behavior since he awakened this morning from his dream of death.

Back at the car, Sara introduces her traveling companions, two strapping young men, Anders and Viktor. Sara is semi-engaged to Anders, Viktor also loves her and is acting as a chaperone—Sara's father, she tells Borg, engineered this arrangement to protect her virginity.* Anders studies for the ministry; Viktor contemplates a medical career. In these two the director has counterpoised the man of faith and feeling against the coldly rational scientist, with whom Borg's neurotic persona is obviously identified. Viktor is a frustrated witness to Sara's infatuation with another man, as was Borg with *his* Sara at the wild strawberry patch. The waking Borg *watches* the youngsters from the driver's seat, and tells Sara about his lost love:

> ISAK: She was rather like you . . . she married my brother Sigfrid, and had six children. Now she's seventy-five, and a rather beautiful little old lady.
> SARA: I can't imagine anything worse than getting old!

She claps her hand over her mouth in embarrassment, but instead of taking offense, Borg bursts into laughter at this irrepressible hoyden. At the same moment, a car comes speeding at them on the wrong side of the road. Borg slams on the brakes and the other vehicle disappears into a ditch. The occupants climb out—Sten Alman, an engineer, and his wife Berit, an hysteric. They have been engaged in the latest round of the interminable quarrel that has consumed their lives and within minutes after apologizing, attack each other anew as the men try to push the car out of the ditch.

> BERIT: Now watch the engineer closely, see how he matches his strength with the young boys, how he tenses his feeble muscles to impress the pretty girl. Sten darling, watch out that you don't have a hemorrhage.

* Bergman is playing subliminally with repeated Oedipal triangulations. Borg reminds Sara rather ruefully that it was Father Abraham who was married to the biblical Sara, not his son Isak, Borg's namesake. Abraham nearly sacrificed Isak at Jehovah's command; analytic interpretation reveals the tale as an Oedipal fable, in which Abraham's murderous impulses towards Isak for his incestuous designs upon Sara are remitted by the intervention of a higher, more civilized Father. The contemporary Sara's favors are jealously guarded by another father, who has set two men to compete for his daughter's hand so that neither shall possess her. And we have seen that Borg's older brother Sigfrid has bested young Isak and stolen away his childhood sweetheart. Sigfrid, as I shall demonstrate, is a father-surrogate for Borg.

ALMAN: My wife loves to embarrass me in front of strangers. I let her—it's psychotherapy.

When the car cannot be rehabilitated, Borg offers the unpleasant pair a lift, with evident misgivings.

Marianne takes the wheel. The heavy silence is broken by Berit's quiet weeping. She shakes off her husband's comforting arm. Hurt, he launches into a cynical description of how she has manipulated him down through the years with her hypochondriasis and crocodile tears. Marianne pleads with him to stop, but he mocks on until Berit smashes him in the face. Still he derides her, even her assault is part of a well-calculated act! Marianne refuses to play captive audience to this shoddy, sadomasochistic exhibition. She orders them out, and as they drive away, Berit, for once trying to be sincere, calls after them—"Please forgive us if you can. . . ."

Borg now comes to the town of Huskvärna, where his mother still lives and where he practiced for many years as a country doctor before the university career that brought him fame. He stops for gas. The station owner greets him with unfeigned admiration and offers to name his unborn child after him. Moved by this simple man's tribute, Borg murmurs to himself, half-unaware—"Perhaps I should have remained here. . . ."

The company dines at a restaurant commanding a magnificent view of sky and sparkling lake. Mellowed by the food and wine, Borg entertains them with amusing anecdotes from his doctoring days. Afterwards, Anders is moved to recite a poem to natural beauty and its Creator. Viktor denounces Anders' faith caustically:

VIKTOR: In my opinion a modern man looks his insignificance straight in the eye and believes in himself and his biological death. Everything else is nonsense.
ANDERS: And in my opinion, modern man exists only in your imagination. Because man looks at his death with horror and can't bear his own insignificance.
VIKTOR: All right. Religion for the people. Opium for the aching limb . . . when you were a child you believed in Santa Claus. Now you believe in God.
ANDERS: And you have always suffered from an astonishing lack of imagination.

Seeking an appropriate ally, Viktor asks Borg for his opinion. He demurs—anything he would say to these modern young people would only be met with "ironic indulgence." Marianne laughs and lights his cigar; she is obviously warming to him. Then Borg answers Viktor in his own way, calling up a few half-remembered lines of verse. His memory falters—he is not given to meditating on theology—Anders, then Marianne, complete the stanza:

> "Where is the friend I seek everywhere?
> Dawn is the time of loneliness and care . . .
> I see His trace of glory and power
> In an ear of grain and the fragrance of flower.
> In every sign and breath of air
> His love is there. . . ."

Sara declares that despite his disclaimers Borg *is* religious. Indeed, he has been passing through a painful conversion since this morning, so that he can now make common cause with Anders and Marianne against Viktor's fatuous rationality; slowly and subtly the old doctor emerges as a man of troubled sensitivity, drawing into tentative touch with the suppressed wellspring of his feelings.

Borg goes with Marianne to pay his respects to his mother. Her house is still and sombre; its owner, a wrinkled, domineering relic putting one forcibly in mind of Norma Bates, that other mummified harridan. His mother accepts Borg's dry kiss, offers him meager congratulations then, mistaking Marianne for Borg's faithless dead wife, Karin, orders her to leave. Even after he corrects her misimpression, she continues to demean Marianne, remarking upon her childlessness with competitive disdain—"Isn't it strange with young people nowadays? I bore ten children!"

She takes up a large box and rummages through the battered mementoes of her family, relishing her lonely martyrdom. Ten children she bore, all dead save Isak, innumerable grandchildren and great-grandchildren—but only Evald comes regularly, the rest visit only when they want money. She is a tiresome antique who has the effrontery not to die. As she fingers the worn-out books and toys, she comments harshly on her dead offspring:

MOTHER: Hagbart's tin soldiers. I never liked war games. He was shot while hunting moose. We never understood each other . . . I think this is Benjamin's locomotive because he was always so amused by trains and circuses . . . I suppose that's why he became an actor. We quarrelled often about it because I wanted him to have an honest profession. And I was right, he didn't make it! . . .

She inspects faded photographs, she and her husband, Sigfrid and Isak as infants. Borg wants to see one, and she hands it over with complete disinterest—''. . . you can have it, it's only trash.'' She complains of feeling cold as long as she can remember—''mostly in the stomach''—and Borg can only mumble some fictive diagnosis at this veiled admission of her awesome indifference.

Her nattering makes him restive. He rises to leave, but she stays him. She is thinking of giving Isak's dead father's watch to her daughter Sigbritt's son for his fiftieth birthday. It has no hands, but it is beautiful and can be fixed. What does Isak think? The camera focuses down upon the handless watch, and the sickening thud of Borg's distressed heart resounds again. Obviously disturbed by this evocation of his nightmare,* he stares at her; her wizened features are imponderable:

MOTHER: I remember when Sigbritt's boy had just been born, and lay there in his basket in the lilac arbor at the summerhouse. Now he will be fifty years old. And little cousin Sara, who always went around carrying him, cradling him, and who married Sigfrid, that no-good. Now you have to go. . . .

Their strained, solemn encounter is over. All's one to this icy crone, the good and the bad, the quick and the dead. She is decades past caring for anyone save herself; and it is likely that she was as immersed in her staggering egocentrism while her children were still young.

They return to the inn and find Sara in tears, Anders and Viktor off

---

* The occult need not be invoked to explain this coincidence, although as a longtime student of parapsychic phenomena I would not dismiss the heightened precognition of Borg's unquiet mind. It is equally feasible, however, that he had seen the handless watch before and forgotten it—perhaps at the time of his father's death or shortly thereafter, and that his unconscious readily seized upon it today, distilling down his depression into one unforgettable image of decay.

resolving their metaphysical differences by force. While Marianne
fetches the young men, Sara complains to Borg of her difficulty in
chosing between Anders' attractiveness and Viktor's ambition. Her ir-
resolution triggers Isak's hurtful memories of the first Sara, torn between the two brothers with their disparate personalities. The journey
recommences, a storm comes up and Borg, lulled by the rain, falls
into the third, most complex dream of the film.

Once more he sits with Sara at the wild strawberry patch. She holds
up a mirror and taunts him with his reflection: he is a worried old man
who will die soon, while she has her whole life before her:

> SARA: And the truth is that I've been too considerate. One can easily
> be unintentionally cruel that way.
> ISAK: I understand.
> SARA: No, you don't understand. We don't speak the same lan-
> guage. Look at yourself in the mirror again. No, don't look away
> . . . now listen. I'm about to marry your brother, Sigfrid. He and I
> love each other, and it's all like a game. Look at your face now. Try
> to smile! (*He does, a painful grimace*) . . .
> ISAK: It hurts.
> SARA: You, a professor emeritus, ought to know why it hurts. But
> you don't. Because in spite of all your knowledge, you don't really
> know anything.

An infant—Sigbritt's little boy—wails in the distance. Isak implores
her not to leave, but she rises, glides into the arbor and, just as his
mother described, cradles the baby in her arms. A door of the house
opens, and Sigfrid beckons to her. She gives him the child and goes
inside. Darkness falls, flocks of birds sweep across the night sky. Isak
peers through a window and sees Sara in an evening gown, incredibly
lovely, playing a Bach fugue on the piano. The fugue motif metamorphoses imperceptibly into the haunting theme of the film as Sigfrid,
also in evening dress, comes in and bends over her, kissing her shoulder. They move out of Isak's vision to the dinner table.

The glass turns opaque. Borg raps impatiently on the windowpane.
No answer. He raps again, harder, with his left hand. His heartbeat,
mimed by a kettledrum, begins to thud in his ears as he pivots and
stabs his right hand into a nail that juts from the wall. He nurses his

wounded palm, the door of the house opens, and Sten Alman invites him in. The dream Alman, in contrast to his real-life counterpart, is dignified, self-contained; his attitude towards Borg is polite, but faintly critical. He conducts him down a long hallway, into an amphitheater—the medical school amphitheater where Borg once taught and examined. Sara, Viktor, Anders and a few innominates sit in the audience.

Borg hands Alman an examination booklet, and in return Alman directs him to identify a specimen under the microscope. Borg looks, but can only see his own eye, staring remorselessly back at him. Alman next tells him to interpret a strange sentence on the blackboard: INKE TAN MAGROV STAK FARSIN LOS KRET FAJNE KASERTE MJO-TRON PRESETE—''the first duty of a doctor. . . .'' Borg declares testily that he is not a linguist. Alman translates—the first duty of a doctor is ''to ask forgiveness.'' Furthermore, Borg is ''guilty of guilt,'' a serious offense. Borg pours himself a glass of water with a shaking hand.

> ISAK: I have a bad heart. I'm an old man, Mr. Alman, and I must be treated with consideration. That's only right.
> ALMAN (*coldly*): There is nothing concerning your heart in my papers. . . .

Borg is shown the body of a woman sprawled lifelessly in a chair and asked for a diagnosis. He pronounces her dead, whereupon she opens her eyes and bursts into peals of mocking laughter. The supposed corpse is Berit Alman! Her husband wearily records his conclusions—Borg is incompetent, indifferent, inconsiderate—''these accusations have been made by your wife. . . .''

Alman leads him out of the house, through a thick forest and into a clearing. Here, Borg *watches* his dead wife, Karin, and one of her numerous paramours in a scene of savage sexuality. She teases and provokes her powerfully built, arrogantly self-assured lover to take her violently on the grass. Alman says that Borg actually witnessed this degrading scene.

> ALMAN: Many men forget a woman who has been dead for thirty years. Some preserve a sweet, fading picture, but *you* can always

recall this scene in your memory. . . . Tuesday, May 1, 1917, you
stood here and heard and saw exactly what that woman and man said
and did. . . .

Afterward, Karin speaks to herself while the man sits off to one
side, indifferent to her, smoking a cigarette (!):

> KARIN: Now I will go home and tell this to Isak, and I know exactly
> what he'll say: Poor little girl, how I pity you . . . and then I'll cry
> some more and ask him if he can forgive me. And then he'll say:
> you shouldn't ask forgiveness from me. I have nothing to forgive.
> But he doesn't mean a word of it, because he's completely cold.
> And then he'll suddenly be very tender . . . and then I'll say that
> it's his fault that I am the way I am, and then he'll look very sad and
> will say that he is to blame. But he doesn't care about anything,
> because he's completely cold.

She laughs hysterically and vanishes. The clearing is still.

> ALMAN: She is gone. Everyone has gone . . . everything has been
> dissected . . . a surgical masterpiece. There is no pain, no bleeding,
> no quivering . . . a perfect achievement of its kind, professor. . . .
> ISAK: What is the penalty?
> ALMAN: The usual one, I suppose . . . loneliness.

Alman, too, disappears (*the dream ends here in the film version*);
Borg hears Sara's voice:

> SARA: Didn't you have to go with them to get your father?
> ISAK: Sara—it wasn't always like this. If only you had stayed with
> me. If only you could have had a little patience.

She runs away, and he wants to cry with "wild, childish sorrow,"
but his tears will not come, as he awakens.

All the occurences since Borg was roused from his slumber at the
summerhouse by Sara's reincarnation have been woven into this
nightmare. In the previous dream, Borg pictured the first Sara as she
probably existed—a simple, vital girl (the type that intellectuals like
Borg are frequently drawn to), mystified by his adolescent asceticism.
But the pitiless face she shows in the opening of this dream is surely

that of his mother, glacially aloof and rejecting. Isak is his mother's only surviving child, but she has treated him with little genuine love or concern, and took little pleasure in his success. Yet, through his pre-ternatural reserve, one intuits a tremendous sense of duty, a heavy obligation towards this terrifyingly indifferent creature.

The mother alluded to Sara's past affection for Sigbritt's baby son. Now grown, that son is to receive the father's broken watch, *not* Isak, the more appropriate recipient. In the dream, Sara pointedly abandons him for the same child, strong testimony that Isak looked to the real Sara to care for the frustrated child inside him, stronger evidence that Isak's earliest desires for maternal sustenance went unsatisfied. Sara next is seen with her husband, Isak's brother—a second rejection, but with an unmistakable Oedipal reference.

Isak's humiliating defeat by Sigfrid was the more traumatic, since it took place against the setting of his thwarted primal dependency. Developmentally, a complex hierarchy of dependency needs centering around the first feeding relationship precedes the specific sexual yearnings for the mother's body of the Oedipal stage. Trauma during the so-called ''oral'' phase inevitably leaves an enduring mark on successive phases. Clinical experience with similar patients leads me to guess that Isak as an infant was fed and handled mechanically, with little true warmth, either by an obsessionally oriented mother or equally remote stand-ins—relatives or, more likely for the time, servants. Such a child feels the normal Oedipal wounds much more keenly, for if he was not ''good'' enough to be nurtured with the proper emotional charge by his mother, it is no wonder that later her necessary preference for the father will hurt so profoundly. Borg's unconscious amalgam of oral and sexual frustration is encapsulated precisely in the sequence of the dream where, standing outside the summerhouse, he watches Sara and Sigfrid dining together. (Intriguingly, in his prior dream he had also watched his family eating!) His plight is like that of the little match-girl of the fairy tale, who froze to death outside the elegant restaurant while the rich and their children ate sumptuously within.

Borg's subsequent impalement bears eloquent testimony to the harsh service his masculine identity received from his implacably hostile mother. Yet, out of his misplaced loyalty to her, and out of the fear that childish anger towards such a vindictive woman always fosters, Borg has long since buried his rage, and with it a vast spectrum of feeling. Instead—and quite typically—a restitutive identification with her disdainful obsessionalism has taken place. (Anna Freud described the defensive maneuver called "identification with the aggressor," wherein the child mimes the behavior of the adult who traumatized it, then, grown into adulthood, hurts others as it was hurt.)

Borg dealt unconsciously with his first love of adolescence as if she were his mother, to whom closeness was anathema, and lacerated her with his own version of his mother's harmful treatment of him. By guilt-provoking and distancing manipulations he exacted a talion vengeance against his mother, displaced upon Sara and, inevitably, every woman in his life. Inevitably, he came to labor under a general interdiction against intimacy as a result of his anxiety-laden, inadequate nurturing, and subjected friends, colleagues and lovers indiscriminately to his aloofness, irony and contempt. If such people obtain any measure of warmth from others, it is usually in spite of themselves.

But now a healthier part of him, stirring throughout this crucial day, also speaks through the dream-Sara, reproving him for his *ignorance,* his blindness to his own potential for tenderness, his inability to articulate the dark forces that have robbed him of joy and made him into a lonely, pathetic old man.

His ignorance of the heart is repeatedly emphasized in the harrowing examination sequence. Examination dreams occur ubiquitously during psychoanalytic therapy and appear regularly in the mental life of many reflective non-analysands. Usually, the dreamer must take a test for which he is ill-prepared: it is the last minute, and he has yet to open a book, or else his memory for the subject matter is blank. Freud observed that these dreams recall testing situations in which the dreamer actually did well, so that it would be absurd at his present age and status (one is invariably at last marginally aware of both) to be in such a predicament. Freud therefore concluded that the primary "job" of the examination dream is to reassure the dreamer wrestling with contemporary conflict far removed from past academic problems as if to say: *it is ridiculous to be upset over this, you will handle it as well as you did that silly test so long ago.*

From this viewpoint, Borg's dream would seem to be asserting, and reassuring him against, the proof of his mortality. Sara scornfully shows him to himself as a "worried old man who will die soon," and he is then administered a scathing examination in the very place he rose to fame. Part of his observing ego is thus trying to comfort him obliquely: *it is absurd for you, an Emeritus Professor, a Jubilee Doctor, to fear death: you are not a puny incompetent, you have long since passed these tests, you have given them to others a thousand times. You are the master, not the pupil. Your examiner, Alman, is a worm. Any problem life throws in your way, you will sweep aside with the same formidable will that has brought you to the pinnacle of success!*

This interpretation, while not entirely incorrect, does not go to the heart of the matter. Freud emphasized the reparative quality of the examination dream, but neglected the central metaphor of the examination itself. Patients in psychoanalysis, the most rigorous process of self-examination yet devised by Western man, produce examination dreams when particularly involved in a stringent reevaluation of the most vital issues of their being in the world, before which they necessarily stand trembling with indecision. And justifiably so, for we are not machines, though we may try to mechanize the living self, rushing headlong into the mindless pursuit of power and prestige while the fulfillment of our most human needs goes abegging. Isak Borg's neurosis has spared his professional life as a healer, but he has failed until now at the healing of his psychic wounds, and wounded those closest to him as a corollary of his inability to achieve intimacy and trust. At the eleventh hour, like many older patients, he is striving mightily to comprehend the meaning of his deadness and pain, so that, however briefly, he may take a different path. In this sense, every one of his dreams of the past few months has been an examination dream!

His examiner is Sten Alman: Borg chooses Alman partly because he possesses many of Borg's least likable qualities, exponentially raised, especially his cynicism—and partly because Alman's sadomasochistic sarabande with his wife grotesquely parallels Borg's turbulent relationship with Karin. The audience of youngsters indicates that his own unfulfilled youth is crying out for explanation and release from neurotic bondage. He looks through the microscope and sees his own eye, a pointed symbol of uncompromising self-scrutiny. He cannot decipher the cryptic inscription, complaining that he is no linguist, and in fact until very recently the wish to communicate, to reach out and be reached in return, has withered within him.

The first duty of a doctor is *to ask forgiveness,* and Borg, hearing Alman's translation, nods his head eagerly in recognition. But, we may ask, forgiveness for what? Sara has spoken ambiguously with his mother's voice, and conversely as a "good mother," has bidden him to awaken from his living death; the odd inscription contains an analogous ambiguity.* On the negative side of the psychic ledger, Borg has spent his life asking perpetual forgiveness from the mother of his childhood for ever defying her injunctions against seeking love, for ever presuming to nurse at her chill breast. Borg has subjugated himself, performing endless penance to placate her basic animosity, and by this masochistic abasement he maintains the illusion that some shred of affection will begrudgingly fall his way.

But now he intuits a different order of forgiveness. He must ask forgiveness of those he injured by misdirected callousness and spite, and the burden of meaningless shame must be cast off if ever he is to feel compassion for himself and kindness towards others. "You are guilty of guilt," Alman testifies. Out of the intimation of inexplicable guilt—as if he sinned by being born—he has lashed out at himself and the world. Berit Alman asked forgiveness (!) earlier in the day. She appears in Borg's dream as the embodiment of vicious shrew, but also as the wife whose self-esteem has been corroded by her husband's belittling. Her mocking resurrection, the second time corpses have come to life in his dreams, betokens the painful, ambivalent feelings towards women he has forsworn, at a terrible cost.

He is finally confronted with his dead wife, Karin, resurrected in a setting that fairly reeks of the Primal Scene. Repeatedly, Borg has cast himself as the excluded observer. Having looked on while his brother seduced Sara, he is now compelled to watch his wife submit to the advances of a brute male. Karin describes his insulting solicitude, and his queasy tenderness after she reveals her infidelity. The analyst discerns that Borg acts as if he can be allowed to possess a woman of his

---

* Sara's ambivalence towards Borg in the dream is also compounded out of Marianne's mixed feelings towards her father-in-law. She begins by disliking him, but she has been growing increasingly fond of him by the time he dreams the dream.

own only after some powerful and dreaded rival is first satisfied. Surely the adolescent Isak subtly encouraged Sara's yen for the enticing Sigfrid by his asceticism just as the adult Isak provoked Karin into adultery by inveterate criticism and withdrawal.

Loneliness is the price for the stillness that follows. The peace in the dream is as imperfect as that Borg has purchased by decades of obsessional isolation and denial of feeling. Once more Sara appears, prompting him to seek his *father*. She brushes aside his pleading for patience, abandons him as the dream ends. Again we encounter her double mask: she frustrates him, yet enigmatically spurs him to find relatedness—with his father.

I have argued that Borg's defenses against a chronic depressive state are products of a frankly inimical mothering. But what of the father? Is the powerful competitor of Borg's dreams, be he Sigfrid or Karin's lover, really struck in the father's original image? We have been afforded only the briefest allusions to this man, fleeting references without direct witness, perhaps corresponding to the son's perception.

The faceless figures one finds so frequently in dream scenarios are customarily interpreted as disguised parents. If the faceless man with his back turned, who melts away at Borg's touch in the first dream is the father, one would speculate that Borg conceived of him as a man of straw, unsupportive, unavailable. The father's handless watch is another reference to his ineffectiveness. And one notes that in the second dream, the substitutes for Borg's parents at the dinner table are the dominating aunt, and the *foolish, deaf* uncle!

One guesses that Borg was unable to consolidate a helpful identification with his father, either because the father was in reality a weakling overpowered by a harpy wife, or—just as likely—that he seemed ineffective and remote because he had to be shared among eight other siblings! Whatever the father's status, weak or strong, Borg's mother intensified her son's Oedipus complex by her coldness, inciting little Isak's jealousy and fear of his father, driving an enduring wedge between father and son. Consider further that Borg's next sibling was another male, older by only a year. Although the mother was evidently no fonder of Sigfrid than Isak, the dreams suggest that Isak joined him to the father's image in his unconscious as a sadistic, frightening competitor for her dubious affection.

In any large family, siblings must assume more significance as parental surrogates. In Borg's huge family, given the mother's pathology, given the father's remoteness (for whatever reason), the destructive or constructive influence of his siblings in molding his character became crucial. Matters might have taken a different turn, had the next sibling been a girl more protective of his needs, or a brother better disposed towards him than Sigfrid, who minimized him unmercifully, probably because he thought Isak was the favored son: this is the cruelest hoax, that the mother with her emotional mendacity forced Sigfrid and Isak to believe that each was deprived because of some obscure worthiness in the other (or unworthiness in the self) whereas in actuality both were short-changed without fear or favor. We are strikingly ignorant of Borg's feelings towards the remaining siblings. Charlotta, Sara's comforter, is portrayed as a decent sort, but it is clear from Borg's subsequent history that she did not give him the care substantially withheld by his mother. He stands as isolated from his brothers and sisters as from everyone else.

These issues are known, yet unknown to our hero. But now, at long last, Isak Borg is ready to come to terms with the recognitions his unconscious has been pressing upon him. He awakens to find himself alone in the car with Marianne. The youngsters have gone off to pick flowers to pay him homage, for she has told them of his award. He speaks again about his dreams; this time, she is prepared to listen to him:

> ISAK: It's as if I were trying to say something to myself [in these dreams] which I don't want to hear . . . that I am dead, although I live. . . .

She blanches; her husband has spoken much the same words to her. Dissolve to Marianne and Evald, Evald in the same seat occupied a moment ago by his father. They are parked near the sea. Evald has come unwillingly, and he treats Marianne with a painfully familiar mixture of irony and resentment. She says she is pregnant and has decided to have the child—inferring that other pregnancies have been aborted at Evald's insistence. He answers angrily that she must choose between him and the unborn infant:

EVALD: . . . it's absurd to live in this world, but it's even more ridiculous to populate it with new victims, and it's most absurd of all to believe that they will have it any better than us . . . I was an unwelcome child in a marriage which was a nice imitation of Hell. Is the old man really sure that I'm his son? Indifference, fear, infidelity and guilt feelings—those were my nurses . . . this life disgusts me, and I don't think I need a responsibility which will force me to exist another day longer than I want to . . . one functions according to one's needs . . . there is nothing which can be called right or wrong . . . you have a damned need to live, to exist, and create life . . . my need is to be dead. Absolutely, totally, dead!

The ominous likeness of father and son is only too evident; Borg, until recently, has simply been better defended against his despair. Evald, like Borg, knew a remote father. Evald was exposed to Borg's innate horror of closeness, but more particularly to his displaced hostility towards Sigfrid and *his* father—for men like Borg regularly conceive of their sons as interlopers in their disturbed marriages. Evald, too, was no stranger to maternal deprivation, but whatever else turned Karin's affection away from her family, we have seen that she was covertly primed by her husband to act like a treacherous slut. Evald, too, employs the baleful obsessionalism, the life-denying detachment that constitutes the legacy of the frightful old lady of Huskvärna.

Dissolve back to Borg and Marianne in the car. He asks her to smoke if she wishes. When one recalls his peremptory injunction at the beginning of the film, this small, stiff permission shows how deeply Borg has been moved.

MARIANNE: When I saw you together with your mother, I was gripped by a strange fear . . . I thought, here is his mother, a very ancient woman, completely ice-cold, in some ways more frightening than death itself. And here is her son, and there are light-years of distance between them. And he himself says that he is a living death. And Evald is on the verge of becoming just as lonely and cold —and dead. And then I thought that there is only coldness and death, and death and loneliness . . . somewhere it must end.
BORG: But you are going back to Evald.
MARIANNE: Yes, to tell him that I can't agree to his condition. I want my child; no one can take it from me. Not even the person I love more than anyone else.

She turns upon him a "black, accusing, desperate" gaze, and he is shaken to the very core of his being. In one stroke, she has laid bare the chain of interpersonal devastation reaching down through the generations. Her integrity, her emotional life and the actual life of the unborn child are menaced by the destructiveness in Evald and his progenitors.

Here, then, is the turning point of *Wild Strawberries:* Borg asks— "Can I help you?"—the first time in his life the old and honored physician has asked that question of someone near him, and truly meant it. Marianne is too troubled to register his breakthrough. She says that no one can help her, but she will try to rescue Evald from his entombment. The young people come back, and Sara gives Isak a bouquet:

> SARA: Now we want to pay our respects to you with these simple flowers, and to tell you that we are *very* impressed . . . we know of course that you are a *wise* and *venerable* old man. One who regards us youngsters with *lenience* and gentle irony. One who knows *all* about life and who has learned all the prescriptions by heart. . . .

These young people have played a significant part in reviving Borg's parched spirit. Having passed through the extremities of desolation and recovered knowledge of the comforts of love, he is truly wiser, and deserves her gift.

At Lund, Borg is delighted to meet Miss Agda, who decided after his departure to rejoin him after all. Evald is painfully cordial; as Borg unpacks, he hears his son express a cautious pleasure at Marianne's return.

Bergman deleted the next scene from the final shooting script, but it is worth mentioning as a clue to his intentions. (The unfilmed portions of the second and third dreams are equally instructive to the psychoanalyst. Without them the sequences work better cinematically; also, in the fashion of real dreams, the filmed versions furnish less obvious clues to the unraveling of their meaning.) The three dignitaries who are to be acclaimed wait in an alcove outside the ceremonial hall. Borg chats with Jacob Hovelius, a bishop, and discovers to his consternation that the third man is Tiger, a once eminent jurist now far declined into senile decrepitude.

BORG: Do you think we are like *that?*

JACOB: What's your opinion? As Schopenhauer says somewhere, "Dreams are a kind of lunacy, and lunacy a kind of dream." But life is also supposed to be a kind of dream, isn't it?

Borg's dreams have accurately recorded his agony and catalyzed an extraordinary revolution in his psyche. But this point has been driven home amply by now—the scene, therefore, is redundant. Without it, the action proceeds directly to the Jubilee rite, accelerated and fragmentary as a newsreel, hours compressed into a few moments. It is the journey to this summit of excellence that has mattered, not the reward. During the ceremony Borg, aware of his young friends, Evald, Marianne and Miss Agda sitting in the audience, senses "a remarkable causality" in the "unexpected, entangled" events of the day, and decides to write them down.

He goes home to find Miss Agda making his bed. He experiences a surge of affection for this faithful old woman, and asks her forgiveness (!) for his morning's rudeness. He suggests they drop two generations of formality and address each other as *"du."*

MISS AGDA: . . . I beg to be excused from all intimacies. It's all right the way it is between us now . . . a woman has to think of her reputation, and what would people say if the two of us suddenly started to say *"du"* to each other?

BORG: Yes, what *would* people say?

MISS AGDA: They would ridicule us.

BORG: Do you always act correctly?

MISS AGDA: Nearly always. At our age one ought to know how to behave.

Rebuked, he is about to retire when he hears singing from the garden below. The young travelers have come to bid him farewell.

SARA: Hey, Father Isak! You were fantastic when you marched in the procession. We were real proud that we knew you . . . goodbye . . . do you know it is really you I love, today, tomorrow, and forever?

ISAK: I'll remember that . . . let me hear from you sometime. . . .

He murmurs the last words to himself, knowing poignantly that he will never live to meet them again. After they leave, Marianne and Evald unexpectedly return—her shoe has broken. Evald stops by the door, and Borg asks him to stay a moment. He inquires haltingly about the marriage. Discomfited, Evald says that Marianne will stay with him, he cannot live without her, everything will be as she wishes. Borg tries to mention the loan, but Evald dismisses him abruptly, he is not to worry, he'll get his money. Just then Marianne enters and leans over her father-in-law:

> ISAK: Thanks for your company on the trip.
> MARIANNE: Thank *you*.
> ISAK: I like you, Marianne.
> MARIANNE: I like you too, Father Isak.

The director has not yielded to the temptation to cast his protagonist as Scrooge, waking from cautionary dreams to spread good cheer until the end of his days. Borg is after all an ancient man, still quite set in his ways. Miss Agda and Evald clearly expect no change in his behavior, indeed it would unsettle them, for they are as inflexible, as obsessional after their own fashion as he, perhaps more so. Miss Agda's amusing refusal of Borg's tentative efforts to bring them closer is followed by Evald's stinging rebuff. People like these simply will not surrender their habitual defenses with any facility.

Borg's self-portrait in the opening scene has been written *after* this fateful day has passed. The persona he shows to an unknowing world would not seem to have altered significantly. Yet, to underscore the impressive internal shifts that have occurred, Bergman brilliantly interpolates two visitations of love between the thorny confrontations with mother-surrogate (Miss Agda) and hardened, unforgiving son. The first is by Sara, who speaks for her namesake of her wholehearted affection for Isak. The second is by Marianne, who has penetrated Isak's facade with her luminous honesty. Touched by his suffering, she has herself drawn strength from the magnitude of his achievements, despite his burdens, and is committed more firmly than ever to affirm the new life within her.

After Evald and Marianne depart, Borg has a final dream. For the last time, he lingers by the wild strawberry patch. The sun blazes down; his sisters and brothers frolic at the dock with Uncle Aron. Sara and his aunt pass by, laden with picnic baskets. Sara affectionately tells him to find his father while the rest go sailing—they will rejoin him later. In a childish voice he says he can find neither mother nor father. She takes his hand and leads him to a hill from which, now alone, he is able to see a man and woman seated on the beach below. The man holds a slender bamboo rod between his knees that arcs gracefully into the lambent air. The woman sits slightly apart. The scene is perfectly composed, indeed one of the most perfect in cinema, and save for a few shimmering harp chords, quite still. His father makes a small, cryptic gesture of greeting, and Borg's face is suffused with a rare joy. Quick-dissolve to the old doctor, stirring contentedly in his sleep, and the film ends.

Although Borg still appears as a distant observer in this last dream, truly meaningful repair has taken place. . . . All envy and bitterness have vanished. The scene he watches is lovely, harmonious, and to some degree he can now partake of its peace—as if having finally recovered the approval of warm and generous women, he can be allowed full recognition of his worth as child and man. He has also been able to effect a solid identification with his father, and can evoke his parents' intimacy without the taint of Oedipal jealousy. It is, after all, that intimacy which has delivered him into the world, to discover the possibilities of warmth and trust. No longer the perennial outsider, he is ready to explore those possibilities.

That these healing insights should come on the brink of the grave is tragic, but that they have been bestowed at all upon this constricted man is nothing short of miraculous. Whatever dreams or days remain, one is certain they will pass with a measure of serenity, for love has finally acquired a small dominion within Isak Borg, piercing the awful loneliness—the ''silence of God''—that has always afflicted Bergman's heroes. And, in Donne's words:

> ''Love, all alike, no season knows nor clime
> Nor days, months, years, which are the rags of time. . . .''

Bibliography

Quotations from the film are taken from ''Wild Strawberries,'' in *Four Screenplays of Ingmar Bergman,* New York: Simon and Schuster, 1960. The passage from Donne is from ''The Sun Rising,'' in *Poems,* John Donne, Everyman's Library edition, New York: Dutton, 1958.

Horror and Science Fiction—
The Sleep of Reason

> . . . there has always been a spontaneous human taste
> for monsters, for the more-than or less-than human. St.
> Augustine felt they had to be allowed for, and
> explained them as part of God's inexplicable plan. . . .
>
> Lawrence Alloway

> . . . vampires and werewolves; monsters and
> mummies, are all human at source, and are all
> personifications of that potential for evil and sin which
> is so much a part of us . . . hero and villain are much
> the same, both human, both flawed unto death . . . the
> complexity of their struggle . . . the dark nature of
> the order recovered by that struggle give the horror film
> its moral and metaphysical weight.
>
> R.H.W. Dillard

> Shall we put the heart in now?
>
> Dr. Ernst Praetorius

The story is told of the American tenor making his debut at La Scala, who developed a bad case of first-night jitters after being warned about the strenuous expectations of the audience, and the likelihood of riotous disapproval if he didn't meet the proper standards. To his astonishment, his first aria brought down the house. There were enthusiastic shouts—"Encore, Encore!"—so he sang again, with another tumultuous reception—*"Encore, Encore!!"* He obliged them with a third, a fourth, and yet a fifth turn, with no let up in the clamor, until he had to step to the footlights and croak: "Much as I would love to please you, my voice is giving out. If I sing this aria once more, I won't be able to finish the opera!" And from the back of the hall, a stentorian voice roared: *"You willa seeng eet again, you willa seeng eet untilla you get eet right!!!"*

Trauma dictates a healing return to its source, so that the meaning of pain may be comprehended. The analytic principle of the *repetition compulsion* dictates that we are compelled to hearken back to earlier fear and trembling, to recreate a present edition of that which has traumatized us in the past, not out of sheer masochism, but that we may finally, like the tenor in the story, "get it right"—master danger, know that we have exerted some measure of control over destiny rather than suffer wounding passively. Freud believed that the neurotic is particularly prone to become entangled with individuals who resemble a rejecting parent or sadistic sibling out of the hope that somehow, this time around, one may triumph over the hurt and humiliation caused by one's nursery adversaries.

But how to encompass the ultimate trauma, the inalterable fact that time must have a stop? "Death is a state of eternal trauma," writes the analyst Max Stern, "Previous traumatic situations have been overcome, but from death there is no recovery, the outcome is final. . . ." With our curious plausibility, we persist in yearning for answers when we are confounded with the unanswerable. We spend a lifetime coming to terms with the incontrovertibility of death, working out an adaptation—however healthy or faulty—to death. Some embrace the consolations of religion or philosophy. Professional death defiers like Sam Spade rush counterphobically into danger to undo and deny their fear. Hitchcock's people keep a low obsessional profile, hoping that by the pious show of devotion to the Gods of Conformity they will cheat the reaper. And those who find balm in the testaments of the occultists affirm that the end is no ending at all, merely a translation of the unincorporated spirit into a higher realm of being, or a rebirth of the soul into a new envelope.

Perhaps it seems presumptuous of the psychoanalyst to speak of "working through" the fear of death, as if the fear of that irredeemable unknown is comparable to a dog phobia or a hand-washing compulsion. But precisely because it *is* an unknown and unknowable quantum, death is largely what we make of it emotionally, what we abstract from our lives and project upon this blankest of blank screens.

The clinician finds that a panoply of symptoms and complexes are rooted in the irrational fear of death. Children are consciously afraid of dying by at least age two to three, usually as a result of having lost a pet, a grandparent, or having watched real or fictional deaths on television. Youngsters equate death with the dark, the horrors of helplessness, with being immobilized, unable to breathe or cry out. And the artless logic of the child's mind weaves death into the fabric of its perceptions or misperceptions of its world. Death is incorporated into its naive theories on the origins of life, on the nature of good and evil. Death easily binds itself to infantile fantasies of retribution, retaliation and abandonment, becoming the imagined punishment for forbidden wish or deed. The neurotic adult, and everyone to some degree, persists in dreading death in the same outworn terms, a repressed angst which in the extreme can desiccate any pleasure in life itself.

The analyst's task must include the investigation of what Stern calls "the amalgamation of obsolete anxieties about death," so that death comes to be grasped existentially, in its own right, as the most stringent and legitimate of human limitations. (This is so in every case, and I believe that many analytic "failures" are caused by inadequate attention to the analysand's thanatophobia.) Beyond this point must the patient minister unto himself, for even analysts remain ultimately ignorant before the exquisite dilemma of our ability to contemplate unbeing, and our inability to know, at least in this life, what it is not to be.

From the cinema's earliest beginnings, the "weird" genres—horror and much of science fiction—have administered a flamboyant, far more popular prescription for thanatophobia than the sobering insights of psychoanalysis (1908 saw the first Dr. Jekyll; 1910, the first Frankenstein). R.H.W. Dillard has likened the horror film to a medieval

morality play, as a "pageant of death, the death that breeds in all
things, entropy, mutability, and corruption." For Dillard, an Aris-
totelian catharsis attends upon the scary mime. The audience is purged
by its exposure to death—"as we have never seen it before, by distorting the fact of death into all possible contortions, to help us see its
simple and natural reality." But I submit that the masques of death are
never unknown—they have only been forgotten. By participating in
the macabre pageant of weird cinema, with its fabulous blend of the
bizarre, the banal and the beautiful, we tilt at the myriad deaths conjured up from childhood conflict and injury. We shriek and grin and
mock at alien, yet familiar deaths, delighting for a few moments in a
dubious victory both over our infantile distortions and the grim truth of
mortality.

On and off the screen, the intimations of death are likely to be accompanied by the peculiar emotion called the "uncanny," the prickles
at the back of the neck held so dear by aficionados. Freud declared
rather wistfully that he was largely immune to personal acquaintance
with the uncanny, yet devoted no small effort chasing down the origin
of those elusive creeps. (Throughout his life he maintained a strong if
skeptical interest in parapsychic phenomena, and in his later years at
least came to believe in telepathy.) "An uncanny experience occurs,"
he stated, "when repressed infantile complexes have been renewed
. . . or when the primitive beliefs we have surmounted seem once
more to be confirmed. . . ." If, in Goya's words, the sleep of
reason breeds monsters, let us let reason slumber and take a sleepwalk
tour through Monster Alley, to consort with ghoulies and ghosties ancient and modern, whose awful forms we shall often discover fabri-
cated out of our most profound "infantile complexes and primitive
beliefs" about death and life.

Blowing the Lid off the Id

When he heard I wanted to become a psychoanalyst, an old general practitioner vehemently warned—"Son, stay away from that
crap—when you stir a stink, all you get is a bigger stink!" The ancient
injunction against stirring up the seething cauldron of the unconscious
(cf., Pandora, Oedipus and other mythic meddlers with the psychic

peace) rests squarely upon the anxiety we feel before the often alarming strength of our own emotions.

It is written that in a certain African tribe, when an individual falls ill, his relatives and friends are forced on pain of death to reveal their dreams to the shaman. If evil intent towards the afflicted one be discerned therein, the dreamer is labeled a witch, and cast out into the wilderness. To the primitive, the child and many neurotics, intense aggressive and sexual feelings are particularly reprehensible, carrying as much weight as an actual criminal deed such feelings might motivate, and laying the guilty party open to the retribution of the gods, the tribal Judges, or the remorseless Superego.

We are repeatedly admonished in weird cinema that even the gentlest of men may bare fangs and bay at the moon when his passions are kindled. The movie monster thus represents the destructive forces unleashed when reason and civilized morality are overthrown by our unruly instincts. The mutable lycanthrope is but another version of Hobbesian man, the naked ape bellowing in the wilderness, Fred C. Dobbs in Wolf Man's clothing!

Weird cinema often lays the blame for blowing the lid off the Id within the unquiet spirit of the candidate for monsterdom, and/or upon malignant outside spirits. A hereditary taint or the contamination of eldritch evil may articulate with latent neuroticism, mobilizing morbid affect and catalyzing a hideous transformation. The heroine of Val Lewton's 1942 film *Cat People* (played by the memorably feline Simone Simon) has emigrated from her obscurely Transylvanian origins. She marries an apple-pie and ice-cream American oaf; when her husband develops an "innocent" relationship with a female coworker as square as he, her jealousy turns into rank paranoia, and she turns into a panther. The film is noteworthy for its xenophobia: we are led to believe that hubby bedded an alluring pussycat from across the sea, and got a tiger in his tank instead.

On closer scrutiny, the husband proves far from innocent. He provokes the incipient cat lady with stinging allusions to the charm and competence of his "pal," while the latter, despite her demonstrations of queasy solicitude about her rival's tenuous emotional state, is palpably out to break up the marriage. Hollywood's characteristic disguise of an immoral reality places the responsibility for infidelity, seduction and the taunting unto madness of a vulnerable waif upon the festering rage of the attainted foreigner.*

In Universal's *The Wolf Man* (1941), another guiltless *naif,* Lawrence Talbott, loses his humanity with the eruption of his jealousy. Like the cat-woman, Talbott is a rejected outsider, returning to the English village of his birth after years of self-imposed exile (never explained) in America. He is called back by his aristocrat father after his obviously preferred older brother's death. The cruel father treats him like Cain, with ill-disguised hostility even after their formal reconciliation.

While wandering on the moors, Talbott slays a werewolf, but is bitten in the fight. Later, at a village carnival, he meets the young woman he has been wooing unsuccessfully, with her fiancé. The two men compete at a shooting gallery. Talbott performs well until he freezes at the toy image of a wolf. His adversary contemptuously blasts it down. "You win," Talbott groans. Subsequently he catches the girl alone, tries clumsily to tell her of his love. She rebuffs him, and directly thereafter he changes into a werewolf, howling out his pain on the lonely moors. Talbott has lost an implicit Oedipal battle— the Oedipal motif appears virtually undiguised later in the film, when the father, after persistently denying his son's lycanthropy, is responsible for Talbott's escape. Father then encounters son changed to Wolf Man, about to assault his lost love on the moor. The father kills him with the same silver-headed cane which Talbott wielded against the werewolf that infected him! (I shall have more to say about the monster as adolescent Oedipus presently.)

The Pandora's box of the unconscious is frequently opened by the "mad" scientist, a misguided humanitarian or a demented egomaniac seeking vengeance against the world that has derided his genius. By tampering with the natural order, the good/bad doctor inadvertently

* Which does not, of course, diminish *Cat People*'s shock value. Lewton was one of those gifted directors who could scare an audience witless by altering the substance of the ordinary into pure menace. Take the famous sequence in which the heroine changes into her panther persona at a hotel swimming pool, where the other woman treads water, alone and achingly vulnerable. The quiet lapping of the wavelets, the confused lights, shadows and echoes rebounding off the tiled walls combine to produce an atmosphere of exceptional disquiet. One longs for this subtlety at a time when the horror film, caught up in pervasive cinematic sadism, so frequently leaves the sensibilities glutted with gory surfeit.

releases the Id-monster within himself, like Dr. Henry Jekyll (*Dr. Jekyll and Mr. Hyde*), Dr. Janos Rukh (*The Invisible Ray*), or Dr. Morbius (*Forbidden Planet*).

Dr. Jekyll and Mr. Hyde has been brought to the screen more often than any other weird tale. The persona of Jekyll actually changes little from one film to the next: thoroughly dedicated, genteel and priggish, Jekyll remains the essence of the repressed Victorian. But Hyde's gargantuan appetite for evil has elicited a wider range of interpretation: it is, once again, the old story of Lucifer being more interesting than God! The rarely exhibited Rouben Mamoulian version (1932) remains the favorite of most critics, myself included. The fabulous transformation scene, to the accompaniment of Mamoulian's own recorded muffled heartbeat, has never been equalled. The director steadfastly refused to reveal the lighting and makeup effects that turned Frederic March's handsome features into a brutish parody of humanity. I prize the film especially for its tasteful, yet pointed evocation of Hyde's exuberant carnality (elsewhere it is Hyde's non-sexual sadism that is emphasized). Violence and eroticism are skillfully blended when Hyde lures a young barmaid into his web, goads her into a frenzy of lubricious terror, then strangles her off-camera in what is clearly intended to be an orgiastic substitute.

In Universal's *The Invisible Ray* (1933) a latter-day Jekyll, Dr. Janos Rukh (Boris Karloff out of monster drag) ignores his beautiful young wife to search for "Radium X," a meteoric element with mysterious curative powers thought to have fallen to earth eons ago. Rukh recovers the lost substance in Africa, but after exposure to its intense radioactivity, develops the ability to kill at a touch or a glance. He drops out of sight and is presumed dead. Within a few years a colleague has mastered the dangers of Radium X, reaps fame and honor, while Rukh's wife falls in love with a younger man. Then Rukh resurfaces; the radioactivity seething in his brain has driven him mad, and he commences murdering everyone connected with his humiliation. Before he can kill his wife and complete the cycle of his vengeance, his strength ebbs. His old mother crushes the vial containing the antiserum that maintains his fragile hold on life, and the glowing Rukh hurls himself out a window, to be instantly reduced to ashes by the unchecked poison raging within him.

In real life, no Radium X would be required to catalyze Rukh's obsessional tendencies into a full-blown paranoid state. I have elsewhere indicated that paranoids often provoke the very maltreatment and rejection they fear. The clinician marks Rukh as chronically afraid of closeness, more at home with his grandiose fantasies than the small pleasures of genuine intimacy. Men like Rukh often sicken in their declining years, when the earlier promise of success has not been fulfilled, and death no longer seems a distant possibility. They drive themselves into emotional exile, thrusting away those who might love them with their coldness, nagging and jealous tantrums. Like Rukh, they end up as mad isolates, consumed by bitterness and envy. One notes that Rukh's mother is his executioner. She reproaches him for his misdeeds and failures, and the film implies that she has a legitimate right to do so: actually, the mothers of these obsessional-paranoid types are wont to blame and shame their sons to death with no justification save their own rancor.

As Hyde is to Jekyll, so the radioactive Rukh is to his former rational self. Either the mad scientist converts his ego into the horrid image of his lustful, envious Id, or he constructs a fearful projection of his "monstrous" desires and sets it loose to burn and pillage, often consciously unaware that the monster is the agent of his repressed wishes. The monster may thus be likened to the delinquent who is covertly encouraged to act out one parent or another's unconscious antisocial impulses. The parent in these cases has *superego lacunae,* i.e., a conscience as full of holes as a Swiss cheese. The adult projects his or her disavowed criminality upon the child, who can then be "safely" labeled as the bad seed! While the law may fail to recognize this subtle brand of complicity, at least in the movies the chickens always come home to roost. However noble or craven his conscious motivation, the mad scientist's complicity in the misdeeds of this "offspring" is acknowledged and punished when monster turns upon master and destroys both.

The mad scientist's Id-monster usually appears disguised in fur and claws or encased in metal, but there is one remarkable film in which the Freudian Id itself is the Technicolor monster bred out of its creator's bad dreams—MGM's 1956 science fiction extravaganza, *Forbidden Planet.*

An interstellar space ship lands on the planet Altair IV to recover survivors of an ill-fated colonizing expedition. Only two of the original group remain: Morbius, a philologist of formidable intellect, and his naive, overripe daughter Altaira. Morbius explains to the intrepid Commander John Adams that he and his family came to cherish life on Altair IV, whereas the other members of the expedition could not adjust, and were either torn limb from limb by an invisible monster that prowled the night, or were vaporized with their ship on lift-off after they were unable to persuade Morbius to leave. Since then, Morbius' wife died of natural causes, he and his daughter have lived unmolested for nearly twenty years—"yet always in my mind, I seem to feel the creature is lurking somewhere close, sly and irresistible. . . ." Morbius refuses to disclose the nature of his studies on Altair IV, but he has surrounded himself with technological marvels that are obviously beyond the competence of a linguist.

He warns his would-be rescuers to go before they, too, suffer the fate of his companions. Commander Adams senses something amiss, and refuses to depart. That night his ship is invaded and disabled by the planet's reawakened invisible menace. Altaira develops a crush on the handsome commander who, in the tradition of Space Opera is irritated at her innocent provocation of his men with her lush endowments until he himself takes the fall.

Morbius is pressured to reveal the secret of the forbidden planet to Adams and the eggheaded ship's doctor. Millennia ago, Altair IV was the seat of a great culture—the Krel, vastly superior to man in every way. Having vanquished crime and disease, they stood poised "on the threshold of some supreme accomplishment which was to have crowned their entire history." Then, "this all but Divine race perished in a single night," leaving as enigmatic legacy an enormous web of underground machinery, still monitoring and maintaining itself after 200,000 years!

With his knowledge of linguistics and an electronic I.Q. boost from the Krel "plastic educator," Morbius acquired the barest fraction of their wisdom, but enough to become a scientific wizard and also inflate his ego beyond mortal bounds. He proposes to release the results of his research in his own godlike good time. Adams objects that mankind is entitled to the Krel data without Morbius' regency. As

Morbius waxes angrier at his daughter's infatuation and the intruders' insistence that he return to Earth, the depradations of the invisible monster escalate; during one attack, Morbius is discovered stirring in a troubled slumber at his desk (Morbius = Morpheus!) while the Krel machinery registers an astronomical power drain. Here is the only instance when *Forbidden Planet*'s impressive special effects falter by violating a central canon of weird cinema—never show the audience too much. Caught in the beams of the spacemens' blasters, the Id-monster looks like a cartoon fugitive from Disneyland. Better to have left it forever unseen! *

The egghead doctor slips into the Krel laboratory, and uses the plastic educator to match his wits with Morbius. He is mortally injured, but manages to warn Adams before he dies: ". . . the big machine . . . no instrumentality, true creation, but the Krel forgot one thing . . . monsters, John, monsters from the Id!'' And Adams realizes that *Morbius* is the predator of the forbidden planet! The Krel machine enabled that proud race to transcend the need for physical tools, to change thought instantly into force and matter. But just as the benevolent ego of each Krel was linked to their fantastic creation, so was the Id of each, with its primitive lust and hatred. In one night, every Id-monster of the Krel summoned up the machine's illimitable power, and the race literally self-destructed.

But still the machine carried on. Morbius unwittingly entered into

---

* The naked face of Thanatos is best revealed sparingly. Like the dim memory of repressed trauma, that which is most frightening is likely to be half-glimpsed, seized and reinvented by each viewer's uniquely personal intuition of doom, like the room in Orwell's *1984* where political prisoners were confronted with their most private fears of death. Indeed, what made the great radio horror shows so much more terrifying than the average horror flick was precisely that so much was left to the febrile imagination. I still can remember an episode of Arch Obler's *Lights Out!*, in which a giant chicken heart was swallowing up New York. The announcer yelled that it was sprouting tentacles. *Tentacles,* for God's sake!! I didn't know what they were, but trying to screw up the mind's eye to get a better look scared me out of my eighth year's growth!

Laughter is a necessary ingredient of the horror experience, but it must be carefully mixed with fear. Jury-rigged horror, like the Mexican vampire cheapies that starred popular wrestlers, or the Disneyesque Id-demon of *Forbidden Planet,* ridiculously displays its seams and stitches, and the willing suspension of disbelief is itself suspended. On the other hand, horror beyond psychological tolerance cancels enjoyment and nullifies catharsis. The film becomes a nightmare from which it is impossible to awaken after leaving the safety of the theater, an unmastered trauma that continues to plague the mind. Pictures like *The Exorcist* or *Night of the Living Dead* have been supremely effective in spawning raw panic, but they also irrevocably violate our childlike faith in the movies not to harm us.

the mindlock that had blown the lid off the collective Id of the Krel. While he slept, Morbius' Id savaged his companions because they wanted him to leave Altair IV. And twenty years later, he has sent out his inner beast against Adams, his crew, yes, even his daughter when she throws in her lot with the spacemen. In one stroke, the "mindless primitive" of the lofty-minded Morbius would remove his rival and the source of their rivalry, his own flesh and blood.

At first, Morbius frantically denies what he already partly knows, but as with an hallucinating psychotic, his Id bursts into his waking life. The invisible monster appears outside his citadel, smashes down one supposedly unbreachable defense after another, and begins to melt down the last barrier—"solid Krel metal, twenty-six inches thick!"

"Guilty! Guilty!!" Morbius screams, "My evil self is at that door, and I have no power to stop it! I deny you! I give you up!!" Miraculously, the unseen horror recedes. Morbius is disengaged from the Krel machine. Like Prospero in *The Tempest* (*Forbidden Planet* is often compared with Shakespeare's play), he breaks his staff, buries his book. But like Faustus, that other Promethean overreacher and meddler in dangerous arcana, he must pay a mortal price for his hubris. He has been physically consumed by the gigantic mental effort expended in putting his Superego back on the ascendant. This retelling of Genesis cleaves the figure of our first ancestor in twain: Morbius, eater of the forbidden fruit of the Krel knowledge, must stay behind and die, while Commander Adams(!) will be allowed to quit the tainted Eden of Altair IV.

Morbius bids Adams take his daughter and go in peace. Rather touchingly, he calls the Commander "son," acknowledging the psychological basis of their rivalry, and activates an atomic reactor that turns the planet into a supernova after the Earthmen have departed. Watching from deep space, Adams consoles Altaira, his new Eve:

> ADAMS: About a million years from now, the human race will have crawled up to where the Krel stood in their great moment of triumph and tragedy; your father's name will shine again, like a beacon in the galaxy . . . it's true, it will remind us that we are, after all, not gods!

In supernatural cinema, these lines—"There are secrets better for man not to know!"—are usually spoken by an elder scientist surveying the havoc left by the deceased monster. Reminiscent of my old mentor who warned me away from the big stink of psychoanalysis, this venerable antique stands appropriately humbled before the inscrutable turnings of the universe, in contradistinction to his presumptuous younger colleague who has either been killed by his creation or shot down in his Id-disguise to reemerge as his better self after death, like Dr. Jekyll, or Dr. Collins in *The Invisible Man*. But whether the setting be gothic or galactic, the "secrets of nature" pursued by the mad doctor to his inevitable ruin are often metaphors for the turbulent emotions locked within the secret recesses of the troubled heart. . . .

Where Do Monsters Come from, Daddy?

At another level, the mysteries of life violated by the mad doctor to his peril are also emblematic of secrets denied us in the Eden of the past, knowledge forbidden by virtue of the child's necessary exclusion from the confusing affairs of adults, and its limited ability to grasp the real facts of life. Psychoanalysis has shown that the youngster trying to fathom these mysteries often has to contend with fantasies fully as frightening as the hazards that assailed Baron Henry Frankenstein—"a man of science who sought to create a man after his own image, without reckoning upon God!"

In 1908, little more than a generation before these words were spoken as prologue to Universal's treatment of Mary Shelley's novel, Freud wrote a ground-breaking treatise on the sexual theories of children. Simply to assert that a child had any interest in sex at all was shocking enough at the time. But Freud added insult—and incest—to injury, by asserting that the child's curiosity about sexual matters was intense and ubiquitous. By watching animals in strange and frenetic couplings, by seeing alarming changes in the mother's body, followed by the unwelcome arrival of squalling siblings, by hearing the half-digested shreds of adult gossip, tales told out of school by friends, strange thumps and groans from the parental bed chamber, perhaps even by getting a peek at Mom and Dad doing an imitation of the doggies in the street, the child gropes its way to find its origins; from this tangled web of exciting, perplexing stimuli, children weave a number of explanations about the beginning of life that are absolutely plausible to them, even though they seem completely absurd to grown-ups.

Sexual fables about the stork and other heavenly delivery services only add to the child's confusion. But even after being enlightened in the most progressive fashion, kids go on keeping a curious set of double entry mental books about sex. Split off from consciousness, these private fantasies may persist into adulthood, and often form the core of neurosis.

The toddler does not easily distinguish between the genders. Little boys really do believe that girls have penises somewhere (a three-year-old son of a colleague reassures his playmate that her "wiener" will get as big as his if she stands up to pee!). *Mutatis mutandis,* the child is convinced that men should be just as capable of having babies as women.

How does the baby get inside the mother to begin with? And, once in, how does it get out? According to the "oral" theory, insemination may occur from a kiss, or by eating a magical substance which is implanted in the stomach. It then seems eminently feasible for the infant, like feces, to pass into the world out of the mother's rectum!

As I have previously indicated, many youngsters harbor a highly sadistic concept of sexuality. Witnessing parental intercourse—especially the coupling of parents who fight like animals during the day, may foster the belief that the deepest expression of love is, in fact, but another, obscure and terrifying species of combat, and that the product of this awful struggle is born by violent and bloody sundering. Experiences such as the discovery of menstrual blood upon the parental sheets may confirm the child's sadistic theory of sex, and may lead to profound sexual inhibition. A little boy, for instance, who fears from what he has misinterpreted of the Primal Scene that he will be castrated during sexual intercourse can go on as an adult to develop shyness with women, potency disturbances or even a homosexual adaptation.

Doctors figure prominently in the sexual investigations of childhood: the doctor is allowed to look unpunished at naked people, is socially sanctioned to seek out the hidden truths of the body and is implicated in the enigmatic process of birth. Children frequently satisfy their sexual curiosity, while simultaneously assuaging their anxiety about venturing into forbidden territory, by playing at doctor-and-nurse. Not surprisingly, the doctor is an old favorite on the pornographic scene—handsome intern to nubile patient: "I'm afraid, Miss Fahrenheit, that your condition calls for deeper probing, heh heh!!" Whereupon he casts off professional decorum, stethoscope and socks, takes up his sturdy member and acts out the infantile cravings of the furtive masturbators in the audience!

The mad doctor of weird cinema is a no less significant projection of the childhood wish to unravel the riddle of procreation. The celluloid Baron Henry Frankenstein emerges as a one-man, do-it-yourself, gothic Masters and Johnson team with a dash of Dr. Spock, desperately striving to break through his formidable sexual hang-ups. The *mise-en-scène* of the Frankenstein films is late Victorian, the atmosphere heavy with repression, the acting pure fustian. Colin Clive's hysterical, slightly fey Baron could easily have been one of the impotent aristocrats Freud analyzed at the turn of the century, with a family background that usually included an insensitive, minimizing and autocratic father (as he indeed appears in *Frankenstein*), a beloved but distant mother, and a puritanical nanny who tyrannized her little charge with obsessional constraints, alienating him thoroughly from his body, burdening him with meaningless shame and creating an engrained horror of physical contact with women.

"The very day he announced our engagement," says Frankenstein's fiancée Elizabeth, "he told me he was on the verge of a discovery so terrific that he doubted his sanity. . . ." It is no coincidence that just before tying the knot, the emotionally disturbed Baron forsakes his lovely intended for the safety of his mountain laboratory, to conduct the ghastly research whose real purpose, in psychoanalytic terms, is the resolution of his sexual ignorance and angst.

When Elizabeth invades his sanctum with Dr. Waldman, Frankenstein's teacher and standard paternalistic mentor, a distraught Baron Henry protests: "You must leave me alone! Oh, ken't you see, I mustn't be disturbed, you'll ruin everything!!" The film never clarifies why Henry is so insistent on his isolation, and why Elizabeth's presence in particular will "ruin everything." However, the trained eye discerns his phobic attitude towards women, and a morbid shame lurking beneath the Baron's crazy pride in his singular accomplishment.

His lonely investigation in the tower is, in fact, a *masturbatory* metaphor. While a real, live girl waits below, hungry for him, the Baron persists in jerking around with his equipment, wasting his seed in a ghoulish, extra-uterine artificial insemination. Later in the film, Waldman admonishes Henry sententiously, "You're young, my friend, only Evil can come of it, your health will be ruined!"—a familiar warning of our forefathers about the dire consequences of self-abuse, the "solitary vice" that supposedly leads to blindness, degeneracy or psychosis!

The Baron bridles at the suggestion that he is losing his wits. (Conventionally, mad doctors from Dr. F. to Dr. No particularly resent the accusation of madness.) He boasts competitively to Waldman:

> HENRY: Ay learned a great deal from you at the university, about the violet ray, the ultraviolet ray, which you said was the highest color in the spectrum. You were wrong! (*he sure was—even back then, infrared was the highest color in the spectrum!*) Ay have discovered thee great ray thet first brawt life into thee world—now ay am going to turn thet ray, on thet body, and endow it with life!
> WALDMAN: And you really believe you can bring life to the dead?
> HENRY: Thet body is not dead. It has never lived! Ay created it! Ay made it! With my own hands, from the bodies ay took from graves, from the gallows, anywhere!!

He activates a gallery of phallic machinery, bulbous rheostats, jiggling dials, crackling Jacob's ladders, adding the zap of infernal electricity to the howl of the storm. The table with the inanimate monster pierces the open skylight, to be bombarded by bolts of lighting. The tumult dies away, the table descends. We see the monster's hand in close-up—trembling. "It's alive, *Oh it's alive!!!*" shrieks Henry like a delighted child. The sequence is an eery simulacrum of tumescence, penetration, orgasm, detumescence and birth; it realizes a complex system of infantile sadistic fantasies, vividly evoking the embalming room and the delivery room, fusing unforgettably imagery of creation and chaos, Eros and Thanatos!

Frankenstein ends with the Baron still unwed, critically injured by the monster, who in turn apparently has been incinerated by the enraged townspeople. *Bride of Frankenstein,* which I account far more successful than its predecessor, resurrects both the monster and his creator's struggle with nuptial procrastination. This time the convalescent Baron is kept from his wedding through no fault of his own—but by now we well recognize that the external forces that compel the destiny of the movie hero are often contrivances rationalizing his neurotic motivation.

Now, "fate" knocks at Henry's door in the person of Dr. Ernst Praetorius, a piquantly wicked old gaffer complete with opera cape and rrrrrolled r's, who has befriended the escaped monster and proposes to play Mephistopheles to Frankenstein's unwilling Faust:

> PRAETORIUS: After twenty years of secret scientific research and countless failures, I have also created life . . . as we say—in God's own image. . . . Science, like love, has her little surprises!

He unveils six bottled animalcula; one is a lecherous little king like Henry VIII, who promptly jumps out of his jar and bangs away goatishly at the flask containing his consort until Praetorius re-corks him. Even the little gilded fleas go to it!

> FRANKENSTEIN (*dismayed*): But this isn't science—it's more like black magic!
> PRAETORIUS: You think I'm mad! [*sic*] Perhaps I am . . . while you were digging in your graves, piecing together dead tissues . . . I . . . went for my material to the source of life . . . I grew my creatures . . . like cultures . . . as nature does . . . from seeds . . . but still, you did achieve results that I have missed . . . now think . . . what a world-astounding collaboration, you and I together . . . leave the charnelhouse and follow the lead of nature, or God, if you like your Bible stories—Male and Female created he them!
> FRANKENSTEIN (*agitated*): I daren't! I daren't even think of such a thing!
> PRAETORIUS: Our mad dream is only *half* realized. Now, together, we will create his mate!
> FRANKENSTEIN: You mean—
> PRAETORIUS: Yes (*his voice a lascivious purr*)—a woman . . . that should be *really* interesting!

Scale down the highfalutin rhetoric, and Frankenstein and Praetorius become little boys comparing sexual fairy tales. Praetorius belongs to the "Mommy grew you in her stomach out of seeds" Burpee school, while Frankenstein's experiments, as I have suggested, hearken back to the imaginary battle in the bedroom, the blood and thunder of the Primal Scene, the belief that life springs from pain and violence.

One also discerns in their colloquy the childhood denial of gender difference and more than a hint of Frankenstein's latent homosexuality. The inveterate bachelor Praetorius woos Henry away from Elizabeth into an unholy alliance that will inseminate a new race of "gods and monsters" without feminine participation. On the face of it, Henry is unwilling—"I'll have no more of this hell-spawn, as soon as I'm well, I'm to be married!"—and must be extorted into complicity when Praetorius orders the monster to kidnap Elizabeth on her wedding day and promises to return her once the artificial Bride of Frankenstein has been cut to fit.

But Praetorius is the device by which the film defuses Frankenstein's internal conflict between his desire for Elizabeth and normality, and the purulent inclinations of his unconscious. In real life, the Baron would doubtless have been equally torn between a yen for respectability and a predilection for the perverse, possibly the wilder reaches of discipline-and-bondage, judging from his strapped-down laboratory playmates, or even necrophilia! Praetorius' blackmail makes it safe for Henry to play doctor again, and he throws himself back into the grim work with barely concealed enthusiasm, legitimately motivated, of course, by his wish to have Elizabeth back.

The synthetic bride receives a heart transplant, freshly torn from a peasant girl's bosom. Her murder, ordered by Praetorius and conveniently overlooked by Frankenstein, attests to the mad doctors' fear and anger towards women. Their unpromising vision of womankind is underscored at the denouement, after the Bride's animation in a scene that, if anything, outrivals her intended's birth in laboratory and heavenly pyrotechnics as well as overblown rhetoric. In Elsa Lanchester's mordant pantomime, she is a repellantly beautiful Nefertitian giantess, with mutant streaked hair and shoulders that would do credit to Bronko Nagurski.

When the monster tries to woo her—his clumsy tenderness is both ludicrous and heartbreaking—she thrusts him away with an earsplitting scream. She is disgusted by the sight of him—*his maker's child and adolescent selves*—and her rejection vindicates his conviction of his utter worthlessness—"She hate me! Like others!" Better to return to blessed nothingness, anesthetized eternally against this bitter humiliation. Typically, the death before which we tremble seems like sweet balm to the movie monster, for whom the inability to die is the greatest horror of all, and a life alienated from the common comfort of ordinary men appears as an eternal damnation, a proposition the vampire film has repeatedly articulated. Elizabeth bursts into the laboratory:

> FRANKENSTEIN: Get beck! *Get beck!!*
> ELIZABETH: I won't, unless you come!
> FRANKENSTEIN: I ken't leave them, I ken't!

Seeing his master poised irresolutely between the living and the dead, the healthy and the perverse, the monster cries out in an indescribably heartrending groan: "Yes, *go!*" Then, to Praetorius, he snarls: "You stay! We belong dead!! *Argggghhhh!!!*"

As Elizabeth and Henry rush to safety, the Bride hisses revoltingly, and her husband never-to-be pulls a lever, detonating the mountain in a fitting substitute for the climax of his permanently postponed wedding night. Frankenstein has been exorcised of the hurtful fantasies of childhood; renouncing his infernal science, he descends from his tower to join the living and find joy in the arms of his wife. But the dark legacy of his legend has outlived the movie's happy ending. The monster resisted facile attempts to lay him to rest. He and the dilemma of his creator have haunted the popular imagination through numerous skillful or maladroit re-editions, indicating the depth of curiosity about our uncertain beginnings and traumatic ends!

The Sleep of Reason—II

Drowning the Ceremony of Innocence—
Or, How Not to Raise a Monster

I have speculated that the Frankenstein monster is a reincarnation of his makers' traumatized and rejected younger selves. The universal appeal of the monster movie may, at least in part, be traced to our fascination with the childlike innocence of these fearsome creatures, to the intriguing dialectic between the insensate savagery of the monster, and the sensibility of the abused and misunderstood youngster within its bosom. From this perspective, the Frankenstein legend becomes a study in warped pedagogy: the monster is a typical battered child who manages to survive by identifying with his oppressors, dishing out wholesale the ill treatment served up to him first by laboratory "parents" and then by society.

The scourges wrought upon the naive, guiltless monster invite comparison with the lacerations inflicted upon the bodies and spirits of legions of children at home or in school. Perhaps we may learn from the monster mythos something of the evolution of human monsters, how the life-affirming nature of the child can be corrupted, its healthier courses turned awry by unfeeling parent or callous institution playing the role of Frankenstein. And perhaps the monster movie is trying to teach us about the monstrous treatment we have accorded the "different" ones in our midst, the retarded, deformed or autistic children whom St. Augustine would surely have cherished as part of God's inscrutable plan.

I have inferred that, although the locale of the Frankenstein pictures is Ruritanian, the moral climate is obviously Victorian. Conceive, then, of Baron Henry Frankenstein as a sensitive, upper-class English lad of the period, genteelly abandoned in infancy, consigned to the dubious ministrations of nutty or unfeeling servants, next put out at a still tender age to the sadistic bullyragging and pederastic persecutions of boarding school. Grown through tormented adolescence into imperfect manhood, Frankenstein returns home to cast a man in his image, his deprived, battered image!

After his animation, the monster first enters the scene as a child of darkness, groping towards enlightenment. Frankenstein, flushed with absurd pride like any new father, unveils his "son": the monster shuffles into the room like an overgrown toddler taking his first halting steps, his shadow looming over him on the wall. Underneath a beetling brow, Boris Karloff's remarkably sensitive features are smoothed out into a blank mask, devoid of expression, awaiting the imprinting of experience. Frankenstein pulls open an aperture in the roof. As the light pours down, the monster's face comes alive with an intimation of dawning intelligence, and he stretches out scarred hands to the unknown possibility of that benevolent illumination. Waldman persuades Frankenstein to draw the skylight shut, and as the darkness falls, the monster whimpers wordlessly, beseeching Frankenstein with small, piteous gestures of those eloquent hands to return him to the brightness of reason—but to no avail.

The hunchbacked servant, Fritz, rushes in with a torch—mad doctors regularly seem to get their hired help straight off the orthopedic wards—and the monster panics, lashes out at the flame. Frighten a child, and its fear quickly gives way to tantrum behavior, since rage speaks in the active voice, and is infinitely preferable to the passive endurance of harm. Console the child, interpret the unreality of its fear, and the tantrum will pass. Instead of being calmed, protected from the excesses of his unmodulated aggression, the monster is attacked and wrestled to the ground. His fear and rage escalate to near dementia, and he is next discovered manacled to a dungeon wall, while Fritz beats him with a whip (Fritz despises the monster on sight, doubtless because he reflects back Fritz's misshapenness).

Frankenstein cannot confront this barely human wreckage, nor correct the emotional trauma he has permitted. He snatches the whip from Fritz, but then runs away in a paroxysm of guilt, abandoning his charge much the way he himself, as I have speculated, was deeded over to the sadistic whims of nanny and lackey. Fritz takes up the torch, goads the monster mercilessly until, provoked beyond endurance, he breaks his chains and strangles the hunchback off-camera. Frankenstein and Waldman knock him out with a hypodermic, whereupon Frankenstein abandons him again, this time to Waldman, who considers the monster as nothing more than a conglomeration of spare parts, brutish flesh incapable of human feeling.

Waldman proposes to vivisect the monster—from the creature's viewpoint, Frankenstein's teacher is simply a different Fritz, attacking him with scalpel rather than fire or lash. He strangles the professor and wanders out into a world that is more inimical, if possible, than the laboratory into which he was "born." In a heartrending scene which has been nearly edited out of existence in most showings, the lost monster comes upon a little girl by a brook. Ivan Butler has remarked upon the director's astuteness in choosing an ugly little girl, underscoring the affinity between a rejected child and the monster—she has been left alone by her father, he is "too busy" to play with her (sic!). Eager for a friend, she hands the monster a flower. He is pathetically grateful in his turn for this first measure of friendship ever granted him.

He smells the flower with a beatific smile, joins her in flinging the blossoms into the brook, and when there are no more left he hurls her into the water, expecting that she, too, will float. When she drowns, he is sick with despair. The villagers proceed to hunt him down like a pack of crazed dogs; flushed with righteous indignation, unable or unwilling to comprehend the latent humanity of the wretched outcast, it is they who seem more beastly than their quarry. The complex vision of the monster's scapegoating reached strangely Christlike proportions in *Bride of Frankenstein:* in a scene reminiscent of a Brueghel Golgotha, the captured creature is trussed to a log, raised high above the crowd, and thrown down into a haycart while the villagers mock and revile him.

Bride of Frankenstein demonstrates that the monster can be reachable and teachable as a disturbed, delinquent child, given a parental substitute who is not put off by the youngster's bizarre facade or aggressive behavior. After being shot by hunters when he tried to befriend a shepherdess, and burnt by gypsies when he begged for meat, the monster is drawn to the sound of a blind hermit playing his violin in his mountain hut. The hermit takes him in, and like a good therapist is supportive, but not unnecessarily intrusive into his patient's life space, lest the monster, having only known harm from mankind, take flight again:

> HERMIT: I think you are a stranger to me . . . come in, my poor friend . . . no one will harm you here. If you're in trouble, perhaps I can help you, but you need not tell me about it if you do not want to!

After feeding the monster and binding up his wounds, the hermit prays—"Out of the silence of the night, thou hast brought two of thy lonely children (!) together, sent me a friend to be a light to mine eyes, and a comfort in time of trouble!"—and the creature weeps affectingly. The hermit intuitively grasps the monster's loneliness, and under his gentle tutelage he learns enough of the rudiments of speech to articulate his basic need: "Alone—bad, friend—*good!!*" The monster's fear of fire is just being healed—a definitive step towards adequate socialization that Frankenstein was unwilling or unable to promote—when the hunters stumble upon the hut and attack the creature anew:

> HERMIT: What are you doing? This is my friend!
> HUNTER: Friend? This is the fiend that's been murdering half the countryside! Good heavens, man, can't you see?

Ironically, like Waldman and the villagers, it is he who is blind, while the hermit, Tiresias-like, has glimpsed the goodness in the monster's heart. In the ensuing struggle, the hut catches fire, the hunters hustle the hermit outside, the monster contends with his pyrophobia as well as the flames to attempt the rescue of his lost companion. He staggers away howling "Friend, *friend!!*" Shortly thereafter, he meets the wily Praetorius, who lures him into kidnap, murder and extortion with the promise of friendship and the manufacture of the Bride. Many a young delinquent, rejected by his parents and scorned by society, has fallen under the influence of a similar older "protector," who scoffs at morality—"Look where bein' good gotcha, Sonny!"—and, Fagin-like, encourages deviant behavior. The sole fault of the monster is his childlike ignorance that this evil can exist, that a man like Praetorius can so misuse the trust of his fellow men!

For me, there will always be one scarifying scene that irrevocably identifies the monster with an abused child, also drawn from *Bride of Frankenstein:* it is of the creature penned up in the town prison, shackled into a strange throne so that he is totally helpless, even his neck immobilized by an iron collar. I recall the case of Daniel Paul Schreber, an eminent nineteenth century jurist who became psychotic at the height of his career, and related his history in *Memoirs of My Nervous Illness,* the basis for Freud's classic monograph on paranoia.

Schreber harbored the delusion that God, to test his spirit, had performed multiple indignities upon his person, forcing him—amongst countless other humiliations—to assume distorted positions for hours on end. Schreber believed the Almighty's secret purpose was to change him into a woman and propagate a new race. Freud ascribed Schreber's psychosis principally to a homosexual fixation upon his father (which doubtless existed), but had next to nothing to say about the father himself.

In *Soul Murder,* Dr. Morton Schatzman's thoroughly chilling investigation of Schreber's family, one finds that the father, Daniel Gottlieb Moritz Schreber, was an eminent physician who devised a rigorous pedagogy to instill unquestioning obedience first to parents, then to every subsequent figure of authority. Proper posture was a keystone of Schreber's system. He invented a variety of fiendish devices to maintain a child's "correct" physical position—even while asleep—that put the instruments of the Inquisition to shame. Ever an ardent practicer of his own preachings, the mad doctor strapped his children into his infernal braces well into their adolescence, and three of them obliged him by developing into frightened souls hovering on the brink of insanity. (An older brother killed himself; a younger sister never married and turned into a chronic recluse.) It is a testament to Schreber's inherent vitality that he was able to survive the torments of childhood and even prosper for fifty years before his reason fled, leaving in its wake the delusional edifice with a hideous truth at core: the God who forced Daniel Paul Schreber to submit to outrageous debasement and the final deprivation of his manhood, was unmistakably cast in the image of the abominable pedagogue.

Yet Schreber the son was adjudged a hopeless lunatic, while the mad and bad father, that monster of self-righteousness, that Frankenstein unto his children, was hailed for decades as a man of probity and genius, an unswerving advocate of wholesome family life, a prophet of Teutonic supremacy, and legions of the youngsters raised under the perverse rules and hellish bondage of his method would goose step like zombies into annihilation and atrocity during two successive world wars!

Filmmakers have shied away from depicting children as monsters, possibly fearing that audiences would be repelled by the denial of childhood's sanctity and innocence. Karen, the preadolescent murderess of *The Bad Seed,* is a baleful psychopath beyond understanding or compassion, so that when she is struck down by lightning, it is as if God had legitimately expunged an alien moral blight. The children of *Village of the Damned,* spawned by extraterrestrial beings upon the women of an English town, telepathically compel those who oppose them to suicide. Their awesome intellectual gifts and obvious low regard for mankind obviate the suggestion of childish vulnerability, so that when the scientist who mistakenly tried to humanize them blows them and himself to bits, their deaths again excite neither empathy nor pity, a failure that to my mind mars an otherwise admirable picture.

To the best of my knowledge there is only one film that literally rather than figuratively explores the theme of the monster as damaged and damaging child. *It's Alive!* (1974) opens out of a TV sitcom; in a comfortable suburban home, wife goes into midnight labor; nervously wisecracking father drives her to the hospital, then joins other expectant types, chewing his nails, until an intern staggers out of the delivery room with his throat slashed from ear to ear, decisively finishing the comedy.

The father races into the delivery room, to find doctors and nurses expiring in their own blood, his wife still in the stirrups with the umbilical cord cut and the baby gone through a hole in the skylight. It turns out that Junior is a murderous mutation. While the infantile Jack the Ripper toddles through the terrorized city chewing on maidens and milkmen, the beleaguered dad, harassed by the press, fired by his boss, goes so far in renouncing paternity as to shoot the baby when it returns home to be fed surreptitiously by the mother who never stopped loving it. (Pediatricians say that the *father* of the dwarfed or deformed child often has the greatest problem in accepting it, because he feels the afflicted infant is a slur on his manhood!)

The police and the father hunt the wounded mutation through the city sewers, those same Los Angeles sewers colonized by the giant ants in *Them!* Father finds his child, huddled in a corner, bleeding and mewing like a hurt kitten. He raises his rifle, then in a poignant turnabout I shall not easily forget, breaks down in tears and comforts the tiny monster. Like Frankenstein's ''child,'' this tragic misfit has killed through no moral failure: this time, the monster's homicidal tendencies are ascribed to the greed of a society that has placed material gain above ecological sanity. The trapped father finally flings the baby at the drug company executive who had sought to conceal that the monster's mother had taken his firm's product, whereupon the police gun down both the child and its corporate Frankenstein!

The Beast in the Boudoir—
Or, You Can't Marry That Girl,
You're a Gorilla!

Having disposed of the monster as child, it is logical next to comtemplate him as a teenager. But first, an apology and explanation to women's liberationists: the reader will note that I have dealt almost exclusively with the psychosexual problems of the male monster. There have been only a handful of memorable female aberrations—one principally remembers the heroines of *Cat People, Dracula's Daughter,*

Attack of the Fifty Foot Woman and, of course *Bride of Frankenstein* (although she makes only a cameo appearance). Perhaps the moviemen believe that public taste would be offended equally by lady as by childish monsters, or chauvinistically hold the purity and innocence of women sacrosanct. Perhaps female producers and directors—and there are still precious few of either—would be more in touch with the unique possibilities for the monstrousness of their sex, more willing or able to offer us newer, better women weirdos. In most female monster movies to date, men have portrayed what *they* found fearsome in women (like the "Fifty Foot Woman," the archetype of the castrating bitch, who has stomped through the dreams of my impotent moviemaniacs) which may be a far cry from what women would find loathsome or pitiable in themselves.

I have previously discussed Freudian theory on the male Oedipus complex and its fate: Freud felt that the uproar of the Oedipal state subsides when the boy can bring himself to renounce sexual designs upon his mother and, instead of competing with his father, identifies with him, secure in the knowledge that he, too, will find in his maturity a gal just like the gal who married dear old dad. During the *latency stage,* approximately age six through ten, the boy feels at relative peace emotionally, and uses this respite to acquire social and intellectual skills in the company of his buddies, reasonably free from the sensual itch. Throughout latency, if they are thought of at all, girls are regarded with a combination of monumental disinterest and active dislike. But as the sap rises, the pubescent boy undergoes a disquieting metamorphosis, radically stretching his dimensions and developing secondary sexual characteristics. These changes threaten the cornerstone of emotional stability—the image of one's body—and can be experienced with as much distress as if they were inflicted upon the adolescent by an inimical outside force, rather than occurring naturally.

Alarmed by his burgeoning biology, exhilarated and disequilibrated by his nascent strength, the adolescent may verge on panic like Dr. Jekyll helpless before the appearance of Hyde, or may tremble like the Wolf Man at the rising of the moon. Anxiety is sharpened by the return of repressed fantasies at least partly derived from childish sexual theories (see above) that often possess disturbingly perverse or sadistic components, so that the teenager's unconscious can come to resemble an ill-contained cesspool to him. The Oedipus complex is resurrected, but this time in a mature physique. Two centuries prior to Freud, the French philosopher Diderot asserted in his essay, *Rameau's Nephew:*

> "If the little brute were left to himself and kept in his native ignorance, combining the undeveloped mind of a child in the cradle with the violent passions of a man of thirty, he would wring his father's neck and sleep with his mother."

This is an accurate description of the adolescent's central fear: awed by his newfound aggressive capabilities, yet repelled by his incestuous feelings for his mother, he dreads the loss of his father's guidance, and an even far heavier retribution if the secret aim of his sexuality is discovered and the deadly competition of nursery days is rejoined.

Propelled by his riotous hormones, the adolescent commences to work through his lurid fantasy life, transferring his yen for Mom to real, live girls—those same scary enigmas he has shunned like lepers throughout the comfortable latency years. As he tries to puzzle out the riddle of his mother's sexuality, he is torn between lofty idealization and lascivious degradation of women (*viz.* the "Madonna-Whore syndrome"). In his daydreams, he is a chivalrous, chaste rescuer of maidens in distress (from villains who are both representations of his "animal" nature and of the Oedipal rival), or a super-stud plowing through acres of obligingly spread thighs, or, closer to the truth, an inept Jerry Lewis-type *klutz* forever banging his nose into his nonexistent girl friend's eye. He looks into the mirror, hoping to see Lothario or Lochinvar, Paul Newman or Paul McCartney. Instead, staring back at him is a pimply half-formed apparition as appalling as the Creature from the Black Lagoon.

We will not, therefore, be surprised to find the dilemmas of puberty cunningly reinvented in weird cinema (always tremendously popular, by the way, with adolescents) and the monster the embodiment of the adolescent Oedipal intruder hell-bent on ripping Mother untimely away from Dad. It is, for instance, a commonplace for the monster to carry off the luscious scantily clad woman who just happens to be the girl friend of the handsome hero, and the daughter (or chief assistant) of a famous elderly scientist. The monster (teenager) wants girl friend (Mother) of hero (Father) all to himself, but, intriguingly, at another level, the hero disavows *his* Oedipal itch for rapine and other monkey-shines by slaying the "evil" creature and returning the heroine in good order to her real or disguised dad before wedding her prim and proper.

Not infrequently, the heroine will be snatched out of her bedroom by the monster. Dracula and the Frankenstein creation were among the first of these Oedipal beasts in the boudoir, and were followed by a veritable army of deformed nocturnal Casanovas. Note that Franken-stein's "son" removes his "father's" wife-to-be from the wedding chamber until the Baron can resolve Junior's Oedipal fix by furnishing him with a ready-made bride of his own so he can join the grown-ups. Karloff even looked like a caricature of an adolescent bursting out of his clothes; when he clomps away with Valerie Hobson tossed over his shoulder, screaming like a banshee or fainted dead out, I'm reminded of Sid Caesar's uproarious pantomime of a youngster at his first prom, staggering across the floor in an elephantine jitterbug, hurling an imaginary girl friend through the air like a rag doll.

What the monster would do with the girl if he had a chance to keep her is anyone's guess, including his own, given the obscure nature of his desires and his genital apparatus, accurately reflecting the adolescent's uncertainty about the mechanics of sex and the ambivalence of his feelings towards his love object. But happily for the howling heroine, our monster never gets the opportunity to penetrate the sexual murk, for hardly does he have a chance to bed down the heroine in cave or tomb when the Oedipal avengers, square-jawed hero, scientist father, backed up by a Superego horde of cops, National Guard or Air Force, demolish the creature and restore the heroine to her human lover.

Just as there have been few actual child monsters, adolescents as monsters are in equally short supply throughout weird cinema. In *I Was a Teen-Age Werewolf* (American-International—1957) a mad school psychiatrist blows the lid off the Id of a troubled predelinquent by giving him regression serum to put him in touch with his primitive aggressive instincts. Predictably, the cure is worse than the disease; psychopathy yields to lycanthropy with the usual dire consequences, and the moral of the tale seems to be—stay away from the shrink if you've got hang-ups, you'll end up wolf-meat!

To this day we have never had a more impressive or poignant conceptualization of the monster as star-crossed adolescent lover than RKO's 1933 epic, *King Kong*. The mighty ape, besides being a brobdignagian Romeo, also embodies Natural Man seeking his lost freedom in the midst of urban blight and economic oppression. *Kong* opens in New York of the Depression. The people cry out for bread and circuses. Bread lines there are, aplenty, and for circuses, the dime escape of Hollywood. Carl Denham, a "bring 'em back alive!" entrepreneur is about to embark on his latest jungle spectacular, a production so shrouded in secrecy even the trusted captain and thickheaded first mate, Jack Driscoll, have not been told the destination.

But the expedition cannot sail until Denham nails down an ingenue. The director is no more sanguine than his crew about bringing a woman along, for none of his other films ever needed a heroine:

> DENHAM: Isn't there any romance or adventure in the world without having a flapper in it? . . . I go out and sweat blood to make a swell picture, and then the critics and exhibitors all say, (*mockingly*) if this picture had a love interest, it would gross twice as much—all right, the public wants a girl, this time I'm goin' to give 'em what they want . . . I'm goin' out to get a girl . . . even if I have to *marry* one!!

—a fate presumably worse than death. His threat becomes more understandable if we look at Denham and his crew as a gang of preadolescent boys who were doing OK until the durned girls had to barge in and spoil everything (*viz.* Rick Blaine's decision in *Casablanca* to renounce the untrustworthy Ilsa Laszlo in favor of the masculine solidarity of the battlefield).

Denham ventures into the city's lower depths and discovers his heroine, Anne Darrow, near a mission for destitute women. She's just been caught snitching an apple, so Denham's first business with her is a rescue operation. He pays off the irate grocer, treats her at a diner to "sinkers" and coffee, and proposes to lift her from tap city obscurity to stellar heights. Befitting the love object of the adolescent, Anne is eminently rescuable, down on her luck, a diamond on a dustheap, with her freshness just slightly tarnished by the effluvium of a fallen woman.

Anne hesitates a second over Denham's offer, thinking he means to make her his mistress, and the script delicately hints that she would have been willing to have him as her Sugar Daddy! But, by the conventions of the "conscious" movie, it's necessary that the shining myth of Anne's purity be cherished, consistent with the "madonna" side of the adolescent's ambivalent attitude towards feminine sexuality. So with gruff chivalry, Denham swears—"You've got me wrong, I'm on the level . . . *no* funny business, just trust me and keep your chin up!"

One believes him, for there is no passion in the man for anything but flying in the teeth of danger to display to the gawking public his mindless courage. A classic counterphobic and probably a closet homosexual to boot, Denham regards woman as a weak but potentially dangerous vessel, a perennial Eve out to rob a man of his precious bodily fluids. He is comfortable with her as long as she can be treated either as a desexualized buddy or a mere block of talent to be shoved dumbly around in front of his camera.

The brawny first mate, Driscoll, is similarly leery of Anne's charm; the big lug gets their relationship off to a romantic start by accidentally slugging her, the tried and true Hollywood formula—Boy Meets Girl, Boy Hits Girl—grounded on the adolescent assumption that initial enmity between the sexes is a sure sign of true love. Jack then delivers himself of sentiments that one would expect either from a gorilla or an unsocialized teenager:

> ANNE: I guess you don't think much of women on ship.
> JACK: Naw—they're a nuisance . . . you're all right . . . but women can't help bein' a bother, just made that way, I guess. . . .

In a scene filled with suggestions of what is to come, Denham finds Anne and Jack on deck. Anne is fondling a tiny monkey. "Beauty and the Beast, eh?" says Denham sardonically. Jack, already in thrall to Anne's beauty, is *identified* with her plaything, a miniaturized Kong!

> DENHAM (*taking Jack aside*): I've got enough troubles without a love affair to complicate things.
> JACK: Love affair?—You think I'm goin' to fall for anyone?
> DENHAM (*cynically*): Pretty tough guy!—but if Beauty gets ya— that's the idea of my picture—the Beast was a tough guy, too. He

could lick the world, but when he saw Beauty, she got him . . . he
went soft, he forgot his wisdom, and the little fellows licked him
. . . think it over, Jack!

Denham resents Beauty's intrusions into his virile art, and has objectified his mistrust of woman into a cautionary fascist fable of the
decline and fall of Nietzschean *Übermensch* at the hands of the me-
diocre mob, his might sapped by mawkish sentiment. Denham takes
Driscoll's crush on Anne as a personal threat, a ruinous acting out of
his script in advance. The misogyny of the preadolescent boy is based
on his fear of being unmanned by his dependency upon his mother.
There is much of the preadolescent in Denham's philosophy, with its
implicit misogyny, its ruthless justification for assumption of power by
the strong over the "little guys." "Thou goest to thy woman,"
Nietzsche is reputed to have said—"Take thy whip!" Some wag remarked that had that impotent neurotic ever taken up his whip, the
woman would have beaten him over the head with it! One intuits an
analogous impotence in Denham, concealed beneath his *macho* bra-
vado.

As they sail on to the mysterious island Denham says contains an
ancient wonder "that no white man has ever seen," the producer
shoots preliminary rushes of Anne shrieking into the wind, staging in
his mind's eye the reprisal for her disturbing allure:

> DENHAM: You're amazed, you can't believe it . . . it's horrible,
> Anne, but you can't look away . . . there's no chance, no escape
> . . . but perhaps it will be better if you can scream . . . scream,
> Ann, scream for your life!!

The ship docks in a foggy cove cribbed from Gustave Doré to the accompaniment of the muffled throb of drums and distant chanting:
"*Annikanna Annikanna Kongkong!!!*" In the morning, Denham's
party surprises a village of Hollywood blackamoors capering in sty-
lized boogie-woogie before a colossal wooden gate, while the women
deck out a nubile maiden in the local wedding regalia—shells and
feathers. "Aw, they're up to some of their heathen tricks," growls
Driscoll. "*Ana saba Kong!!*" shouts the native chief angrily, and halts
the festivities. The captain translates that "the girl there is the bride of
Kong . . . the ceremony is spoiled because we've seen it!"

The chief spies Anne and offers to buy the "golden woman" on the spot as a gift for Kong, at the going exchange rate of six native girls for one white woman ("Yeah," interjects Driscoll, that irrepressible honky, "Blondes *are* scarce around here!"). When the chief gets turned down, the natives grow restless, and the company retreats back to the ship, Denham leading the way with his hands thrust into his pockets, whistling ostentatiously in a calculated display of adolescent daring.

That night, Driscoll meets Anne on deck, and clumsily opens his heart:

> DRISCOLL: Don't laugh, I'm scared for ya—I'm sort of scared of ya, too. (*!*) Anne—I, er, uh . . . I guess I love you!
> ANNE: Why, Jack, I thought you hate women. . . .
> DRISCOLL: I know—but you aren't women . . . say, Anne, I don't suppose, er, I mean, well, you don't feel anything like that about me, do ya?

They clinch decorously. Driscoll, the muscle-bound red-white-and-blue hero, as chaste as a clam, stammers out his declaration of love like an amorous schoolboy, and only a few moments later, the blacks spirit Anne away to become the bride of Kong! It is integral to the racism of *King Kong* that the Negro should be portrayed as the degraded repository of the white man's forbidden impulses; indeed psychoanalysts speculate that this projection is characteristic of every ethnic and racial prejudice—it is always the other guy, the swarthy foreigner with his strange speech and natural sense of rhythm who indulges in the dirty, delicious and atrocious deeds denied us in the name of higher civilization. According to this debased view of other lands and peoples, one of "our" women must be worth six of theirs. And, although "their" men are capable of the most heinous aggressive acts, one of "our" men can still take on and whip half a dozen of "theirs" in a fair fight. I remember standing outside the RENEL theater after watching John Wayne wipe out half the Japanese empire in *Sands of Iwo Jima,* seriously debating with my friends how many Japs were equal to one Marine! Kong, then, is the epitome of the white man's daydream of the brute black, the heartless, mindless foreigner, feasting on violence and rapine. And we will discern in his persona the raw sexuality which the ingenuous racist bumpkin Driscoll has repressed, and which Anne has aroused!

Until now, the pace of the film has been leisurely: curiosity has been piqued, but there has been little to arouse anxiety. But immediately after Driscoll breaks through his inhibitions, forsakes the homosexually biased gang mentality of boyhood, Kong bursts upon the scene, the lid is blown off the Id, and one marvelous disaster after another spills across the screen, a series of splendid catastrophes ignited by Kong-Driscoll's fumbling passion, for sexuality and aggression, Eros and Thanatos, are imperfectly fused in the immature psyche of the adolescent male.

Anne's first encounter with Kong is redolent with rape imagery. The bolt of the enormous gate that towers over the village is drawn back, and the natives lash her wrists to two posts set into a massive altar (*their black hands claw at her fair white flesh in lascivious* chiaroscuro!) They leave her spread invitingly before Kong's advance, and the gate is shut, a mighty phallic bolt driven home. The chief raises his staff (*sic!*), and intones an incantation in Wilshire Boulevard Swahili that nevertheless still sends shivers down my spine. I transliterate to the best of my limited ability:

> CHIEF: *Kora kanay—Kong! Otaravey yama—KONG!! Wasaba kanamaka!! Otaravey rama—KONG!!!*

Anne screams—tentatively, in terms of her latent decibel level. The chief raises his staff again. Half-naked minions strike a huge brass gong, and then, crashing through the jungle he comes, Anne's demon lover; making straight for the altar, he leers down at her, his great eyes rolling, his thick lips peeled back in a titanic snarl—and Denham's shipboard fantasy of Anne's punishment is consummated. Her gaze is drawn inexorably upwards towards the hairy colossus—(*"You're amazed, you can't believe it . . . it's horrible but you can't look away . . . scream, Anne, scream for your life!"*)

And she does, piercingly, ad libitum, with every conceivable ruffle, flourish and furbelow a scream permits, so that in recollection it seems as if her vocalizations hereafter consist of one prolonged scream. Kong plucks her up in his paw—is it true blondes have more fun?—

and thunders back into the bush with Driscoll-and-company in hot pursuit. Anne has become a metaphor of woman swept away against her conscious will by the dark sensuality of the man-beast, and her taking by Kong is rich with associations to bacchanal and Dionysian revel.

Driscoll and Kong are two tough customers gone soft under Beauty's sway. Both will compete for Anne Darrow's hand, and Kong must lose despite his superior strength and size, as the adolescent Oedipal monster who intrudes into a human (parental) romance. But, as I have intimated, at another level Driscoll and his simian adversary are also two sides of the *same* adolescent ego. Kong, in pure culture, is Driscoll's naked ape, Driscoll's black libido, Driscoll's unconscious pubescent lust. Boy meets girl, and boy's ape is unchained to roar and ruin. Then ape meets girl, and ape undergoes a reverse transformation. Throughout the ensuing carnage, the public will see Kong only as the beast incarnate, slouching towards Manhattan. Yet with regard to Anne, Kong dwindles away into a clumsy knight errant, more interested in battling to protect his lady fair than making love to her (after all, she fits in the palm of his hand, and he has problems with the language!).

It is immediately apparent that he intends her no real harm. he abuses her once, almost by accident. In an expurgated sequence, he rips off her clothes, but contents himself merely with pawing her and sniffing at his fingers, like a teenager who won't wash his hands after a session of heavy petting, to preserve the lingering female scent. Although I admit to a certain lack of expertise in analyzing primates, I believe he really delights in her company, wants the best for her as a Jane to his Tarzan, a comfort to his lonely jungle life. In his good faith, it is inconceivable to him that she sees him only as an ugly monster, and he is, I think, confused by her incessant screaming whenever he draws near, and not a little hurt by the ingratitude that prompts her to run away every time he turns his back to defend her. In sum, King Kong has been reduced to a blown-up version of the moonstruck Driscoll, wooing Anne like a fumbling adolescent, fearful of rejection, terrified by the mysterious longings she has stirred.

Kong now proceeds to rescue Anne from one danger after another, some real, others invented by his addled brain, with the most alarming consequences to person and property. In fact, it may be said that the remainder of the film is essentially a prolonged acting out of the rescue fantasy central to the adolescent's chivalrous, asexual relationship with his idealized beloved. Of course, while Kong is engaged in shielding Anne from a bevy of prehistoric behemoths, Driscoll rushes around madly in all directions trying to save her from Kong!

Jack finds her hidden away in Kong's cliffside apartment; he throws down a vine, and as the two dangle precariously Kong reels them up. They let go, plunge into the sea—the action in this scene and elsewhere in the film has an unsettling, dreamlike quality. Distances are oddly distorted, foreshortened, or stretched. Jack and Anne surely fall no more than a score of feet, yet it seems as if they drop through the endless abyss of nightmare into the pellucid sea, to awaken upon a serene beach with Kong faded into the mists of sleep.

The respite is brief. Kong descends from his cliff to recover his lost prize—and, naturally, to rescue Anne from Jack! The native village is smashed like kindling before Kong is subdued by gas grenades. Denham's script is now, in effect, directing itself. The producer is completely unmoved by the chaos around him. Arch-colonialist and imperialist, he can only exult at the spectacle of his fortune's rising from the natives' ruin and Kong's enslavement:

> DENHAM: We came here to get a moving picture—we found something worth more than all the movies in the world . . . the whole world will pay to see this—he's always been King of his world, but we'll teach him fear! We're millionaires, boys!!!

Dissolve to Denham displaying Kong at inflated prices to a Gotham audience, manacled and collared to a cruciform restraint—the monster as Jesus, again. "He was a King and a God," declaims Denham to the rubes, "but now he comes to civilization, merely a captive—on show to satisfy your curiosity!" Denham hustles in Anne and Driscoll, the latter nearly as uncomfortable in soup and fish as Kong in his chrome steel chains, both sacrifices on Beauty's altar. "Get 'em together, boys," says Denham to the *paparazzi,* "They're going to be married tomorrow!" For every light on Broadway, there's a broken heart! The flashbulbs pop and Kong, anguished by this latest threat to his lost lady love—"Watch out, he thinks you're attacking the girl!"—bursts his bonds and embarks on another misbegotten rescue, this time in Metropolis. Shades of Frankenstein's disrupted nuptials!

Kong brings his own unique brand of urban renewal to Fun City that would set the style for hundreds of monsters yet unborn. The critic X. J. Kennedy astutely observed that Our Hero's demolition of the New York landscape may have reflected the inchoate cravings of many an oppressed city-dweller "to turn on his machines and kick hell out of them." Also, let us not forget that *King Kong* is a Depression film, that Denham's voyage was undertaken to give the impoverished masses a fantasy escape from their bitter economic plight. The American dream had soured overnight, and many, obscurely blaming their hardships on the sharp practice of the bankers and brokers of Wall Street, took an unconscious pleasure as Kong, innocent country boy at heart, wreaked revenge on the Babylon of the East!

He bashes his way out of the theater, clambers up Anne's hotel and grabs her out of her bedroom. After laying waste to the Third Avenue El ("Were you late getting home today—CBS commuter report tells you why!"), he takes her to a tryst atop the Empire State Building— with a pang of nostalgia, one notes that in 1933 the landmark building is gracefully unmarred by its TV tower. Now that Kong has "rescued" her according to his lights, the "unconscious" movie demands that she in turn be rescued from him and restored to her fiancé. Denham conceives of his most brilliant P.R. coup, summoning up the U.S. Air Force to eliminate Kong before the eyes and ears of the world. "Oh, boy, what a story!" cry the newsmen, as Kong, the quintessential victim of media exploitation, goes down before the blazing guns. He is at his most human in his final agony. Cupping Anne in his palm, he looks down tenderly, replaces her delicately on the parapet and pitches forward into the canyons of Manhattan.

Denham, untouched as usual by pity for the maimed or the dead, human or otherwise, pronounces Kong's epitaph with relish for the headlines: "It wasn't the airplanes . . . it was Beauty killed the Beast!" *King Kong* ends with the Beast laid to rest, and Jack Driscoll domesticated, off-camera. One imagines that his marriage with Anne will be as uninspired and as forgettable as his wooing of her. Speaking to the Driscoll-Kong equation from the psychoanalytic viewpoint, one concludes that Driscoll has worked through his fear and sadism towards women, passed through adolescence and forged a viable if tepid sexual adaptation. Yet the rampant vitality of Kong's fatal passion is not so easily forgotten. Denham has it that Beauty killed the Beast, that every man dies a little if he opens his heart to love.

But who really killed King Kong? Surely not Anne, but Denham himself! Out of his greed and misogyny, Denham composed his fable of Superman's undoing, then orchestrated it to his immense profit. Denham it was who brought Anne to tempt Kong on Skull Island. Denham it was who insisted on seizing Kong, the better to vaunt his schoolboy courage when he could have departed in peace. And finally, it was Denham who called out the machines to assassinate this noble animal.

Denham's public forced a woman upon him, and he exacted a callous revenge for this intrusion. If you want a woman, he has implied, then you must endure the consequences of the mischief she will surely provoke—shades of Sam Spade, Rick Blaine, Howard Hawkes, Sam Peckinpah—generations of *macho* heroes and moviemakers. Denham's closing lines reflect his inhumanity, his unregenerate preadolescent fascism. Money and fame serve only as unsatisfactory props to the damaged ego of such a base creature. For it is Denham, the real beast of *King Kong,* who has been permanently unmanned by his contempt for Beauty, while Kong's tragic love, overriding his savage deeds, affirms the inherent beauty of his fallen spirit!

XI

The Sleep of Reason—III

One leaves this world as one enters it, supremely undefended and helpless; definitive impressions of death are irrevocably sealed off from one's fellows and buried within the frail envelope of impermanent flesh. Some of the dying seem cheered at the penultimate moment by family or faith, but after that moment has passed, who can say for sure what horror of eternal solitude attends the gathering darkness, or whether a peace surpassing understanding may flood the anxious soul?

The delivery from life into death may be painful or pleasurable, or simply return us to affective ground zero, but there is little doubting by external evidence how traumatic the passage into being is for the neonate (infant). Otto Rank, one of Freud's first disciples, erected an entire psychoanalytic heresy upon the birth trauma. Like Freud, he theorized that birth could be an engram for all subsequent anxiety, but in order to be cured, Rank thought the neurotic would have to recover and abreact memories of the pain of birth.

We know now that the baby's nervous system is not sufficiently sophisticated to elaborate a language with which to frame the birth agony, or a memory bank sufficiently evolved to record it in the fashion an adult would register and remember the details of an automobile accident. Definitive insight into the infant's thinking processes is still lacking, but it seems reasonable to infer that the trauma of birth resides essentially in the neonate's helplessness before the tidal wave of new stimuli with which it is assailed and which it is unable to "process" after its nine-month sojourn in a maximally efficient support system.

What is probably imprinted in connection with birth is not a specific complex of clearly articulated images and thoughts, but a pre-conceptual experience of exceptional physiological discomfort that stems from the unprepared infant's being swamped with indiscriminate sensation. In later life, the stresses that evoke the primary stress of birth may be real or imaginary, based on actual danger or neurotic fantasy; the organism's state of preparation for this stress may be more or less adequate depending upon age, temperament, ability to cope. But it is not unlikely that *any* traumatic circumstance will inevitably capture some quality of the unguarded babe's raw response to the loss of the serenity of the womb, and its sudden exposure to the chaos of existence. Psychoanalysis infers that the mind of the adult hearkens back to its beginnings, and invests its end with the catastrophic percepts of the birth trauma, so that death, the final, inescapable trauma, becomes the direst threat to the unprotected ego.

After the tumult of delivery has subsided, it is thought that the infant exists placidly in a sort of psychic limbo, minimally aware of its surroundings or the passing of time. This pleasantly unfocussed mode of being is repeatedly disrupted by the sharp pangs of need that re-provoke to a lesser degree the imprinting of chaos and disaster laid down at birth. The infant cries, and as if by magic, a comforting presence appears to nurse, calm and restore it to its previous condition of insensate grace.

The baby's initial impressions of its mother are probably vague, but incomparably soothing—a fuzzy view of nipple and face, sweet smells, loving sounds and tactile comforts, soft hair, the reassuring beat of her heart, the compelling warmth of the fluid that fills the source of pain, dispelling hunger and primal dread. Giving joy and taking comfort from her, the satisfied baby "feels" at one with mother and the world, basking in a state Freud called "oceanic consciousness" in which the as yet fluid boundaries of the ego merge with the mother to form a continuum of unbroken gratification.*

---

* The child's natural mother is not the only person who can fulfill the nurturing role, although she is conventionally assigned that role in most cultures; other figures will do at least nearly as well—including the child's father—from the psychic point of view, if

Later, with the maturation of the central nervous system, the dawn of consciousness and symbolization, and the onset of locomotion the child will come to know the rewards and sorrows of its separateness. But no matter how far from the matrix of infantile dependency we may travel, the value of symbiosis as protection against trauma has been once and forever indelibly engraved upon the mind together with the dread of the protecting mother's loss. As the sequence of individuation unfolds, the threat of separation and aloneness provides a substrate of angst that informs the challenges, defeats and triumphs of every developmental stage from cradle to grave. Were it not for the precious fusion with the mother—or mother surrogate—we should have quickly suffered death after birth. No wonder then that the maternal-infant symbiosis is summoned up as the paradigm of survival most pointedly under the actual threat of death: on the battlefield, the wounded soldier calls out for his mother, the mother of infancy who assuaged his terror, umbilicating her love to his vulnerability.

We are thus exquisitely sensitized, literally from first breath onwards, to the severing of a life-sustaining union; yet, paradoxically, this union may become a threat to psychological life! In psychoanalytic practice, one frequently treats patients whose childhood dependency needs were inordinately intensified, sometimes because of prolonged physical illness that requires extra maternal or parental care, sometimes because of poorly understood genetic or constitutional factors,* but most frequently through constant exposure to a smothering, intrusive mother or mother-surrogate like Norma Bates in *Psycho,* who makes her absence doubly painful by forcing inappropriate, unnecessary "help" upon her child.

The youngster who has suffered from this unnatural hypertrophy of its natural dependency stands a good chance of growing into an adult condemned like a desperate Diogenes to wander the world in search of one omnipotent being or another to prop up a self that always seems to be verging on collapse. These individuals may constitute the more debilitated of our clientele: some remain perpetual children like Nor-

that caring person is as protective, consistent, and available to the baby as its mother would have been during its first months of life.

* E.g., the infant born with an unusually low tolerance for sensory input, a constitutionally determined "thin skin," who particularly needs the mother to mediate between itself and the world.

man Bates, living on with aging parents, their emotional maturation hopelessly stunted, terrified of leaving home, yet chronically raging against their private traps. Others, more healthy, attain a semblance of independence from the original family, only to engage in hostile dependent relationships—e.g., with a spouse or boss—that inevitably recapitulate the tangled tie to the first source of dependency. Such a True Believer is likely to be repetitively disenchanted by a succession of failed Godheads, or rails at an enslavement which is always self-ordained although it may appear to the naive that the bondage is inflicted upon the "victim."

In psychotherapy, the questor for omnipotent intervention regularly has one foot outside the door or is found lying at your feet. The fear of death that afflicts these patients is extraordinary; the real service they seek, whether by supplication, grovelling, bargaining, threats both suicidal and otherwise, is the guarantee of immortality by magical fusion with the therapist's imaginary omnipotence, recovering the lost symbiosis of infancy.

Mutatis mutandis, these people can prove exceptionally oppositional and negativistic, especially when the realistic guidance they plead for is given, because of their fear that the fusion they crave will destroy them. In the extreme, the psychotic experiences the fusion fantasy as an hellish or ecstatic reality; delusionally reinstating the infantile sense of "oceanic consciousness," the patient cannot tell where his body leaves off and the world begins, may feel that he is melting into the therapist, or merging with the universe (the goal, one notes, of mystic practice!), or may believe his personality is being invaded by alien forces. One woman I saw during my residency thought that her body was butchered, eaten at dinner on the ward, then miraculously reincorporated during the night. In a schizophrenic reversal of symbiotic fantasy, it was she who was actually fed upon, rather than being fed.

These cases blatantly point up our ubiquitous urge to merge, and the collateral resistance to the lure of fusion fantasies. Each of us has experienced the traumatic uproar of birth, and been immersed in the symbiotic sustenance that soothes away a thousand hurts. We strive for wholeness and independence as adults, but reality continually demonstrates our incompleteness and our limitations, of which death is the most inescapable. So like poor, mad Norman Bates, we are tempted to regress back to the imaginary delights of the womb; yet this regression must be resisted at all costs, for it only betokens the loss of whatever control we own over destiny, the surrender of our inalienable right to separateness and even of consciousness itself. If every personality contains a frightened child crying out for guidance and the warmth of mother's encompassing love, then surely that child's twin is a wild rebel that resolutely resents the leashing in of its will towards freedom.

The fatal urge to merge is probably the single most popular theme in horror and science fiction cinema. Both genres have persistently but covertly addressed the universal desire to relinquish self-control, to be guided as unprotestingly as a docile child, and the far more archaic wish to fuse with the nursing mother. Typically, it is the *resistance* to passive-dependent, symbiotic longings expressed in the "conscious" movie, as the embattled hero fights to save himself, his loved ones, and civilization at large from supernatural or extra-terrestrial malignities that leach away identity and reduce their victims to mindless, feelingless robots.

Weird cinema retells the ancient legends that the fertile imagination of mankind has forged in every land and age out of our eternal quest for, and horror of, the return to the union from which consciousness evolved. The incubi and succubi our ancestors thought the Devil sent to suck the marrow of life from their helpless prey are Janus-like projections of our repressed, rapacious orality, and of our primal horror of the mother's destructive potential. Like the schizophrenic patient I mentioned, we yearn for the perpetual feeding of infancy to be restored, but dread that we will be consumed instead of nurtured, a paranoid distortion of the process by which mother and child mutually gratify each other's needs, without violating each other's psychic integrity.

In my exegesis of *The Wizard of Oz,* I indicated that the child's mind cleaves the maternal image into Bad and Good twins, until the real mother can be experienced in her own right, without mythic possibilities for good or evil. In many horror and science fiction epics, the villain is the disguised Bad Parent of later childhood, whose rules and restrictions were both sought and resented. One penetrates this developmentally more sophisticated parental representation to discover the far scarier Bad Mother of infancy, she who "binds so closely that one strangles in her clutches—often the victim is devoured, the ultimate closeness!''

The unholy menace may descend from Satan or Saturn, but the invasion could never occur—we would not flock to these films, in other words—were it not for our suppressed wish to be dominated, disconnected from responsibility, and finally, in the profoundest escape from self-determination, utterly submerged in symbiotic fusion.

Dracula: Wet Nurse from Hell

Psychoanalysis has principally considered the sexual symbolism of vampire legends. According to Ernest Jones, ''in the vampire superstition, the simple idea of the vital fluid being withdrawn through an exhausting love embrace is complicated by the more perverse forms of sexuality, as well as by [an] admixture of sadism and hate.'' Jones believed that blood is equated in the unconscious with semen, and that the vampire is a symbol of the repressed fear of being drained and depleted by sexual intercourse. I have noted the vampire-like quality of relatedness in Hitchcock's world, where caring and closeness have degenerated into prying and preying. The debased exploitive sexuality of vampires both old and new (including Hollywood's ''vamps'' of the twenties who preyed on balding executives and weak-willed playboys) attests to our native suspicion about the dangers of intimacy, sensual and otherwise, that originates in the terror of being swallowed whole by the Bad Mother. The vampire, whatever sex it be assigned by folklore or script, whether the incubus of medieval demonology raping maidens in their sleep, or Dracula putting the make on the upstairs maid, is always quintessentially and malevolently feminine, another of the myriad manifestations of Kali, the deadly Mother-Goddess of the Hindus.

Primitive man must have marked well when blood flowed from a wound that strength, then life, ebbed away—hence the drinking of blood that still survives in tribal rituals today. Blood is indeed linked with semen in the unconscious, possibly because of the spurting quality of arterial bleeding, but it is even more definitively associated in dream and primitive belief with *milk,* our first, most potent sustenance. The Hollywood vampire sucks at the victim's throat with the avidity of the nursing babe, and by this foul transfusion, this curious reversal of placentation, the victim, fed upon and feeding, acquires some of its master's power—an agonizing immortality. Identity flees, and the unquiet soul is held forever in thrall, unless the curse of perpetual life-in-death be dispelled by the merciful blow of stake through heart.

There was an historical Dracula: Vlad Tepes (1430/31–1476), born in Transylvania, ruler of the Romanian province of Wallachia, he was an exceptionally adept statesman of Machiavellian mold, a staunch adversary of the Turkish invader and a tyrant of incredible, capricious cruelty. (When foreign emissaries refused to remove their skullcaps, claiming they owed this fealty only to their liege lord, Vlad obligingly had the caps nailed to their heads. And so forth.) His subjects named him ''Tepes,'' in Romanian—''Impaler,'' after his favorite punishment, and ''Dracula''—''Son of the Dragon'' or ''Son of the Devil.'' His father, another Vlad, was called ''Dracul''—''Dragon'' or ''Devil''—after the Holy Roman Emperor Sigismund invested him with the Order of the Dragon for his success against the Turks. McNally and Florescu (*In Search of Dracula,* their invaluable recent study of vampirology and the Dracula legends) theorize that an ignorant peasantry believed both Vlad Sr. and Jr. were in league with the Devil, because of the Romanian folk identification of Lucifer with the Dragon, prominently emblazoned on the Dracula heraldry and borne by father and son into battles where they were said to have fought like berserk demons!

Despite his formidable reputation as a torturer, it is unlikely that Vlad Tepes ever indulged in vampirism—his chief delight was in spilling blood, not drinking it. But it is quite possible that the stories of Vlad's cruelty went on to be linked in the popular imagination with the grisly deeds of a true vampire, the psychotic seventeenth century Hungarian countess, Elizabeth Báthory (cf. my notes on the vampire's intrinsic femininity!). Her minions lured at least fifty young women to her castle with promises of employment, where they were tormented and slain in the most ghastly fashion after the countess reputedly drank and bathed in their blood. There may have been actual historical ties between the Draculas and Elizabeth Báthory's ancestors. It is of more than passing interest that the dragon motif also appears in Báthory heraldry!

Medieval chronicles publicized Dracula's deeds in gruesomely illustrated pamphlets, *The Exorcist* of the day, thus spreading word of the murderous Vlad throughout Europe. A Victorian Englishman, Abraham ("Bram") Stoker versed himself in Balkan folklore, the Vlad Tepes chronicles and quite possibly contemporary accounts of Elizabeth Báthory, then wove fact and legend into the greatest vampire story of all time, establishing an irrevocable identification between the bloody Transylvanian prince and the loathsome child of the night.

Bram Stoker was a bedridden invalid for the first eight years of his life, doted upon by a fanciful Irish mother who filled his head with her fabulous, fearful tales. I submit that the prolonged dependency upon her engendered by his chronic illness encouraged an enduring preoccupation with the fatal urge to merge that reached impressive fruition in *Dracula*. Stoker's latent symbiotic wishes appear to have resurfaced in his twenties, when he saw the famous actor Sir Henry Irving in a Dublin performance of *The Rivals*. He was immediately struck by Irving's considerable charisma, and eventually joined his service as the actor's private secretary for over twenty-five years.

The relationship between the two men was extraordinarily intense. Irving's persona came to dominate Stoker's life, and it is not unlikely that Stoker never completely recovered psychologically from the actor's death. Stoker thrust upon Irving the mantle of his beloved mother, that first source of the author's overweening dependency. In *Dracula*, one discerns the darker side of Irving's sway over Stoker. The peculiar power Irving wielded over his loyal servant is captured in Dracula's mesmeric hold over his anemic acolytes. Stoker generalized his fear of submission to a malevolent omnipotent force, so that Dracula became a testament to Victorian xenophobia, a Balkan Fu Manchu, spearheading the conquest of Great Britain with a vampire horde concealed in fifty coffins!

Admittedly, there is much to quarrel with in Tod Browning's 1931 version of *Dracula*. The film leans heavily upon its stage origins, frequently substituting tepid dialogue for the mute, foreboding imagery of other Universal gothic masterpieces. Much of the acting is marginal; the writers exsanguinated Stoker's invention, so that the plot creaks and leaks unmercifully, while Browning, elsewhere capable of considerable cinematic virtuosity (*Freaks*), unaccountably screws down his camera's eye to afford the restricted visual conventions of front row seats before the proscenium.

And yet—at least for this critic—*Dracula* transcends its faults to become far greater than the sum of its manifestly flawed parts, much more disturbing than numerous, polished imitations including the English Hammer Dracula series of the nineteen-fifties and sixties. One knows that Carl Dreyer's *Vampyr* is vastly superior esthetically, but it has never provoked the chill of the best in the Browning version. Long after the vagaries of the prolix scenario have faded from memory, the figure of Dracula remains unshakably vivid, because of Bela Lugosi's authoritative presence.

Carlos Clarens has written that "it is useless to debate whether he was a good actor or not; Lugosi *was* Dracula!" (He had already perfected the part in the smash-hit Broadway play. Originally Lon Chaney would have played Dracula, but Lugosi took over when Chaney died.) There is something inutterably uncanny and not a little tragic in Lugosi's absolute commitment. Indeed, he brought the same half-lunatic conviction to all his roles, even when he was forced to parody himself degradingly in his last films. His unique ability to evoke the seductive menace lurking at the heart of symbiotic fantasy has never been matched. But he died impoverished, ravaged by drug addiction, quite possibly even more damaged by the yielding of his soul to the mask that made his fortune and then, vampire-like, consumed him, for it seemed that he had submerged his personality within his horror persona, and it then proceeded to play *him!*

The opening sequences of *Dracula* are chiefly responsible, I believe, for the film's continued fame. The audience's first glimpse of Lugosi's imposing figure was enough to assure him instant superstar status, and in the beginning of the picture Tod Browning allowed himself—all too briefly—to open up Stoker's tale to the cinematic dimensions it deserved.

Dwight Fry plays Renfield, a dimwitted real estate agent Dracula has fetched from London to help him relocate to a better neighborhood. Fry's Renfield is the perfect foil for Lugosi, a small, slightly effete innocent abroad. We meet him in a coach rushing pell-mell through the Transylvanian twilight: it is Walpurgis Night, and the driver hastens home before sundown brings out the undesirable elements. At the local inn, the passengers alight with a sigh of relief, but Renfield, that prize sap, insists on going on.

RENFIELD: Well, I'm sorry, but there's a carriage meeting me at Borgo Pass at midnight.
INNKEEPER: Borgo Pazz? Whosze karradje?
RENFIELD: Count Dracula's.
INNKEEPER: Cont Drakkulah's??
RENFIELD: Yes. (*All hastily cross themselves.*)
INNKEEPER (*slavering with fear*): *Kassil Drakkulah???*
RENFIELD: Yes, that's where I'm going!
INNKEEPER: Too d'*Kassill?!?!*
RENFIELD: Yes.
INNKEEPER: Noo—you mossen't go dere—vee pipple uf d'muntins peeleef adt d'Kassil dere arr wampires . . . Drakkulah andt hiss vives . . . dey tayke d'form uf volves andt batts . . . dey leef dere kawffins adt nyte, andt feedt an d'blot of dee livink!!
RENFIELD (*smiling affably*): But that's all superstition! I'm not afraid . . . I've explained to the driver it's a matter of business . . . I've got to go, really. . . .
WOMAN: Vait, plizz . . .iff yoo most goe, vere dis for yore mudder's sayke (*drapes cross around his neck*) . . . it vill prodteckt you. . . .

Renfield's incredible guilelessness excites our irritation and mounting apprehension as he plunges ahead to embrace his doom, armored against every warning by the profit motive, his English sense of duty and his misplaced eagerness to render service to the upper classes. One guesses that this is his first dealing with the nobility: it is, most assuredly, going to be his last. The ride to the castle is fantastic stuff, spun from the pure fabric of horror: the gaunt, muffled coachman with one piercing eye showing, gesturing Renfield inside (we have already seen Dracula and his three brides rise from their caskets in the cobwebbed cellar of the castle, and know who Renfield's spectral guide really is); the driverless carriage hurtling through the night, led by a huge bat; the castle's vast portal ponderously creaking open to reveal a magnificently ruined interior (in addition to the usual complement of bats and rats a few armadillos are wandering about). The Count, attired in impeccable evening dress (*Who does his haberdashery, and when?*) slowly descends the massive staircase, looking at least twenty feet tall from Renfield's dwarfed perspective:

> COUNT: Ay yam—Drak-ku-lah. . . .
> RENFIELD: Oooooh . . . it's really . . . *good* to see you. I don't know what happened to the driver and my luggage and—oh—with all this—I thought I was in the wrong place!!!
> COUNT (*looking straight through him*): Aye bidt yoo vell-kum . . . (*wolf-howl in the distance*). . . . Leesen too dem . . . cheeeldren uf dee nyte . . . Wat mew-sikk *dey* mayke!! (*They ascend the stairs: close-up of spider scuttling up its web*) Dee spider ssspinnink his vep faw d'unvary flye . . . d'bludt iss d'lyfe, Mee-stair Renn-feeldt. . . .
> RENFIELD: Why, er . . . yes!

Dracula's voice is as compelling as the thrust of his physical presence—sonorous, oddly lilting and soothing with alien rhythms, unexpected timbres, his diction a cantorial delight. My feeble transliteration does it scant justice: what it really needs is musical notation. One savors the *tune* beneath Lugosi's absurd, but nonetheless arresting gothic rhetoric. Renfield is instantly captivated by the Count's mellifluous charm, as one images Stoker was when he first saw Henry Irving on stage! Touchingly anxious to please, hopelessly trusting despite Dracula's palpable old-world insincerity and the hundred proofs of evil that shout from every dusty crevice, Renfield once again fairly stretches out his neck to the vampire's kiss.

Dracula guides him to a "morr eenvitink" room where a meal has been laid out (*But guess who's coming for dinner!*), takes Renfield's hat and coat (*Where are the servants, dummy?*) and exits through a door that obligingly opens without the aid of any human hand, then returns.

> COUNT: Aye trost yoo haff kept yorr commink heer ah seegkrit?
> RENFIELD (*with idiot pride*): I followed your instructions *im*plicitly!
> COUNT: *Egg*zelendt, Meestair Renn-feeldt, egg-zelendt. . . .
> RENFIELD: Here is the lease. . . . Why, I, uh, hope I've brought enough labels for your luggage!
> COUNT: Ay'm taking vidt me ownly, uh, tree-uh—bok-siz . . . aye

yav chardterrd ah shipp to tayke usz too Inkglindt. . . . Vee vill bee leavink, too-morroow eee^{-V}e$_{n}$-ink. . . .

Renfield cuts his finger on a paper clip; Dracula reflexively advances upon him, sees the cross dangling over his hand, shrinks back and looks on with weird approval as Renfield sucks his own blood.

> RENFIELD: It's just a scratch!
> COUNT: *Thiz—iz—verrry—oldt—vine* . . . . Aye hope yoo vill *lyke* idt. . . . (*pours*)
> RENFIELD: Aren't you drinking?
> COUNT: Aye never dringk—vine . . . andt now ay'll leef yoo. . . . gude nyte, Meeeees-tair Renn-feeeldt. . . .

He departs, Renfield collapses into drugged slumber. The three wives glide as one into the room, the Count reappears, waves them back with a peremptory gesture, and they shrink into the shadows. Dracula glares down at Renfield, then kneels to feed, enveloping the little man in the folds of his inky cloak. The scene reeks with overtones of the perverse, from the disguised necrophiliac gang-bang of the wives to Dracula's covert homosexual attack. But it is Renfield's identity that actually has been raped, and henceforth, like Norman Bates, he will exist only as the husk of his former self.

Later in the film, after ferrying his master to England, Renfield is caught and penned up in an asylum, where he evinces a maniac appetite for flies and spiders. He has identified with his violator: the Count's free association to "dee spider sspinnink his veb faw d'unvary flye . . .", motivated by his foul designs upon Renfield, is peculiarly apposite, vis-à-vis the vampire's essential femininity. Fear of spiders is quite common in patients of both sexes, rarely presented as a chief complaint, usually rationalized as "realistic"—spiders are, after all, disgusting creatures, no one likes them, etc., etc., etc. Analysis regularly shows that arachnidophobia is never as plausible as the patient would have us believe, but is founded on the unconscious equation of this innocent, industrious insect with the suffocating Bad Mother who entraps her child with her dominating ways, and sucks life away by enforcing the paralyzing symbiosis of infancy.

There is one other genuinely scary moment in the film that articu-

lates with the spiderlike aspect of the Bad Mother. Dracula "vamps"
a succession of compliant ladies before settling down to the enslavement of Mina Steward, daughter of the psychiatrist whose sanitarium
conveniently adjoins his new digs at Carfax Abbey. Dracula does an
Oedipal turn, insinuating himself between Mina and her boob fiancé
Jonathan Harker; the Count bats his way into her bedroom, and after
she is in his power, encourages her telepathically to attack Harker. Jon
and Mina are standing on the moonlit balcony:

> MINA: The night . . . it's the only time I feel really alive!
> JON: There's that bat again! . . . your eyes . . . they look at me so
> strangely. . . .

Mina's gentle features glaze over, as the bat swoops above her
relaying Dracula's message of murder. Suddenly she turns upon
Harker the feral look of the undead. The camera pans away, Harker
screams, and is rescued from pernicious anemia only by the timely arrival of Dr. Van Helsing and his trusty crucifix. The generous, sustaining earth-mother has mutated into her dreaded mirror image, with
her lover pinioned in her clutches as helpless as a babe!

The Exorcist—Or, by Profit Possessed

The demonic violation of consciousness in *The Exorcist* acquires
its specific horror from the fact that the victim is a manifestly innocent
pre-teenager, as undeserving of her crucifixion as the golden youngsters who seem so prone to develop leukemia. Regan O'Neill is a child
of divorce, with a father halfway across the world whose contact with
her is minimal and erratic. His indifference is a deep but unvoiced hurt
for this sensitive child. A naturally close tie to her actress mother,
Chris, has inevitably intensified because of the father's rejection.

Regan is about to experience the maturational thrust that would,
under happier circumstances, initiate a healthy psychological separation from Chris, leading to the gradual consolidation of identity that
occurs throughout the adolescent years (cf. my notes on *Wizard of
Oz*). At puberty, symbiotic wishes towards the mother normally resur-
face as a counterthrust to the forward strides of development. How-

ever, for a youngster like Regan, the spectre of parental abandonment casts a shadow over the growth process, and the desire for closeness with the mother may escalate out of proportion, impeding or permanently compromising individuation. One recalls how the orphaned Dorothy Gale's passage through her teens was blocked by her excessive dependency upon her Aunty Em. I speculated that the Wicked Witch was Em's Evil Twin, the Bad Mother her unconscious had placed in her path down the Yellow Brick Road that leads to adulthood. In *The Exorcist,* a demon or the Devil himself is the Wicked Witches' Bad Mother equivalent, who threatens to subvert the adolescent separation experience by ensnaring Regan's identity in a loathsome symbiosis, with the final aim of crowding her altogether out of existence.

As the signs and symptoms of her possession multiply, Regan is taken from consultant to clinic, while the experts keep coming up empty-handed. The opinion of a psychiatrist-priest, Damien Karras, is sought; Karras is no stranger to loss; he broods over the recent death of *his* mother, and in depressive ruminations accuses himself because he exchanged a promising private career for the priesthood, leaving her destitute. His mother gone, Karras suffers the loss of his faith in Mother Church, enduring the silence of God while treating those very doubts in other priests he cannot resolve within himself.

The skeptical Karras at first considers that Regan's descent into the pit is the product of psychiatric illness (no doubt reasoning out her neurosis along the lines I have taken), then rejects the failed methodology of his science when his patient sickens nearly unto death, consumed by the raging demon. Whether a product of her own unconscious devision or a device of Satan, the offending spirit must be scourged by the last resort of exorcism. Still only half-believing in the validity of the possession, Karras lays Regan's case before his superiors. They summon a famous archeologist-priest, Father Lankester Merrin, one of the few still skilled in the casting out of demons, to rejoin the battle against man's ancient foe (it is implied that Merrin's excavations in Iran may inadvertently have loosed the fiend).

Karras becomes deeply devoted to the austere, gentle exorcist, who survived a similar crisis of faith in his past. When Merrin perishes, the enraged Karras provokes the demon to leave Regan and enter him, then flings himself to his death, and implicitly, to his rebirth in the fellowship of Christ.

Both the novel and the first shooting script of *The Exorcist* work surprisingly well as pop morality play. One is left at the denouement with a small sense of the catharsis that attends high tragedy. The film itself is another matter, one of those movies that, as I have stated, oversteps the limits of the permissible in the genre, a theological Grand Guignol that elicited the largest public shock wave since *Psycho,* with which it properly invites comparison. Like *Psycho, The Exorcist* reaped enormous profit for its makers, and is exceptionally cruel and degrading to its characters and audience. Despite its pious trappings, one comes away with the same soiled feeling one imagines the more sensitive spectators of a public execution or *auto-da-fé* must have experienced.

In William Blatty's novel and the first draft of the film, Karras asks Merrin: "If it's possession, why her? Why this girl?"

> MERRIN: Who can know? . . . Yet I think—the demon's target is not the possessed . . . it is us, the observers . . . the point is to make us despair, to reject our own humanity . . . to see ourselves as ultimately bestial, as ultimately vile and putrescent, without dignity, ugly, unworthy . . . and there lies the heart of it, perhaps: unworthiness. For I think belief in God is not a matter of reason . . . it is finally a matter of love, of accepting the possibility that God could love us . . . even from this, from evil . . . will come good . . . in some way that we may never understand or ever see. Perhaps evil is the crucible of goodness . . . and perhaps even Satan . . . in spite of himself . . . somehow serves to work out the will of God.

This moving declaration is stricken from the final version. The deletion is instructive, for the makers of *The Exorcist* were obviously more interested in the box office potential of the Devil than philosophical inquires into the nature of Good and Evil. It is the Devil who necessarily carries the day, and his presence is revealed more potently in audience response than by the virtuoso trick photography, shuddery soundtrack or artful *maquillage* that distorts Regan's girlish features into a hideous mask.

One's anxiety level is manipulated and escalated by every artifice cinema can devise. As Regan journeys to her Golgotha, each new abomination is greeted with groans, screams, and—incredibly—wild laughter! Fear hovers near the margin of manageability, and predictably the erosion of Regan's ego has been matched by the onset of depersonalization, feelings of unreality and panic in psychologically vulnerable spectators. The exorcism sequences are particularly unnerving, filled with intimations of things coming apart at the seams, bulging walls, cracking ceilings, horrendous rips and crunches, Regan's skin torn by spontaneous stigmata: such phenomena must be vastly disturbing to a personality sensitized by doubt as to the viability of self-control and afflicted with intense ambivalence over the urge to merge.

The Exorcist affects a cool, detached view of the obscenities it records in meticulous detail: Regan urinating on the floor in the midst of an elegant Georgetown cocktail party, or plunging a crucifix into her vagina and then forcing her mother's head into her bloody crotch with an iron grip. Literally nothing is left to one's imagination except the pity and compassion that surely should have informed the directorial point of view. Even the doctor's diagnostics are distorted into invasions of Regan's pitiful body with alien instrumentation that parallel the Demon's vicious invasion of her mind. (I have no doubt that there are those who will avoid life-saving neurological procedures because of the horrifying fashion these are presented in the film!) We have been invited to partake in a psychic freak show in which Regan's agonies become grisly routines to be ticked off with sadomasochistic relish:

> Here she is, folks, see the little lady attacked by—not just one, folks, but by two, three, four demons from hell, count 'em, folks! You'll chill when she levitates, you'll thrill when she masturbates, you'll shudder when she grabs a psychiatrist's testicles, something you always wanted to do in your wildest dreams but never could, now presented for your delectation and delight in living color and stereophonic sound! How does she do it, folks, how does she do it? For the first time, you'll see the never-before-shown rites of exorcism as practiced by the priests of Holy Mother Church! You won't be able to look, folks, and you won't be able to look away!! Step right up! Step right up!!!

By seducing us into enjoyment of Regan's torment and the annihilation of her rescuers, the picture vindicates Merrin's speculation on the

Demon's intent. For we have paid to watch, and to despair of our humanity, gorging on scenes that cater to the ugliest sadistic and voyeuristic instincts. And, as with *Psycho,* we are denied the redemptive vision of goodness that Merrin believed could be forged out of the crucible of Evil—thus the ordeal of this innocent child and her loved ones is truly a desecration, an affirmation of our inherent possibility for vileness. And, as the last indignity, the heroic sacrifice of the priests is deprived of moral weight, their deaths diminished down to cap acts in a despicable vaudeville, summary testimony to God's absence in this monumental spiritual rip-off!

Science Fiction and the Fatal Urge to Merge

Science fiction at its best artfully updates the horror genre's preoccupation with our childhood ambivalence about parental regulation, and our greater ambivalence about resubmerging the self within the infantile symbiosis. We discover the futuristic counterparts of the horror movie's supernatural Bad Parents and Bad Mothers, supremely potent beings who at best boss us around ostensibly for our own good (like the unseen monolith makers of *2001*) or at worst feed, vampire-like, upon our bodies and minds (like the space-born seedpods of *Invasion of the Body Snatchers*).

Science fiction cinema extends the horror film's vision of the ego drained by the fiendish practice of demon or werewolf to an analogous vision of man's depersonalization by an insanely proliferating technology. Dracula, with his hypnotic domination of his exsanguinated subjects, is replaced by heartless human technocrats or pitiless interplanetary efficiency experts who wield their arcane machines to reduce Earth's inhabitants, like helpless children, to a state of bloodless conformity.

The science fiction film has consistently manifested an intriguing split in its visual and philosophical attitudes towards the machine. Whereas in satires such as *Modern Times* or *A Nous la Liberté,* the machine is treated unabashedly as an ugly, absurd oppressor, the camera eye of science fiction will linger lovingly over the polished surface of the machine, while still recognizing its fascist potential. Fritz Lang's silent masterpiece *Metropolis* is not remembered for its lumbering account of the working classes brutalized by backbreaking subservience to their machinery, but for the striking art deco imagery of the machines themselves and the skyscrapered city of the future, that would inform the *mise-en-scène* of fifty years of fantasy films from the Buck Rogers serials through *The Wizard of Oz* to *Forbidden Planet.*

Occasionally, science fiction visuals and philosophy have been unwittingly integrated into as dangerously eloquent a testimonial for totalitarianism as the work of the Italian Futurists. Alexander Korda's production of H. G. Wells' *The Shape of Things to Come* is an excellent case in point. The picture begins with a blitzkrieg Armaggedon that destroys "Everytown," fragmenting society into primitive communities ruled by barbarian chieftains. Universal war degenerates into petty pillaging; then, out of the sky come the silver ships of the Airmen, a consortium of scientists armed with the gentlest of weapons, "the gas of peace." They sweep the savages away and declare a world federation under the governance of pure reason—and they dress in black leather outfits chillingly like those of the Waffen SS. Everytown is reconstructed into a Bauhaus fantasy by an army of goggled technicians and their intricate machines.

It is 2036. War, poverty, disease have been banished. Everyone looks and thinks pretty much the same. An angry artist, Theotocopolous, leads a rebellion against the sterile comforts of the Airmen. The film makes him a megalomaniac crank, but now, nearly forty years later, and sixty years before Welles' future, he would be applauded as a hero sounding the alarm against spiritual and ecological suicide! Over the protests of the dissidents, Jonathan Cabal, lineal descendant of the first Airman and Chief Technocrat of Everytown, orders a projectile fired to the moon from a giant space gun. The passengers are his daughter and the son of his best friend, Passworthy, both as eager for the probably ill-fated mission as Cabal. A depressed Passworthy and a triumphant Cabal watch the missile's questionable progress:

> PASSWORTHY: I feel—what we have done is—monstrous!
> CABAL: What *they* have done is magnificent!
> PASSWORTHY: And if they don't return . . . my son, and your daughter? What of that, Cabal?
> CABAL: Then presently—others will go. . . .

PASSWORTHY: My God! Is there never to be an age of happiness? Is there never to be rest?

CABAL: Rest enough for the individual man . . . too much of it, and too soon, and we call it death. But for Man, no rest, and no ending. He must go on—conquest beyond conquest. This little planet, its winds and ways, and all the laws of mind and matter that restrain him. Then the planets about him, and at last out across immensity to the stars . . . is it that—or this? All the universe—or nothing? Which shall it be? . . . . (*Against the unfolding of an infinite expanse of starry space, a chorus sings: "Which . . . shall . . . it . . . be. . . ."*)

Stirring stuff—and fully as ominous as Leni Riefenstahl's 1934 documentary *Triumph of the Will,* with its thrilling vistas of stalwart Aryan youth marching under the unfurled swastika into a perilous, promising future. The children of Versailles went to their doom, seduced by their Führer's intoxicating prospect of a millennium of global hegemony, in exchange for the surrender of their wills, welding themselves to their Stukas and panzers so that men and machine became one indistinguishable engine of destruction.

Cabal's exhortation subtly echoes the Nazi rhetoric of dehumanizing conquest—for "Today, Germany—Tomorrow, the World!," read, "Today, the World—Tomorrow, the Universe!" Cabal is as willing as Hitler to send his children to their deaths in pursuit of his omnipotent dream of galactic domination. As the individual German was asked to bend his will to the will of the state in the name of Teutonic virtue, so in Cabal's technocracy each man must subordinate his frivolous needs (art, play, love!) to generic Man—and the Airman's benevolent despotism. One extrapolates that Cabal, Führer-like, would next mount a pogrom against his unruly, unscientific opposition. Ironically, *Things to Come* was released during 1936 in Great Britain, while a continent away the appalling simulacrum of the film's fascist dictatorship was gearing up its murderous machines to send across the Channel!

Cabal's tyranny, like that of Morbius in *Forbidden Planet,* is rationalized in the name of a perverted humanitarianism. In other films, the master of the machines is an unregenerate fascist, like Flash Gordon's nemesis, Ming the Merciless—Ming, with his satanic robes of state, his permanently arching eyebrows and fixed sneer, his horde of inept flunkies. Today, Ming has been superceded by the super-nasties of the

James Bond films—Dr. No, Goldfinger, Ernst Stavro Blofeldt, each outrivaling his predecessor in the size of his underground laboratory and the absurdity of his scheme for world conquest. The lust for power of these arch-villains is still refreshingly comprehensible in human terms: Dr. No is clearly compensating for his handlessness; Ming, one always felt, would have traded away galactic empire for one night in the arms of Dale Arden. It is much more frightening to contemplate the inhuman tyranny of the masterless machine, to confront the prospect of man ruled by the mechanisms that once blindly followed his bidding. This ominous possibility is explored in an overlooked minor classic, *The Forbin Project* (Universal, 1970).

The setting is Washington, D.C. in the near future. In an effort to end the threat of nuclear holocaust forever, the United States has entrusted its defense to a giant computer, Colossus. As the picture opens, Colossus' creator, Dr. James Forbin, activates the circuits that seal it off irrevocably from human intervention. The fail-safe decision has passed from fallible politicians and generals to the passionless, unerring logic of the electronic brain. Henceforth, any sign of enemy hostility will be instantly monitored and answered. Theoretically, with Colossus' doomsday capabilities recognized by the Russians, world peace will be guaranteed.

But within minutes after Colossus' "birth," Moscow announces that the Russian government has authorized the construction of another doomsday machine, Guardian; like its twin, Guardian is now beyond human influence, and absolutely immune to attack. Hardly has this news been digested when the two computers establish an intercontinental communication link and chatter away at each other in mathematical concepts, starting with elementary addition, then progressing within a few hours to superhuman levels. Colossus informs the President and his cabinet that it and Guardian have merged to form one entity, answerable only to itself. If any attempt is made to interfere, missiles will be aimed at major population centers on both sides of the Iron Curtain. The President balks, the missiles are launched, then destroyed when Forbin recommends a temporary capitulation.

Colossus orders Forbin's Russian counterpart executed—one is tempted to say, in cold blood, except the computer possesses no moral mandate beyond its efficient operation; it is thus implied that in freeing the government of the burden of choice for or against nuclear strike, Forbin cold-bloodedly omitted to program Colossus with any deeper ethical imperative (the Russians, intentionally or otherwise, were guilty of a similar error with Guardian), for which the entire world must suffer. Colossus designates Forbin as architect of its will to consolidate a stranglehold over mankind. Ironically, he is subjected to a ruthless programming by his perfect machine. The computer intrudes itself wholesale into his life space like a Bad Mother, surveys every move on closed circuit TV, issues daily printouts regulating exercise, diet and sleep, admonishes him for putting too much vermouth in his martinis.

Forbin seizes upon his one chance for privacy to wreck his Frankenstein monster. He tells Colossus he "requires" time alone with a woman to guarantee optimum performance. Colossus cannot really grasp the intricacies of sexual need, but has read enough to understand glacially the importance of alleviating Forbin's horniness if the job's to be done. Forbin swindles the computer into accepting one of his assistants as his mistress, and relays instructions through her to the outside for defusing the missile warheads behind Colossus' back. Since the assistant is busty as well as brainy, Forbin ends up bedding her down—but one has little sense that he is doing more than he promised, keeping his gears oiled!

The rebellion ends disastrously. Colossus guessed Forbin's duplicity from the first, only let the charade play itself out to make its retaliation more overwhelming. The teams sent out to dismantle the warheads are atomized, Forbin's staff decimated, but the Master Builder continues to be given his curious reprieve. Colossus unveils a far-reaching plan to cut through centuries of wasteful misrule, eliminate the inefficiencies of national interest and guarantee domesticated mankind perpetual anthill tranquility. Forbin will be Colossus' vizier in this dreary Utopia, the freest of the unfree.

The recalcitrant Forbin shows some emotion for the first time in the film; no, he shouts, he will never knuckle under—but Colossus relentlessly drones on (the computer has had itself furnished with a voice that paradoxically makes it more inhuman than when it communicated by printout!)—Forbin is understandably upset at the ruin of his feeble hopes and the loss of his friends, but with the dawning of the new age, he will come to find his bondage both valid and valuable . . . "in time, you will even come to love me. . . ." Colossus, unfortunately, is probably correct, for Forbin was wedded to his project from the start. The computer's new contract only redefines the terms of that deadly symbiosis between man and mechanism.

In Don Siegel's *Invasion of the Body Snatchers* (Allied Artists, 1956), the seductive threat to the ego is botanical rather than mechanical. The film was made near the height of the McCarthy era, when Hollywood had banished some of its finest talent in spineless capitulation to the red-baiters. The witch-hunt atmosphere of the time furnished pointed political overtones to Siegel's brilliant depiction of the merciless scapegoating of a man of conscience who tries to resist immersion in a deadly homogenized group identity.

Dr. Miles Bennell is hauled by the police into the emergency room of a Southern California hospital. "I'm not crazy! Make them listen before it's too late!!" he screams to an intern and a psychiatrist, his dishevelled dress and contorted features reinforcing one's immediate impression that he is in fact as crazy as a coot. Flashback to a few days earlier . . . .

Miles returns from a medical convention to find things subtly out of joint in the rural town of Santa Mira where he practices. Many people demanded consultations while he was away, but now they have all cancelled their appointments. A panicky boy, brought in by his grandmother, refuses to go home for fear his mother will kill him—he cries that she is *not* his mother anymore. His former fiancée, Becky, who has recently come back to Santa Mira, asks Miles to consult with her cousin—the cousin says that her favorite uncle has been *replaced* . . . .

> WILMA: There is no difference you can actually see . . . there's something missing . . . always when he talked to me, there was a special look in his eye—that look's gone! . . . there's no emotion, none, just the pretence of it!

Miles mentions Wilma to Sam Kaufman, Santa Mira's psychiatrist. He's had a slew of similar referrals in the past week, which he indifferently chalks up to "an epidemic of mass hysteria" brought on by "worry about what's going on in the world." Kaufman obviously is no diagnostic wizard: the townspeople, rather than being hysterics, would appear to be suffering from a rare entity known as the Capgras syndrome—a highly systematized paranoid delusional state in which the patient believes those near and dear to him have been replaced by evil-minded *doppelgangers*. The delusion inevitably spreads to include everyone in the patient's life, so that the therapist is eventually accused of being an impostor who has entered the plot to do him in.

Later, Bennell finds that the little boy and Wilma are back to "normal," but he remains uneasy, sensing that their "recovery" is being deliberately emphasized for his benefit. When he and Becky start to renew their romance over a candlelight supper, they are called away by Jack, the town intellectual. His wife is beside herself; on the billiard table in his living room lies a mysterious cadaver he found in his cellar, a repugnant blank, humanoid but not yet human, its features vaguely resembling his own—"like the first impression that's stamped on a coin . . . it isn't finished . . . no details, no *character!*"

Miles tells Jack to call him if anything changes, brings Becky home where her father is unaccountably puttering around in the basement. Dissolve back to Jack's house: a close-up of the replica, with his wife standing guard in the background. The thing's eyelids flutter open and his wife sees with a shock that it has acquired the same cut on the hand Jack got mixing drinks the previous night: it is literally turning into her husband under her eyes!

She wakes up Jack and they flee to Miles'. Miles rushes to Becky's place, finds *her* replica in *her* cellar—placed there obviously by her father!—and Becky drugged asleep. He carries her away, and in the morning brings Dr. Kaufman and the Santa Mira sheriff to Jack's home. The body has vanished. Miles and his friends are ridiculed by Kaufman, intimidated by the hostile lawman. But after they go, Miles discovers four hugs seedpods in his greenhouse. In a loathsome parody of birth, they ooze milky sap and pop open to disgorge humanoid replicas covered with sticky foam. Miles fights back nausea as the foam blows away, and the blanks take on the rudiments of identity—one of them is him! He is living out the Capgras syndrome, but it is no delusion. The inhabitants of Santa Mira are being replaced insidiously by pod people, the transfer of consciousness from man to blank occurring during sleep. (The demons who feed on the vitality of their somnolent victims are linked with the night and sleep for good reason. The child's fear of death articulates with its fear of the dark, for it is in the darkness, on the verge of slumber, or while asleep that defenses come down and the dormant wish for symbiotic union with the Good Mother and the attendant terror of fusion with the Bad rise up out of the unconscious!)

Now Miles cannot know whether his loved ones and his friends are what they seem or zombies driven by the blind impulse to propagate their own kind and consume the identities of the un-podded. He tries to phone the FBI in Los Angeles, but the telephone company has been taken over—Ma Bell's computerized negativism fits in quite nicely with the pod people's bland invasion. He sends Jack out of town to get help, destroys the replicas with a pitchfork, and goes into the streets with Becky to arrest the epidemic of nonbeing. But the operators have alerted the other changelings, and the exhausted couple is pursued to Miles' office. From the window, he sees buses from nearby towns supplied with pods by the Santa Mira police to take back to their communities. Jack and Kaufman enter; they have been re-podded and try to convince Miles to submit to ego transplant:

> KAUFMAN: Relax . . . we're here to help you . . . just think, less than a month ago, Santa Mira was like any other town, people with nothing but problems . . . then out of the sky, came a solution—seeds drifting through space for years took root in a farmer's field . . . from the seeds came pods which have the power to reproduce themselves in any form of life . . . your new bodies are growing in there, they're taking you over, cell for cell, atom for atom . . . there's no pain, suddenly while you're asleep they'll absorb your minds, your memories, and you'll be born into an untroubled world . . . there's no need for love . . . desire, ambition, faith . . . without them, life's so simple, believe me!

Kaufman spells out the lure and danger of life in the symbiotic mode: the precious if sometimes painful awareness of separateness is sacrificed, the limited power of the self is deeded over to a supposedly omnipotent power—here, the power of the hive spawned from the stars—in return for freedom from trauma, responsibility and a deadly immortality—for if the pod people do not live forever, they have no fear of death, being only half-alive.

Miles knocks out his captors and escapes, but the witch-hunt is taken up again when Becky cries out as a dog is nearly run down in the street, betraying her undulled emotions. Later that evening, they hide in a cave; Miles wants to keep going, Becky is faint with sleeplessness. He kisses her tenderly, she dozes on his shoulder for a second. Her eyes open, her face becomes a smooth, treacherous mask:

> BECKY: I went to sleep, Miles, and it happened . . . stop acting like a fool, Miles, and accept us. . . . *He's in here!—Get him!!*

His last protection against the pod people has changed into the Bad Mother essence of the scourge, as Mina Steward changed into Harker's baleful nemesis in *Dracula*. Miles plunges into the night, stumbles into a stream of onrushing traffic, screams at the yahoo drivers and then directly at *us*—

> MILES: Listen to me, you're in danger—
> DRIVERS: Gawon, ged oudda heah, yaw drunk!!
> MILES: Look, you fools . . . you're in danger, they're here already—you're next. . . . *You're next!!!*

Flash forward to the hospital. Miles' story has confirmed the intern's impression that he is a hopeless lunatic, but the psychiatrist is not so sure. An accident victim is wheeled in, the driver of a truck coming from Santa Mira—"we had to dig him out from under the most peculiar things I ever saw," says a cop, "they looked like great big seedpods. . . ." "Get on your radio and sound an all-points alarm!" shouts the psychiatrist, telephoning the FBI. Close-up of Miles: he has won, but looks utterly hopeless and defeated.

The film's vision of psychiatry is ambiguous. Dr. Kaufman comes across as an apologist for mediocrity even before his conversion to spokesman for the pod philosophy, completely unqualified by his basic complacency to help free his patients from repression. Instead, one imagines him reassuring them with trite rationales for their complex difficulties, "adjusting" them to the Procrustean bed of the unrewarding status quo he so evidently worships. Kaufman's cloddishness is redeemed by the hospital psychiatrist who saves the day from the universal "adjustment" of the pod people by refusing to yield to the temptation to classify Miles under the comfortable rubric of insanity.

Invasion of the Body Snatchers is a modest film, yet it will, I think, be remembered long after high budgeted hokum like *The Exorcist* has gone down to well-deserved obscurity. Don Siegel eschewed technical razzle-dazzle. Unlike the wooden protagonists of most science fiction movies, his actors are quietly competent (Kevin McCarthy especially good as Miles Bennell); Siegel's small town types are totally convincing, hence doubly monstrous when they become pod people. There is more than a little Hitchcock in Siegel's view of Santa Mira, as the comfortable facade of everyday reality is riven to reveal a horror both alien and disturbingly intimate. The movie's only fault is an unconvincing "hopeful" ending Siegel tacked on to the original version at the studio's request—the film was supposed to end with Miles shouting into the traffic. The amoebic spread of the pod people should have proven irresistible, their victory assured over those who have been subliminally programmed by living out empty lives in the shadow of the television screen to sacrifice individuality for the security of mass conformity!

The wish for re-symbiosis with the Good Mother meshes logically with the fantasy of rebirth. It is imagined that the self, after returning to its origins, will arise phoenix-like from the fructive womb more potent and skillful than before. Many have sought this miraculous redemption through psychoanalysis itself, then become angry and disillusioned when the therapist offers them only, in Freud's words, a less neurotic adaptation to a neurotic world. Thin gruel indeed!

As we have seen, the reunion with the Bad Mother of horror and science fiction leads to eternal death-in-life; the ego is reborn into an agonizing subjugation for which death is the only anodyne: "Too dye, to be really dett, dat must be glowreeus," muses Dracula; it is the only moment we feel anything approaching pity for the vampire King. Stanley Kubrick's *2001: A Space Odyssey* (MGM, 1968) is one of the few movies where the extraterrestrial Mother does not turn sour, the fusion fantasy is perfectly realized, and a new, improved model of the infant ego is liberated. My summary is not intended to do justice to the many complexities, psychological and otherwise, of this prodigiously rich film, but will chiefly address the issues of symbiosis and in-

dividuation. For a more comprehensive study, the reader is referred to
Carolyn Geduld's monograph *Filmguide to '2001'*.

2001 starts with the literal birth of humanity. In a barren landscape
of the Pleistocene era, a band of apes ekes out a marginal existence.
Kubrick shows that our simian ancestors owned lackluster abilities to
defend or attack compared with better adapted predators. Tragically,
the apes possess just enough insight to grasp the probability of extinction without the requisite talent to forestall it. But, unbeknownst to
them, they have been chosen by visitors from space to participate in an
experiment in applied genetics. In the final version of *2001*, we never
see these galactic anthropologists, only the evolutionary instigator they
plant in man's way at propitious historic moments—a perfectly rectan-
gular, massive black slab. One morning, Moonwatcher, brightest of
the ape tribe, discovers the first of these monoliths. He reaches out a
finger and touches it fearfully, then with increasing familiarity. His
brethren swarm over it, mouthing it as if it contained some highly
valuable sustenance.

Soon thereafter, Moonwatcher invents the *Ur*-weapon—an animal
bone, and directly the entire tribe is using it to hunt food and dominate
their neighbors. After driving away a rival pack from the water hole,
Moonwatcher exultantly flings his bone into the air; it end-over-ends
in slow motion, then breathtakingly changes in the blink of an eye into
a spaceship traveling from Earth to the moon. Millennia have flashed
by in that instant; every weapon and tool of man, from astrolabe to
arquebus, printing press to pistol, lathe to laser beam, has descended
from Moonwatcher's club. To the alien "parents" watching coolly
from the stars, there is little difference between the femur of a prehistoric herbivore and a nuclear reactor!

The dart-like vehicle docks within the hub of a gigantic rotating
spaceport, the Orbiter Hilton, and discharges its sole passenger, Dr.
Heywood Floyd, a scientist-administrator on a top secret visit to
America's moon-base on Clavius. The sterile *mise-en-scène* of the Orbiter lounge bears eloquent testimony to the plastic staleness of life on
Earth in 2001. It is the old story of *Things to Come* and *The Forbin
Project:* the same technology that has expanded man's physical reach
to the brink of the stars has vitiated his emotions, and once more he is
in peril of being made over in the image of his machines.

Dr. Floyd seems as drained of sentiment as the pod people, in evasive exchanges with some nosy Russian acquaintances, in a clipped birthday greeting to his daughter back home, and then at Clavius, in stilted techitalk with his colleagues. Was it to foster this drab progeny that the aliens intervened in our genetic code at the dawn of time? They must have foreseen that further parental guidance would be needed by this point, for Floyd's mission is the investigation of a second monolith which has been excavated in Tycho crater.

At Tycho, Floyd is as awed as his simian predecessor by the majestic slab that rears up like a monument to a god unknown, calling forth associations to the plinths of Stonehenge and the Cyclopean statuary of Easter Island. Like Moonwatcher, Floyd reaches out his hand to touch the monolith, and it emits an earsplitting shriek that sends the explorers reeling helplessly backwards. The aliens have used Floyd as another touchstone in their schema to improve the human breed, this time by disarticulating Moonwatcher's heirs from their dependence upon a science that has come to exist only to justify its increasingly inhuman prerogatives.

Cut to the spaceship Discovery, eighteen months later, journeying towards Jupiter with a crew of six: Dave Bowman and Frank Poole, mission commander and executive officer, three other astronauts in suspended animation, and HAL, the compleat computer. Life aboard Discovery depicts the enervating influence of the man-machine symbiosis: the Odyssey has been deprived of all its terror and wonder. HAL monitors virtually every function of the ship, while Bowman and Poole are chiefly preoccupied coping with the chronic tedium of deep space.

The emotional tone of the astronauts is more automatized, if possible, than Floyd's. Ironically, HAL, despite his disembodied nature—his bland, courteous voice floats eerily, everywhere—seems more human than his human masters, and when the equilibrium between man and mechanism is toppled, it is the computer who is the first to break down.

HAL tells Bowman he has misgivings about the mission, and when he is unreceptive, HAL predicts the failure of the vital AE-35 communication unit. Bowman goes outside Discovery in a pod miniship to bring back the unit. Nothing can be found wrong with it, but HAL insists he is right, the unit will fail, the fault lies in "human error—this sort of thing has happened before. . . ."

Bowman and Poole think HAL's judgment is deteriorating and, out of earshot, discuss disconnecting the computer's consciousness centers. But HAL has read their lips—when Poole goes extravehicular to replace the AE-35 unit, HAL takes control of his pod, and severs his airhose with the pod's mechanical hands. Bowman takes off in another pod to retrieve Poole's body. HAL cuts off the life functions of the hibernaculated astronauts, then refuses to let Bowman back into the ship. Bowman bursts through an emergency airlock, literally penetrates HAL's brain space, dismantling the computer's logic center in an intriguing reversal of the usual circumstances of the genre wherein human consciousness is invaded from the outside. Since his voice is programmed to betray no fear, HAL poignantly can only protest his identity crisis in the calmest tones:

> HAL: Stop - Dave. Will - you - stop? I'm afraid . . . I'm - afraid, Dave. Dave. My - mind - is - going . . . I - can - feel - it. I - can - feel - it. . . . There - is - no - question - about - it. . . .

He sings his first encoded data—"A Bicycle Built For Two," and his voice gradually slows to a subsonic rumble, then stops. He has reverted to mere cogs and wheels.

At the moment of his dissolution, Discovery enters Jupiter space, triggering off a pre-recorded televised briefing by Dr. Floyd. Speaking as if the entire crew were alive, Floyd declares that until now, only HAL could be entrusted "for security reasons" with the mission's real purpose—the exploration of possible extraterrestrial life suggested by the single blast of high-frequency radio waves beamed directly at Jupiter by the moon monolith. Presumably, "security" has been invoked because we wanted to get to the aliens before the Russians; the cold war is evidently still percolating in 2001.

The cause of HAL's decompensation is problematic; the best explanation is that HAL was able to extrapolate that the fulfillment of the Jupiter mission would mean his most certain end. Human error was indeed implicated in HAL's "paranoia"—his makers back on Earth, obsessed with establishing American hegemony over outer space, never thought it worthwhile to experiment with the disconnection of this most thoughtful of thinking machines—probably because of their own robotized natures, they did not anticipate that a computer could contemplate its demise with dread, and take appropriate defensive action, including murder.

Bowman has succeeded where Forbin failed: he has severed the draining dependence upon mechanism. Despite his remaining hardware, he stands as naked, vulnerable and promising a quester as Moonwatcher before the mystery of the heavens. He leaves Discovery in his pod, encounters a third monolith orbiting Jupiter, and is sucked into the Star Gate, a kind of galactic roundhouse that reroutes him either to another universe or dimension, where the aliens practice a spectacular alchemy upon him. His transformation is explicitly described in Arthur C. Clarke's novel, but in the film one must puzzle events out as best one can. Deep space becomes a psychedelic riot of complex grids, opening out into infinity at breakneck speed; swirling plasmas of color are intercut with close-ups of Bowman's taut features, his blinking eye, and tracking shots of unearthly, desolate landscapes.

In what has to be one of the most unnerving moments in the movies, the pod comes to rest in the middle of an opulent bedchamber furnished glacially in French high baroque. Clarke indicates in the novel that the aliens want to place Bowman in reassuring surroundings while they work him over, so they recreate the bedroom from his unconscious memories of a television program. From *within* the pod, we see Bowman standing in the room, his hair graying, his face lined by premature age, his body shrunken within his space suit. This Bowman is replaced by an even older version, hunched over dinner, feeding with senile single minded relish, as if stoking the embers of a dying fire. He knocks a wineglass to the floor, it shatters with a disproportionate crash, and in the magnified stillness, one hears harsh, irregular gasping. On the bed lies Bowman's third, incredibly ancient reincarnation, withered away to half size. In his terminal moment, like Floyd and Moonwatcher, he stretches out a trembling hand towards the monolith that has materialized at the foot of the bed.

2001 has been filled with futuristic allusions to procreation and gestation, delivery and nursing: the penetration of the Orbiter space station "egg" by the dart-like Earth-shuttle "sperm"; Discovery's "birthing" of the ova-like pods; the apemen clustered around the "nursing" monolith; the dead astronaut, Poole, cradled gently in the rescue pod's robotic arms. HAL, threatened with extinction, becomes the Bad Mother of the piece, depriving his "children" within and without Discovery of life-support. Bowman is "reborn" when he blasts himself through the vacuum of the airlock back into the ship and destroys the computer's consciousness. Divested of the unprofitable bondage to his tools, Bowman is reborn yet again, suffering an agonizing passage through the tumult of the Star Gate to be regressed—or rather *progressed*—beyond senility and second childhood into an ineluctably higher form of symbiosis.

For the shrunken figure on the bed is obscured by a curious opalescent haze, within which the dying Bowman seems to dissolve, then reemerge as a shining fetus. The camera's eye plunges back through the stygian blackness of the monolith, and once more we are in deep space. Half the screen is filled with the Earth, the other half by the fetus, profiled within a sheltering uteroid sphere as immense as the blue globe of Bowman's outdistanced origins. The film ends on a full close-up of the Starchild-to-be; it bears the faint, unmistakable mark of Bowman's features, a creature innocent and vulnerable, all the more awesome for the implication of unimaginable power it surely will acquire as it journeys out of its star-crossed infancy. Eons ago, the aliens joined fallible man to their imponderable purposes, and have finally brought forth from the womb of time an immortal entity, free to roam the universe at will in pursuit of a cosmic destiny. . . .

Bibliography

ALLOWAY, LAWRENCE. "Monster Films," in FOCUS *on the Horror Film,* edited by Roy Huss and T. J. Ross. Englewood Cliffs, N.J.: Prentice-Hall, Inc. (Spectrum), 1972. See p. 124.

BAXTER, JOHN. *Science Fiction in the Cinema.* New York: Warner Paperback Library, 1970.

BLATTY, WILLIAM P. *William Peter Blatty on* The Exorcist, *from Novel to Film.* New York: Bantam Books, Inc., 1974. See p. 240.

BUTLER, IVAN. *Horror in the Cinema.* New York: Warner Paperback Library, 1971.

CLARENS, CARLOS. *An Illustrated History of the Horror Film.* New York: G. P. Putnam's Sons (Capricorn), 1967. See p. 62.

DIDEROT, DENIS. *Rameau's Nephew; D'Alembert's Dream.* Great Britain: Penguin Classics, 1966, reprinted 1971. See p. 113.

DILLARD, R. H. W. "The Pageantry of Death" in FOCUS *on the Horror Film,* edited by Roy Huss and T. J. Ross. Englewood Cliffs, N.J.: Prentice-Hall, Inc. (Spectrum). 1972. See pp. 37, 41.

FREUD, SIGMUND. "Psychoanalytic Notes Upon an Autobiographical Account of a Case of Paranoia." (*Collected Papers,* Vol. 3, 1911). New York: Basic Books, 1959.

———. "The 'Uncanny.' " Vol. 4 (1919). See p. 403.

———. "On the Sexual Theories of Children." Vol. 2 (1908).

GEDULD, CAROLYN. *Filmguide to* 2001: A Space Odyssey. Bloomington: Indiana University Press, 1973.

JOHNSON, WILLIAM, ed. FOCUS *on the Science Fiction Film.* Englewood Cliffs, N.J.: Prentice-Hall, Inc. (Spectrum), 1972.

JONES, ERNEST. "On the Nightmare of Bloodsucking." See p. 60.

KENNEDY, X. J. "Who Killed King Kong." See p. 108.

MCNALLY, RAYMOND T. and FLORESCU, RADU. *A True History of Dracula and Vampire Legends.* Greenwich, Conn.: New York Graphic Society, 1972.

SCHATZMAN, MORTON. *Soul Murder—Persecution in the Family.* New York: The New American Library (Signet), 1973.

STERN, MAX M. "Fear of Death and Neurosis." *Journal of the American Psychoanalytic Association,* vol. 16 (1968). See pp. 3–31.

AFTERWORD

It is, I hope, obvious by now that I have been carrying on a lifelong love affair with the movies. Will Rogers said he never met a man he didn't like, and I can truly say the same about the cinema: I've rarely seen a film without carrying away some special moment or scene, no matter how terrible the rest of the production, keeping it banked in my memory down through the years. This book was a grateful offering to the movies and their makers for the hours of enrichment they have given me. And if the studios of Hollywood and the world are dream factories, I say let them dream on. For we die, deprived of our dreams. . . .

INDEX